Lecture Notes of the Institute
for Computer Sciences, Social Informatics
and Telecommunications Engineering

David Simplot-Ryl   Marcelo Dias de Amorim
Silvia Giordano   Ahmed Helmy (Eds.)

Ad Hoc Networks

Third International ICST Conference, ADHOCNETS 2011
Paris, France, September 21-23, 2011
Revised Selected Papers

 Springer

Volume Editors

David Simplot-Ryl
Université Lille 1, INRIA Research Center
59658 Villeneuve d'Ascq, France
E-mail: david.simplot-ryl@univ-lille1.fr

Marcelo Dias de Amorim
Université Pierre et Marie Curie, CNRS/LIP6 Laboratory
75252 Paris Cedex 05, France
E-mail: marcelo.amorim@lip6.fr

Silvia Giordano
University of Applied Sciences, SUPSI
6928 Manno, Switzerland
E-mail: silvia.giordano@supsi.ch

Ahmed Helmy
University of Florida
Computer & Information Science & Engineering (CISE) Department
Gainesville, FL 32611, USA
E-mail: helmy@ufl.edu

ISSN 1867-8211   e-ISSN 1867-822X
ISBN 978-3-642-29095-4   e-ISBN 978-3-642-29096-1
DOI 10.1007/978-3-642-29096-1
Springer Heidelberg Dordrecht London New York

Library of Congress Control Number: 2012933852

CR Subject Classification (1998): C.2, K.6.5, D.4.6, E.3, C.2.4, I.2.11

Typesetting: Camera-ready by author, data conversion by Scientific Publishing Services, Chennai, India

Printed on acid-free paper

Springer is part of Springer Science+Business Media (www.springer.com)

Preface

Ad hoc networks, which cover a variety of network paradigms for specific purposes, such as mobile ad hoc networks, sensor networks, vehicular networks, underwater networks, underground networks, personal area networks, and home networks, promise a broad range of applications in civilian, commercial, and military areas. The aim of the annual International Conference on Ad Hoc Networks (AdHocNets) is to provide a forum that brings together researchers from academia as well as practitioners from industry to meet and exchange ideas and recent research work on all aspects of ad hoc networks. AdHocNets is now an established venue in the area of ad hoc networking. The first edition of the conference, AdHocNets 2009, was held in Niagara Falls, Canada, during September 23–25, 2009, and the second edition, AdHocNets 2010, was held in Victoria, Canada, during August 18–20, 2010.

As the third edition of this event, AdHocNets was held in Paris, France, during September 21–23, 2011. The event was very successful, with strong and fruitful interactions among the participants. The technical program of the conference consisted of 15 papers out of 42 submissions, leading to an acceptance ratio of 35%, and two invited papers. These papers covered several fundamental aspects of ad hoc networking, including security, quality of service, radio and spectrum analysis, mobility, energy efficiency, and deployment. The technical program also featured a keynote speech by Hakima Chaouchi, professor at Telecom SudParis, France, on "Can Future Pervasiveness Improve Location and Mobility Management?" and a tutorial on "Experimentation on the WISEBED WSN Testbed Platform," given by Daniel Bimschas from the University of Lübeck, Germany.

This volume of LNICST includes all the technical papers presented at the conference. We do hope that it will be a useful reference for researchers and practitioners working in the general area of ad hoc networking and related fields.

September 2011

David Simplot-Ryl
Marcelo Dias de Amorim
Silvia Giordano
Ahmed Helmy

Organization

General Co-chairs

David Simplot-Ryl   INRIA, France
Marcelo Dias de Amorim   CNRS/LIP6, France

Technical Program Committee Co-chairs

Silvia Giordano   SUPSI, Switzerland
Ahmed Helmy   University of Florida, USA

Local Chair

Hakima Chaouchi   Institut Télécom SudParis (ex INT), France

Publications Chair

Aline Carneiro Viana   INRIA Saclay - Ile de France, France

Publicity Co-chairs

Tahiry Razafindralambo   INRIA LNE/POPS, IRCICA/LIFL, France
Romain Kuntz   Toyota ITC, USA

Web Chair

Antoine Gallais   Université de Strasbourg, France

Table of Contents

Session 4 – Mobile WSNs

Session 5 – Mobile Ad Hoc Networks

Session 6 – Energy

Secure Scheduling of Wireless Video Sensor Nodes for Surveillance Applications

Jacques M. Bahi[1], Christophe Guyeux[1],
Abdallah Makhoul[1], and Congduc Pham[2,*]

[1] Computer Science Laboratory (LIFC), University of Franche-Comté
Rue Engel-Gros, BP 527, 90016 Belfort Cedex, France
{jacques.bahi,christophe.guyeux,abdallah.makhoul}@univ-fcomte.fr
[2] University of Pau (LIUPPA)
Avenue de l'Université, BP 1155, 64013 Pau France
congduc.pham@univ-pau.fr@univ-pau.fr

Abstract. In video surveillance with resource-constrained devices such as wireless video sensor nodes, power conservation, intrusion detection, and security are important features to guarantee. In this paper, we intend to preserve the network lifetime while fulfilling the surveillance application needs. We take into account security by considering that a malicious attacker can try to predict the behavior of the network prior to intrusion. These considerations lead to the definition of a novel chaos-based scheduling scheme for video surveillance. We explain why the chaos-based approach can defeat malicious intruders. Then, by simulations, we also compare our chaos-based scheduling to a classical random scheduling. Results show that in addition of being able to increase the whole network lifetime and to present comparable results against random attacks (low stealth time), our scheme is also able to withstand malicious attacks due to its fully unpredictable behavior.

Keywords: video sensor networks, surveillance, scheduling, mathematical theory of chaos, security.

1 Introduction

Instead of using traditional vision systems built essentially from fixed video cameras, it is possible to deploy autonomous and small wireless video sensor nodes (WVSN) [2] to achieve video surveillance of a given area of interest. Doing so lead to a much higher level of flexibility, therefore extending the range of surveillance applications that could be considered. More interestingly, this scenario can support dynamic deployment scenario even in so-called object and obstacle-rich environments or hard-to-access areas. Such wireless video sensor nodes can in addition be thrown in mass to constitute a large scale surveillance infrastructure. In these scenarios, hundreds or thousands of video nodes of low capacity

---

* Authors in alphabetic order.

D. Simplot-Ryl et al. (Eds.): ADHOCNETS 2011, LNICST 89, pp. 1–15, 2012.

(resolution, processing, and storage) of a same or similar type can be deployed in an area of interest.

Surveillance applications have very specific needs due to their inherently critical nature associated to security [10,13,19]. The basic objective of video surveillance systems is to allow detection and/or identification of intruders. Therefore, in that context, the main goal of a video sensor network is to ensure the coverage of the whole area of interest at any time t. Another issue of prime importance is related to energy considerations since the scarcity of energy does have a direct impact on coverage, as it is not possible to have all the video nodes in activity at the same time. Therefore, a common approach is to define a subset of the deployed nodes to be active while the other nodes can sleep. There are already some techniques that schedule video nodes to work alternatively while maintaining the complete coverage [18,15,14]. The main idea in these techniques is to turn off a redundant node. Here redundancy means that the covered area by a node is completely covered by its neighbors too. However, these techniques usually depend on location or directional information, which is costly in energy and complexity. Usually it is very difficult to determine the redundant nodes without the location information. Fortunately, not all applications need a complete coverage at anytime, and in most surveillance applications for intrusion detection, most sensor nodes can move to a so-called "idle mode" in the absence of intrusions. When an intruder is detected by a node all the network will be alerted. In that context, it is critical to provide an effective scheme for turning off video nodes without degrading the surveillance quality.

In this paper, we present a solution to the joint scheduling problem in surveillance applications using video sensor nodes. We provide a chaotic sleeping scheme and conduct a theoretical and simulation analysis of both performances and security. Until now, only random approaches have been extensively studied in the literature to turn off video nodes without degrading the surveillance quality. Even if such methods present good scores in detecting random intrusions while preserving the lifetime of the network, they do not encompass the situation of a malicious attacker. That is to say, the intruder is not supposed to know something about the surveillance scheme, he cannot observe the WVSN for a while, or he is not authorized to deduce anything from his possible knowledge. In this paper, we intend to tackle with situations where the attacker is not supposed passive: he is smart and does not necessarily choose a random way to achieve his intrusion. In addition of preserving the network lifetime and being able to face random attacks, we show that our scheme is also capable to withstand attacks of a malicious adversary due to its unpredictable behavior.

The rest of the paper is organized as follows. In Section 2, related works related to surveillance applications with WVSN are presented. Smart threats and malicious attackers are introduced in Section 3. Basic recalls and terminologies on the fields of the mathematical theory of chaos and chaotic iterations are given in Section 4, and the link unifying them is explained too. The surveillance scheme based on the chaos theory is detailed in Section 5. We show in Section 6 that our proposed scheme can be used against malicious attacks. Simulation results in Section 7 compare our scheme to the classical random schedule in terms of intruder's stealth time, network lifetime and energy repartition. The paper ends by a conclusion section, where our contribution is summed up and planned future work is detailed.

2   Related Works

In video sensor networks, minimizing energy consumption and prolonging the system lifetime are major design objectives. Due to the significant energy-saving when a node is sleeping, a frequently used mechanism is to schedule the sensor nodes such that redundant nodes go to sleep as often and for as long as possible. By selecting only a subset of nodes to be active and keeping the remaining nodes in a sleep state, the energy consumption of the network is reduced, thereby extending the operational lifetime of the sensor network.

In this context, the coverage problem for wireless video sensor networks can be categorized as:

- *Known-Targets Coverage Problem,* which seeks to determine a subset of connected video nodes that covers a given set of target-locations scattered in a 2D plane.
- *Region-Coverage Problem,* which aims to find a subset of connected video nodes that ensures the coverage of the entire region of deployment in a 2D plane.

Most of the previous works have considered the known-targets coverage problem [7,1,11,8]. The objective is to ensure at all time the coverage of some targets with known locations that are deployed in a two-dimensional plane. For example, the authors in [8] organize sensor nodes into mutually exclusive subsets that are activated successively, where the size of each subset is restricted and not all of the targets need to be covered by the sensors in one subset. In [1], a directional sensor model is proposed, where a sensor is allowed to work in several directions. The idea behind this is to find a minimal set of directions that can cover the maximum number of targets. It is different from the approach described in [7] that aims to find a group of non-disjoint cover sets, each set covering all the targets to maximize the network lifetime.

Regarding the Region-Coverage Problem in which this study takes place, existing works focus on finding an efficient deployment pattern so that the average overlapping area of each sensor is bounded. The authors in [12] analyze new deployment strategies for satisfying some given coverage probability requirements with directional sensing models. A model of directed communications is introduced to ensure and repair the network connectivity. Based on a rotatable directional sensing model, the authors in [17] present a method to deterministically estimate the amount of directional nodes for a given coverage rate. A sensing connected sub-graph accompanied with a convex hull method is introduced to model a directional sensor network into several parts in a distributed manner. With adjustable sensing directions, the coverage algorithm tries to minimize the overlapping sensing area of directional sensors only with local topology information. Lastly, in [15], the authors present a distributed algorithm that ensures both coverage of the deployment area and network connectivity, by providing multiple cover sets to manage Field of View redundancies and reduce objects disambiguation.

All the above algorithms depend on the geographical location information (position and direction) of video nodes. These algorithms aim to provide a complete-coverage network so that any point in the target area would be covered by at least one video node. However, this strategy is not as energy-efficient as what we expect because of the following two reasons. Firstly, the energy cost and system complexity involved in obtaining geometric information may compromise the effect of those algorithms. Secondly, video nodes located at the edge of the area of interest must be always in an active state as long as the region is required to be completely covered. These video nodes will die after some time and their coverage area will be left without surveillance. Thus, the network coverage area will shrink gradually from outside to inside. This condition is unacceptable in video surveillance applications and intrusion detection, because the major goal here is to detect intruders as they cross a border or as they penetrate a protected area.

One direction to solve these problems is to schedule a node to sleep following a probabilistic approach. Each node remains awake with a given probability so that the coverage of the area can be guaranteed. However the probability can be modeled by an observer, who can take benefits from his observations to predict the dynamic of the network. This is obviously a security flaw. These considerations lead us to the introduction of smart threats given in the next section.

3   Smart Threats

Let us suppose that an adversary tries to reach a location X into the area without being detected. We consider that this situation leads to two categories of attacks against WVSN surveillance.

On the one hand, the attacker only knows that the area is under surveillance. He tries to take its chance, for example by following the shortest way or by trying a random path. In this first category of attack that we call "blind elementary attacks", the intruder does not know how the surveillance is achieved as he does not observe the WVSN.

On the other hand, in the second category of attacks, called "malicious attacks" in this paper, the intruder is supposed to be intelligent. He can try to take benefits from his observations to understand the behavior of the WVSN. After having recorded the dynamic of the WVSN for a given time, the malicious intruder can try to determine when video nodes are turned on. This prediction can help the intruder to find a way to reach X without being detected.

In our opinion, the most reasonable way to evaluate the consequences of a malicious attack is to suppose that the intruder has access to the surveillance scheme.

With this supposition, our security model encompasses the case where an attacker can have a physical access to a given node, thus determining the embedded mechanism used for video surveillance. In this Kerckhoffs-based principle, the attacker knows all but the initial parameters of the nodes. Moreover, he can observe the WVSN for a while. To achieve his intrusion, he can use all of the acquired knowledge – the sole difficulty is his lack of a secret parameter (the secret key) used to initialize the surveillance process.

The context of blind elementary attacks is well-known and understood: it has been studied a lot in the last decade, and various solutions have yet been proposed (Section 2). On the contrary, to the best of our knowledge, the case of an intelligent intruder (smart threat) has not yet really been treated. In this paper, we intend to propose a scheme able to withstand attacks encompassing these malicious intrusions, and thus to offer a first solution to the problem raised by the smart threats existence hypothesis.

Technically speaking, the proposed approach offers several benefits. Firstly, the node scheduling algorithm does not need location information. Therefore, the energy consumption is reduced because there is no need to locate the node itself and its neighbors. Secondly, we will show that it performs as well as a random scheduling, in terms of lifetime and intrusion detection against blind elementary attacks (see Section 7). Lastly, due to its chaotic properties, its coverage is unpredictable, and thus a malicious adversary has no solution to attack the network (Section 6).

4   Basic Recalls

In the sequel S^n denotes the n−th term of a sequence S and V_i is the i−th component of a vector V. $f^k = f \circ ... \circ f$ denotes the k−th composition of a function f. Finally, the following notation is used: $[\![1; N]\!] = \{1, 2, \ldots, N\}$.

4.1   Devaney's Chaotic Dynamical Systems

Consider a topological space $(\mathcal{X}, \tau)$ and a continuous function $f : \mathcal{X} \to \mathcal{X}$.

Definition 1. f is said to be topologically transitive if, for any pair of open sets $U, V \subset \mathcal{X}$, there exists $k > 0$ such that $f^k(U) \cap V \neq \varnothing$.

Definition 2. An element (a point) x is a periodic element (point) for f of period $n \in \mathbb{N}^*$, if $f^n(x) = x$.

Definition 3. f is said to be regular on $(\mathcal{X}, \tau)$ if the set of periodic points for f is dense in $\mathcal{X}$: for any point x in $\mathcal{X}$, any neighborhood of x contains at least one periodic point (without necessarily the same period).

Definition 4. f is said to be chaotic on $(\mathcal{X}, \tau)$ if f is regular and topologically transitive.

The chaos property is strongly linked to the notion of "sensitivity", defined on a metric space $(\mathcal{X}, d)$ by:

Definition 5. f *has* sensitive dependence on initial conditions *if there exists* $\delta > 0$ *such that, for any* $x \in \mathcal{X}$ *and any neighborhood* V *of* x, *there exists* $y \in V$ *and* $n > 0$ *such that* $d\left(f^n(x), f^n(y)\right) > \delta$. δ *is called the* constant of sensitivity *of* f.

Indeed, Banks *et al.* have proven in [6] that when f is chaotic and $(\mathcal{X}, d)$ is a metric space, then f has the property of sensitive dependence on initial conditions (this property was formerly an element of the definition of chaos). To sum up, quoting Devaney in [9], a chaotic dynamical system "is unpredictable because of the sensitive dependence on initial conditions. It cannot be broken down or simplified into two subsystems which do not interact because of topological transitivity. And in the midst of this random behavior, we nevertheless have an element of regularity". Fundamentally different behaviors are consequently possible and occur in an unpredictable way.

4.2 Chaotic Iterations

Let us consider a *system* of a finite number $N \in \mathbb{N}^*$ of elements (or *cells*), so that each cell has a Boolean *state*. A sequence of length N of Boolean states of the cells corresponds to a particular *state of the system*. A sequence which elements are subsets of $[\![1; N]\!]$ is called a *strategy*. The set of all strategies is denoted by $\mathbb{S}$.

Definition 6. *The set* $\mathbb{B}$ *denoting* $\{0, 1\}$, *let* $f : \mathbb{B}^N \longrightarrow \mathbb{B}^N$ *be a function and* $S \in \mathbb{S}$ *be a strategy. The so-called* chaotic iterations *(CIs) are defined by [16]* $x^0 \in \mathbb{B}^N$ *and*

$$\forall n \in \mathbb{N}^*, \forall i \in [\![1; N]\!], x_i^n = \begin{cases} x_i^{n-1} & \text{if } i \notin S^n \\ \left(f(x^{n-1})\right)_{S^n} & \text{if } i \in S^n. \end{cases} \tag{1}$$

In other words, at the $n-$th iteration, only the S^n-th cell is "iterated".

Note that in a more general formulation, S^n can be a subset of components and $f(x^{n-1})_{S^n}$ can be replaced by $f(x^k)_{S^n}$, where $k < n$, describing for example, delays transmission. For the general definition of such chaotic iterations, see, *e.g.*, [16].

The term "chaotic", in the name of these iterations, has *a priori* no link with the mathematical theory of chaos recalled previously. However, we have proven in [3] that in a relevant metric space $(\mathcal{X}, d)$, the vectorial negation $f_0(x_1, \ldots, x_N) = (\overline{x_1}, \ldots, \overline{x_N})$ satisfies the three conditions for Devaney's chaos. This result is recalled in the next section.

4.3 Chaotic Iterations and Devaney's Chaos

Denote by Δ the *discrete Boolean metric*, $\Delta(x, y) = 0 \Leftrightarrow x = y$. Given a function $f : \mathbb{B}^N \longrightarrow \mathbb{B}^N$, define the function $F_f : [\![1; N]\!] \times \mathbb{B}^N \longrightarrow \mathbb{B}^N$ such that

$$F_f(k, E) = \left(E_j . \Delta(k, j) + f(E)_k . \overline{\Delta(k, j)}\right)_{j \in [\![1; N]\!]}, \tag{2}$$

where $+$ and $.$ are the Boolean addition and product operations. The *shift* function is defined by $\sigma : (S^n)_{n \in \mathbb{N}} \in \mathbb{S} \to (S^{n+1})_{n \in \mathbb{N}} \in \mathbb{S}$ and the *initial function* i is the map which associates to a sequence, its first term: $i : (S^n)_{n \in \mathbb{N}} \in \mathbb{S} \to S^0 \in [\![1; \mathsf{N}]\!]$.

Consider the phase space: $\mathcal{X} = [\![1; \mathsf{N}]\!]^{\mathbb{N}} \times \mathbb{B}^{\mathsf{N}}$ and the map

$$G_f(S, E) = (\sigma(S), F_f(i(S), E)). \tag{3}$$

The chaotic iterations can be described by the following iterations

$$\begin{cases} X^0 \in \mathcal{X} \\ X^{k+1} = G_f(X^k). \end{cases} \tag{4}$$

Let us define a new distance between two points $(S, E), (\check{S}, \check{E}) \in \mathcal{X}$ by

$$d((S, E); (\check{S}, \check{E})) = d_e(E, \check{E}) + d_s(S, \check{S}), \tag{5}$$

where

$$- \ d_e(E, \check{E}) = \sum_{k=1}^{\mathsf{N}} \Delta(E_k, \check{E}_k) \in [\![0; \mathsf{N}]\!],$$

$$- \ d_s(S, \check{S}) = \frac{9}{\mathsf{N}} \sum_{k=1}^{\infty} \frac{|S^k - \check{S}^k|}{10^k} \in [0; 1].$$

This new distance has been introduced in [4,3] to satisfy the following requirements. When the number of different cells between two systems is increasing, then their distance should increase too. In addition, if two systems present the same cells and their respective strategies start with the same terms, then the distance between these two points must be small because the evolution of the two systems will be the same for a while. The distance presented above follows these recommendations. Indeed, if the floor value $\lfloor d(X, Y) \rfloor$ is equal to n, then the systems $E, \check{E}$ differ in n cells. In addition, $d(X, Y) - \lfloor d(X, Y) \rfloor$ is a measure of the differences between strategies S and $\check{S}$. More precisely, this floating part is less than 10^{-k} if and only if the first k terms of the two strategies are equal. Moreover, if the k−th digit is nonzero, then the k−th terms of the two strategies are different.

It is proven in [4,3] by using the sequential continuity that,

Proposition 1. $\forall \mathsf{N} \in \mathbb{N}^*, \forall f : \mathbb{B}^{\mathsf{N}} \to \mathbb{B}^{\mathsf{N}}, G_f$ *is a continuous function on* $(\mathcal{X}, d)$.

It is then checked in [4,3] that in the metric space $(\mathcal{X}, d)$, the vectorial negation $f_0(x_1, \ldots, x_{\mathsf{N}}) = (\overline{x_1}, \ldots, \overline{x_{\mathsf{N}}})$ satisfies the three conditions for Devaney's chaos: regularity, transitivity, and sensitivity. This has led to the following result.

Proposition 2. *CIs are chaotic on* $(\mathcal{X}, d)$ *as it is defined by Devaney.*

These chaotic iterations have been used to define in [3] an hash function and a pseudo-random number generator (PRNG) able to pass the stringent TestU01 battery of tests in [5].

5   Chaos-Based Scheduling

5.1   The General Algorithm

Network Capabilities. The WVSN is supposed to be constituted by 2^N nodes $V_i, i \in [\![0, 2^N - 1]\!]$. Each V_i is able to wake up on a specific signal, to survey a given area (and to detect intrusions), to send a wake up signal to another node V_j, and to go to sleep when it is required. Furthermore, it is supposed that V_i embeds:

- The mechanisms required by the intrusion detection: a sensing function $c_i(t)$, such as a camera, which returns some digital data at each listening time, and a decision function $d_i(c)$ which returns if an intrusion is detected in this sensing values $(c_i(t))$ or not.
- An internal clock having the time $T_i = r_i T_0$ as a reference.
- A vector of N binary digits, called *the state of the system* V_i, and the capability to swap each bit of this vector $(0 \leftrightarrow 1)$.
- An integer e_i, called *listening time*, initialized to 0.

In other words, each node V_i can achieve CIs. Thus, each node can compute, easily and by using a few resources, a hash value and some pseudo-random numbers as it is recalled in Section 4.2. We will denote by g_i the seed of the PRNG used in node V_i, which is equal to a secret parameter p_i at time $t = 0$.

Deploying the Network. The deployment of video sensor nodes in the physical environment is the first operation (step) in the network lifecycle. It may take several forms. Sensor nodes may be randomly deployed dropping them from a plane, and placed one by one by a human or a robot. Deployment may be a one time activity or a continuous process. These methods have been extensively studied in the literature. In our method, the sole requirement to satisfy is to guarantee the uniform repartition into the region of interest.

Initialization of the WVSN. At time $t = 0$, a subset $\mathcal{I} \subset [\![0, 2^N - 1]\!]$ of nodes are woken up and $\forall i \in \mathcal{I}, e_i^{t_0} = T_i$.

Surveillance. The principle of surveillance applications is defined as follows. At each time $t_j = j \times T_0, j = 1, 2, \ldots$:

1. If a sleeping node V_i has received $n_i^{t_j-1} \geqslant 1$ wake up orders during the time interval $[t_j - 1, t_j]$, then it goes into active mode and sets its listening time $e_i^{t_j}$ to $n_i^{t_j-1} T_i$.
2. If an active node V_i has received $n_i^{t_j-1} \geqslant 1$ orders to wake up during the time interval $[t_{j-1}, t_j]$, then it increments its listening time: $e_i^{t_j} = e_i^{t_j-1} + n_i^{t_j-1} T_i$.
3. For each node V_i having a listening time $e_i^{t_j} \neq 0$:
   - V_i ensures the surveillance of its area during T_0,

- If, during this time interval, an intrusion is detected, then the WVSN is under alert.
- If t_j is the first listening time of V_i after having activated, then:
  - The hash value $h_i^{t_j}$ of the sensed value $c_i(t_j)$ is computed (cf. Section 4.2).
  - The seed g_i of the PRNG of V_i is set to $h_i^{t_j} + t_j$, where $+$ is the concatenation of the digits of $h_i^{t_j}$ and t_j (thus even if $h_i^{t_j} = h_i^{t_k}, k < j$, we have $g_i^{t_j} \neq g_i^{t_k}$).
  - The N bits of the state of the system V_i are set to $E_i^{t_j}$, where $E_i^{t_j}$ is the binary decomposition of i shown as a binary vector of length N.
4. N bits are computed with the PRNG of V_i. These bits define an integer $S_i^{t_j} \in [\![0, 2^N - 1]\!]$. Then the bit of $E_i^{t_j}$ in position $S_i^{t_j}$ is switched, which leads to a new state $E_i^{t_{j+1}}$. By doing so, CIs are realized.
5. Each active node V_i decreases its listening time: $e_i^{t_j} = e_i^{t_j} - 1$.
6. For each active node having its listening time $e_i^{t_j} = 0$:
   - V_i sends the wake up order to node V_k, where $k \in [\![0, 2^N - 1]\!]$ is the integer whose binary decomposition is the last state of the system V_i ($E_i^{t_{j+1}}$).
   - V_i goes to sleep.

6 Theoretical Study

6.1 Scheduling as Chaotic Iterations

The scheduling scheme presented above can be described as CIs. The global state E^t of the whole system is constituted by the reunion of each internal state E_i^t of each node i. This is an element of $\mathbb{B}^{N \times 2^N}$. The strategy at time t is the subset of $[\![0; N \times 2^N]\!]$ constituted by all of the strategies that are computed into the awaken nodes at time t. More precisely, if the node V_k has computed the strategy S_k^t at time t, then the global strategy S^t will contain the value $S_k^t + k \times N$. Lastly, the iteration function is the vectorial negation defined : $\mathbb{B}^{N \times 2^N} \rightarrow \mathbb{B}^{N \times 2^N}$. A subsequence E^{m^t} is extracted from E^t, which determines the changes that occur in the network: nodes whose binary id is into E^{m^t} are nodes that achieve the surveillance at the considered time. Let us remark that S^k and m^k depend both on the outside world, due to the fact that S_i^t are regularly seeded with the digest of some sensed values.

6.2 Complexity

Even if the hash function and the PRNG taken from [3] and [5] respectively can be replaced by any cryptographically secure hash function and PRNG, we do not recommend their substitution. Indeed, all of the operations used by our scheme can be achieved by CIs. Each iteration of CIs is only constituted by the negation of a few binary digits. Obviously, such an operation is fast and does not consume a lot of energy. By doing so, we thus obtain an efficient video surveillance scheduling scheme compliant with WVSN requirements. Section 7 will detail more quantitatively this fact.

6.3   Coverage

The coverage of the whole area is guaranteed due to the following reasons.

Firstly, the scheduling process corresponds to CIs. These iterations are chaotic according to Devaney, thus they are transitive. This transitivity property is the formulation of a uniform repartition in terms of topology. It claims that the system will never stop to visit any sub-region of the whole area, regardless of how tiny the region is.

Secondly, as the choice of the nodes to wake up at each time are done by using CIs, this selection corresponds to the returned value of our PRNG proposed in [5]. This "CI(X,Y)-generator" takes two PRNGs X,Y as input sequences, realizes CIs with X as strategy, the vectorial negation as update function, and selects the states to publish as outputs by using the second PRNG Y. By such a combination, we improve the statistical properties of the input PRNG used as strategy, and we add chaotic properties. The scheduling process corresponds to the CI(X,Y)-generator, with $X=m$ and $Y=S$. As Y is statistically perfect (Y is CI(ISAAC,ISAAC), which can pass the whole NIST, DieHARD, and TestU01 batteries of tests), the uniform repartition of the states is then guaranteed.

Lastly, experiments of Section 7 will show that this intended uniform coverage is well obtained in practice.

6.4   Security Study

Let us suppose that Oscar, an intruder, knows that the scheduling process is based on CIs, i.e. he knows the whole algorithm, except the seeds that have been used to initiate the PRNGs of each node. By doing so, we respect the Kerckhoffs' principle: the adversary has all except the secret key. Oscar's desire is to reach a particular location X of the area without being detected. To achieve his goal, he can choose two strategies. On the one hand, he can try a blind elementary attack, either by following a random way from its position to X, of by choosing the shortest path. The next section will show that such an attack cannot work. On the other hand, Oscar can try to take benefits both from his knowledge and his observations. However, if he can determine the nodes that are awaken at time t, he cannot predict the awaken nodes at time $t + 1, t + 2, ...$ To do so, he should be able to obtain $S^{t+1}, S^{t+2}, ...$, which are computed from the digests of some values that will be sensed in the future. As our hash function satisfy the avalanche effect, due to its chaotic properties, any error on the sensed value lead to a completely different digest.

As Oscar cannot determine the sensed values of each node, at each time and with an infinite precision, he does not have the knowledge of the current state of the global system. He has only access to an approximation of this state. As the global scheduling process is chaotic, this error on the initial condition is magnified at each iteration, leading to the impossibility for Oscar to predict the scheduling process.

7   Simulation Results

This section presents simulation results on comparing our chaotic approach to the standard C++ `rand()`-based approach with random intrusions. We use the OMNET++ simulation environment and the next node selection will either use chaotic iterations or the C++ `rand()` function (`rand() % 2`^{n}) to produce a random number between 0 and 2^n. For these set of simulations, 128 sensor nodes (therefore $n = 7$) are randomly deployed in a $75m * 75m$ area. Unless specified, sensors have an 36° AoV and sensor node captures at the rate of 0.2fps. Each node starts with a battery level of 100 units and taking 1 picture consummes 1 unit of battery. When a node V_i is selected to wake up, it will be awake for T_i seconds. We set all $T_i = T = 20s$. According to the behavior defined in section 5, before going to sleep after an activity period of $e_i T$, V_i will determine the next node to be waked up. It can potentially elect itself in which case V_i stays active for at least another T period. The elected node can be already active, in which case it simply increases its e_i counter. We set about 50% of the sensor nodes to be active initially (each sensor draws a random value between 0 and 1 and if the value is greater than 0.5, it will be active). This initial threshold is tunable but we did not try to vary this parameter in this paper. The results presented here have been averaged over 10 simulation runs with different initial seeds. Figure 1 shows the percentage of active nodes. Both the chaotic and the standard `rand()` function have similar behavior: the percentage of active nodes progressively decreases due to battery shortage.

To compare both approaches in term of surveillance quality, we record to stealth time when intrusions are introduced in the area of interest. The stealth time is the time during which an intruder can travel in the field without being seen. The first intrusion starts at time 10s at a random position in the field. The scan line mobility model is then used with a constant velocity of 5m/s to make the intruder moving to the right part of the field. When the intruder is seen for the first time by a sensor, the stealth time is recorded and the mean stealth time computed. Then a new intrusion appears at another random position. This process is repeated until the simulation ends (i.e. no more sensor nodes with energy). Figure 2 shows the mean stealth time over the whole simulation duration. Figure 3 shows the same data but with a sliding window averaging filter of 20 values. As the nodes are uniformly distributed in the area of interest, there is a strong correlation between the percentage of active nodes and the stealth time as it can be expected. The result we want to highlight here is that our chaotic node selection approach has a similar level of performance in presence of random intrusions than standard `rand()` function while providing a formal proof of non-prediction by malicious intruders.

The last result we want to show is the energy consumption distribution. We recorded every 10s the energy level of each sensor node in the field and computed the mean and the standard deviation. Figure 4 shows the evolution of the standard deviation during the network lifetime. We can see that the chaotic node selection provides a slightly better distribution of activity than the standard `rand()` function.

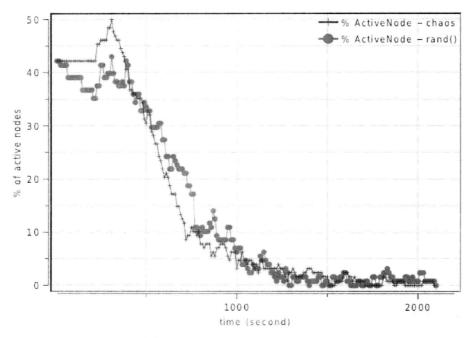

Fig. 1. Percentage of active nodes

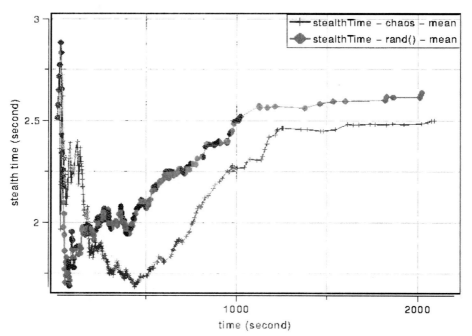

Fig. 2. Stealth time

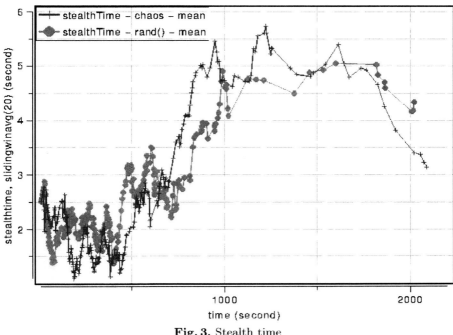

Fig. 3. Stealth time

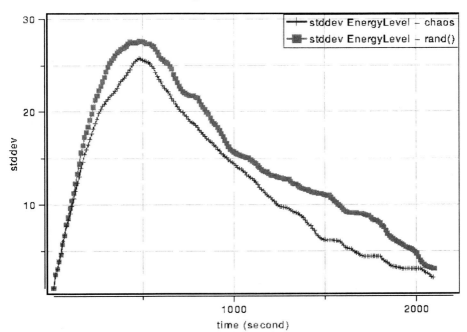

Fig. 4. Evolution of the energy consumption's standard deviation

8   Conclusions and Perspectives

In this paper, a sleeping scheme for nodes has been proposed as an effective and secure solution to the joint scheduling problem in surveillance applications using WVSNs. It has been evaluated through theoretical and practical aspects of performance and security. As opposed to existing works, this scheduling scheme is not based only on randomness, but on the mathematical theory of chaos too. By doing so, we reinforce coverage and lifetime of the network, while obtaining a more secure scheme. We have considered in this paper the case where the intruder is smart and active. Furthermore, we have supposed that he can know the scheme and observe the behavior of the network. We have shown that, in addition of being able to preserve WVSN lifetime and to present comparable results against random attacks, our scheme is also able to withstand such malicious attacks due to its unpredictable behavior.

In future work, we intend to enlarge the security field in WVSN-based video surveillance, by making a classification of attacks that Oscar can achieve depending on the data he has access to. Our desire is to distinguish between several levels of security into each category of malicious attacks, from the weakest one to the strongest one. Additionally, we will study more precisely the topological properties of the scheduling scheme presented in this paper.

References

1. Ai, J., Abouzeid, A.A.: Coverage by directional sensors in randomly deployed wireless sensor networks. Journal of Combinatorial Optimization 11(1), 21–41 (2006)
2. Akyildiz, I.F., Su, W., Sankarasubramaniam, Y., Cayirci, E.: Wireless sensor networks: a survey. IEEE Communications Magazine 40(8), 102–114 (2002)
3. Bahi, J.M., Guyeux, C.: Hash functions using chaotic iterations. Journal of Algorithms & Computational Technology 4(2), 167–181 (2010)
4. Bahi, J.M., Guyeux, C.: Topological chaos and chaotic iterations, application to hash functions. In: IJCNN 2010, Int. Joint Conf. on Neural Networks, Joint to WCCI 2010, IEEE World Congress on Computational Intelligence, Barcelona, Spain, pp. 1–7 (July 2010)
5. Guyeux, C., Wang, Q., Bahi, J.M.: A Pseudo Random Numbers Generator Based on Chaotic Iterations: Application to Watermarking. In: Wang, F.L., Gong, Z., Luo, X., Lei, J. (eds.) WISM 2010. LNCS, vol. 6318, pp. 202–211. Springer, Heidelberg (2010)
6. Banks, J., Brooks, J., Cairns, G., Stacey, P.: On devaney's definition of chaos. Amer. Math. Monthly 99, 332–334 (1992)
7. Cai, Y., Lou, W., Li, M., Li, X.-Y.: Target-oriented scheduling in directional sensor networks. In: 26th IEEE International Conference on Computer Communications, INFOCOM 2007, pp. 1550–1558 (2007)
8. Cheng, M.X., Ruan, L., Wu, W.: Achieving minimum coverage breach under bandwidth constraints in wireless sensor networks. In: IEEE INFOCOM (2005)
9. Devaney, R.L.: An Introduction to Chaotic Dynamical Systems, 2nd edn. Westview Pr. (2003)

10. He, T., Krishnamurthy, S., Stankovic, J.A., Abdelzaher, T., Luo, L., Stoleru, R., Yan, T., Gu, L., Hui, J., Krogh, B.: Energy-efficient surveillance system using wireless sensor networks. In: MobiSys, pp. 270–283 (2003)

11. Liu, H., Wan, P., Jia, X.: Maximal lifetime scheduling for sensor surveillance systems with k sensors to one target. IEEE Transactions on Parallel and Distributed Systems 17(12), 1526–1536 (2006)

12. Ma, H., Liu, Y.: Some problems of directional sensor networks. International Journal of Sensor Networks 2(1-2), 44–52 (2007)

13. Oh, S., Chen, P., Manzo, M., Sastry, S.: Instrumenting wireless sensor networks for real-time surveillance. In: Proc. of the International Conference on Robotics and Automation (2006)

14. Pham, C., Makhoul, A.: Performance study of multiple cover-set strategies for mission-critical video surveillance with wireless video sensors. In: 6th IEEE Int. Conf. on Wireless and Mobile Computing, Networking and Communications, Wimob 2010, pp. 208–216 (2010)

15. Pham, C., Makhoul, A., Saadi, R.: Risk-based adaptive scheduling in randomly deployed video sensor networks for critical surveillance applications. Journal of Network and Computer Applications 34(2), 783–795 (2011)

16. Robert, F.: Discrete Iterations: A Metric Study. Springer Series in Computational Mathematics, vol. 6 (1986)

17. Tao, D., Ma, H., Liu, L.: Coverage-Enhancing Algorithm for Directional Sensor Networks. In: Cao, J., Stojmenovic, I., Jia, X., Das, S.K. (eds.) MSN 2006. LNCS, vol. 4325, pp. 256–267. Springer, Heidelberg (2006)

18. Wang, J., Niu, C., Shen, R.-M.: Randomized Approach for Target Coverage Scheduling in Directional Sensor Network. In: Lee, Y.-H., Kim, H.-N., Kim, J., Park, Y.W., Yang, L.T., Kim, S.W. (eds.) ICESS 2007. LNCS, vol. 4523, pp. 379–390. Springer, Heidelberg (2007)

19. Zhu, Y., Ni, L.M.: Probabilistic approach to provisioning guaranteed qos for distributed event detection. In: IEEE INFOCOM (2008)

A Hierarchical Deterministic Key Pre-distribution for WSN Using Projective Planes

Sarbari Mitra, Ratna Dutta, and Sourav Mukhopadhyay

Indian Institute of Technology, Kharagpur, India
sarbarimitra@gmail.com, {ratna,sourav}@maths.iitkgp.ernet.in

Abstract. We present a deterministic key pre-distribution scheme using projective planes where the nodes are organised hierarchically through a structure of (p^2+p)-nary tree, where p is prime. Our scheme is incumbent to more efficient resilience and connectivity compared to the existing schemes. Each node in our scheme requires to store significantly less number of keys. Furthermore, any number of nodes can be intrinsically inserted in the system by attributing a very few keys to the recently introduced nodes only. Another interesting feature of our scheme is that such node insertions are done without interfering the normal functioning of the existing organised network.

Keywords: t-design, Steiner system, projective planes, key pre-distribution.

1 Introduction

Wireless Sensor Network (WSN) consists of a large number of wireless sensor nodes, which are typically small mobile devices with limited memory and computation power to transmit data within a specified range. Sensor nodes are usually plotted in sensitive regions (e.g. military area, hospital etc.) to gather information through sensors and transmit the collected data by communicating among themselves or with some other source. The process of assigning keys to the nodes prior to their deployment in the target region is termed as key pre-distribution. Usually keys are chosen from a large key-pool and then they are loaded at the nodes.

Key pre-distribution to the sensor nodes has drawn the attention of researchers over the years. Till date combinatorial design is one of the most commonly used mathematical tools for the key pre-distribution. Key pre-distribution in wireless sensor network can be broadly categorized into the following [11]:

- *Probabilistic*: Keys are chosen randomly from the key-pool and are assigned to the nodes so that any two nodes are connected (i.e. share a common key) with some definite probability.
- *Deterministic*: Keys are distributed to the nodes following a fixed manner and it can be determined with absolute certainty that which nodes are sharing common keys.
- *Hybrid*: A combination of both probabilistic and deterministic approaches.

D. Simplot-Ryl et al. (Eds.): ADHOCNETS 2011, LNICST 89, pp. 16–31, 2012.
© Institute for Computer Sciences, Social Informatics and Telecommunications Engineering 2012

A key pre-distribution scheme involves three main steps [8]:

(a) *Key pre-distribution*: The process of loading secret keys to the sensor nodes.
(b) *Shared key discovery*: Any two nodes wishing to communicate between themselves check whether they have a common key or not. This process is known as shared key discovery.
(c) *Path-key establishment*: If two nodes don't share any common key, they look for neighbouring node(s) sharing a common key with both of them. This is known as path-key establishment.

The salient features of a good key pre-distribution scheme includes the following:

(i) Scalability - whether new nodes can be introduced without much disturbance in the existing set-up;
(ii) Efficiency - less memory, less computation and greater connectivity
(iii) Resilience - how the network is affected when some of the nodes are captured.

The above parameters are conflicting to each other. If one common key is stored at all the nodes, the probability of two nodes sharing a common key is 1, which implies the best connectivity. The memory requirement met as well since the nodes need to store only one key. But the network becomes extremely vulnerable as capture of one single node makes the whole network to cease which leads the resilience to become zero. Another possibility is to store a key for each pair of the nodes. In this case, we get desirable connectivity (probability of any two nodes sharing a common key is 1) and significant resilience as capture of any node will destroy the links of other nodes with the compromised nodes. Whereas the rest of the network will remain undisturbed. The drawback of this method is that each node is required a huge memory to store $N-1$ keys for a network consisting of N nodes. Hence one needs to obtain a trade-off between these parameters.

1.1 Previous Work

Eschenauer and Gligor [7] were first to use random key pre-distribution in WSN. Their scheme is known as *basic scheme*. Later Chan, Perrig and Song [5] proposed a modified version of the basic scheme.

Camptepe, Yener [1] were first to introduce combinatorial designs as one of the key pre-distribution techniques. They have considered two combinatorial designs: one is the symmetric $(n^2 + n + 1, n + 1, 1)$-BIBD (or, finite projective plane of order n) and the other is generalized quadrangles. The advantage of this deterministic approach is any two nodes share a common key which improves the connectivity of the network to a greater extent. The main drawback of deterministic approach is that the scheme is not scalable as the network size N should satisfy $N \leq n^2 + n + 1$. If one wants to introduce some new nodes to the network which exceeds the bound, then n has to be raised to the next prime number as the existence of such designs for a non prime power value of n is not certain. This results in a much more larger network than required, and the key-chains at each node have to be changed. It is also observed in [2] that the generalized quadrangles induce better scalable network and provide better resilience than finite projective planes. To improve the scalability, authors have proposed a hybrid scheme in [2]. In this scheme, keys are assigned to the major part of the network according to projective plane, (i.e., following a deterministic approach) and the remaining nodes or newly joined nodes (which could not be accommodated by projective planes) get keys in a completely random manner. This improves the resilience and scalability. However, the probability of any two nodes sharing a common key is reduced.

In 2005, Lee and Stinson [8] proposed a scheme on group-divisible design or Transversal design. It is noticed that the expected proportion that any two nodes can communicate directly is 0.6 and the same for two nodes communicating directly or via intermediate nodes is almost 0.99995. Chakrabarti et al. [3] showed by an example that out of 2401 nodes in a network, if only 10 nodes are captured, then 18% of the links will be destroyed. This is the main disadvantage of this scheme. Later, in 2008, quadratic schemes were developed in [10] based on Transversal designs and the method described in [8] was referred as linear schemes. This work suggests that the quadratic scheme provides best resilience unless the number of compromised nodes is high. Quadratic schemes in general provides better connectivity than linear schemes. Both linear and quadratic schemes are preferred over 2-composite scheme [5] if shared key discovery is taken into consideration.

In 2005, Chakrabarti et al. [3] proposed a probabilistic key pre-distribution scheme. They have constructed the blocks as proposed by Lee et al. [8]. The sensor nodes are then formed by merging blocks randomly. This increases the chance of sharing common keys between two nodes. The scheme in [3] provides better resilience as compared to the Lee-Stinson scheme [8] at the cost of large key-chain size in each node.

3-design is considered to be the underlying combinatorial design of the key pre-distribution scheme proposed by Dong et al. in [6]. Keys are assigned to the sensor nodes in the network by Möbius Planes. This scheme provides better connectivity than the scheme proposed by Lee-Stinson [10] and better memory requirement as compared to Camptepe-Yener scheme [1]. The prime drawback of the scheme is that resilience reduces rapidly with the increasing number of compromised nodes.

Ruj et al. [11] proposed a deterministic key pre-distribution scheme based on Partially Balanced Incomplete Block Design. The authors claim that this scheme gives better resilience than that of [8] storing less than $\sqrt{N}$ keys to the nodes where N is the network size. But to store that many keys to the nodes, for a very large network is also expensive.

1.2   Our Contribution

We propose a storage-efficient key pre-distribution scheme adapting a deterministic approach. We have used a typical Steiner system as our basic combinatorial design for key pre-distribution. We emphasize that apart from storage efficiency, our design also provides better resilience and reasonable connectivity as compared to the existing schemes. Nodes are arranged using a hierarchical tree structure. The whole network is divided into $(p^2 + p + 1)$ sub-networks each of which forms a $(p^2 + p)$-nary tree-hierarchical structure, where p is prime. All the nodes in the same sub-network are connected directly or via a chain of intermediate nodes. Moreover, two nodes from two different sub-networks can establish a key-path via *level* 1 nodes which means that all the nodes in the network are connected.

We claim that our scheme provides much better resilience even in the worst possible condition, which is supported by our experimental results provided in the paper. As resilience and connectivity are contradictory in nature, we choose the order of the projective plane suitably to meet the requirement for both the resilience and connectivity. Consumption of power and memory should be minimal since there will be no external supply of power to the nodes once they are deployed. Increased memory consumption will decrease the power available for computation. Storing significantly less number of keys to the nodes is not only cost-effective but also it leaks less information (in the form of keys) when the nodes are captured. Unlike the existing key pre-distribution schemes, our scheme is flexible in the sense that insertion of a large number of nodes can be done by adding only a few keys to the newly joined nodes without disturbing the previously assigned nodes.

Rest of the paper is organized as follows: section 2 includes preliminaries, we discuss the proposed scheme in section 3, which is explained in detail with a particular example in section 4. Section 5 and 6 provide obtained results and performance respectively followed by concluding remarks in section 7.

2   Preliminaries

Definition 2.01. *A design is defined as a pair* (X, A) *such that (i)* X *is a set of points or elements, (ii)* A *is a subset of the power set of X (i.e. Collection of non-empty subsets of X)*

Definition 2.02. *A t-design is defined as a t - (v, k, λ) block design (with $t \leq k \leq v$) such that the following are satisfied (i)* X $= v$ *, (ii) each block contains k points, (iii) for any set of t points there are exactly λ blocks that contain all these points.*

Definition 2.03. *A t-design with $t = 2$ is known as (v, k, λ)-Balanced Incomplete Block Design[BIBD].*

Example 2.01. *A $(10, 4, 2)$-BIBD has* $X = \{0, 1, 2, 3, 4, 5, 6, 7, 8, 9\}$,
$A = \{(0, 1, 2, 3); (0, 1, 4, 5); (0, 2, 4, 6); (0, 3, 7, 8); (0, 5, 7, 9); (0, 6, 8, 9); (1, 2, 7, 8);$
$(1, 3, 6, 9); (1, 4, 7, 9); (1, 5, 6, 8); (2, 3, 5, 9); (2, 4, 8, 9); (2, 5, 6, 7); (3, 4, 5, 8);$
$(3, 4, 6, 7)\}$

Definition 2.04. *A t-design with $\lambda = 1$ is known as Steiner system.*

Example 2.02. *A $(9, 3, 1)$-design has $X = \{1, 2, 3, 4, 5, 6, 7, 8, 9\}$, $A = \{(1, 2, 3);$ $(4, 5, 6); (7, 8, 9); (1, 4, 7); (2, 5, 8); (3, 6, 9); (1, 5, 9); (1, 6, 8); (2, 4, 9); (2, 6, 7);$ $(3, 4, 8); (3, 5, 7)\}$*

Definition 2.05. *Finite symmetric projective plane of order n is defined as a pair of set of $n^2 + n + 1$ points and $n^2 + n + 1$ lines, where each line contains $n + 1$ points and each point occurs in $n + 1$ lines.*

Example 2.03. *Projective plane of order 2, a $(7, 3, 1)$-BIBD, which is also known as the Fano plane has $X = \{1, 2, 3, 4, 5, 6, 7\}$, $A = \{(1, 2, 3); (1, 4, 7); (1, 5, 6);$ $(2, 4, 6); (2, 5, 7); (3, 4, 5); (3, 6, 7)\}$.*

Example 2.04. *Projective plane of order 3, a $(13, 4, 1)$-BIBD is:*
$X = \{1, 2, 3, 4, 5, 6, 7, 8, 9, 10, 11, 12, 13\}$
$A = \{(1, 2, 3, 4); (1, 5, 6, 7); (1, 8, 9, 10); (1, 11, 12, 13); (2, 5, 8, 11); (2, 6, 9, 13);$
$\quad (2, 7, 10, 12); (3, 5, 10, 13); (3, 6, 8, 12); (3, 7, 9, 11); (4, 5, 9, 12); (4, 6, 10, 11);$
$\quad (4, 7, 8, 13)\}$.

Any design (X, A) can be mapped to a sensor network where the elements of the set X represent the keys and the blocks of the set A correspond to sensor nodes.

3   Our Generalized Scheme

In this section we shall discuss how a projective plane can be mapped to the network. We consider a particular projective plane of order p, (p is considered to be prime so as to ensure the existence of the projective plane), as our basic building block design. Initially we label all the nodes by Node[1], Node[2], Node[3], $\cdots$, Node[N]; where N is the total number of nodes. Similarly we label the keys as key[1], key[2], key[3], $\cdots$, key[K]; where K is the size of the key-pool. A set of $p^2 + p + 1$ keys are chosen from the large key pool and then distributed to a set of $p^2 + p + 1$ nodes so that each node gets $p + 1$ keys and each key is assigned to $p + 1$ nodes. Without loss of generality, we assume that the nodes chosen are given by Node[1], Node[2], Node[3], $\cdots$, Node[$p^2 + p + 1$]. We call these nodes as *level* 1 nodes, the keys used in *level* 1 are termed as *level* 1 keys. The set of nodes and keys used in *level* 1 thus forms a Steiner system. In *level* 2, Node[1] forms a Steiner system with $p^2 + p$ new nodes. We know that total $p^2 + p + 1$ keys are required to form a Steiner system. As there are $p + 1$ keys already stored in the first node, we need only p^2 nodes to complete the Steiner system. In the similar manner, Steiner systems are produced corresponding to each of the *level* 1 nodes. All the nodes that are included in *level* 2 are referred to as *level* 2 nodes and all the keys that are used for the first time in *level* 2 are called *level* 2 keys. Steiner systems are created corresponding to each of the *level* 2 nodes to complete *level* 3. This method is repeated until keys are distributed to all the nodes in the network. This completes the key pre-distribution phase.

4   Fano Plane Scheme

We explain the key distribution procedure described above for a Fano plane. Fig.1 illustrates the 2 - $(7, 3, 1)$ Steiner system i.e. the Fano Plane under consideration.

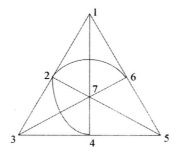

Fig. 1. The Fano Plane

Here seven nodes correspond to seven keys and each line represents a sensor node (key chain of the node). This assigns a set of 7 keys to 7 nodes such that all nodes together contain exactly 7 keys and any two are connected by exactly one common key. We label all the nodes and all the keys by $1, 2, 3, 4, \ldots$ for convenience. In *level* 1, seven keys $\{1, 2, 3, 4, 5, 6, 7\}$ are distributed to the first seven nodes as described above. Thus the key-chains assigned to the nodes $1, 2, 3, 4, 5, 6, 7$ are respectively $\{1, 2, 3\}$, $\{1, 4, 7\}$, $\{1, 5, 6\}$, $\{2, 4, 6\}$, $\{2, 5, 7\}$, $\{3, 4, 5\}$, $\{3, 6, 7\}$.

The Steiner systems corresponding to all the *level* 1 nodes are explicitly described in Table 1.

In *level* 3, each of *level* 2 nodes are attached to six new *level* 3 nodes to form a Steiner system and the corresponding key chain is chosen in the same manner, i.e., keeping the first three keys same as the *level* 2 keys contained by *level* 2 nodes and adding four new *level* 3 keys. This process is repeated until keys are assigned to all the nodes in the network. We provide the algorithm Key Pre-Distribution for assigning keys to the tree hierarchy as explained above. We consider a hierarchical structure using a 6-nary tree for key pre-distribution.

Let us consider a network having maximum N nodes. Let K denote the total key-pool and l denote the maximum level in the hierarchical tree structure. The three keys assigned to Node[i] are stored in Node[i][1], Node[i][2], Node[i][3]. Choose $\{u_1, u_2, u_3\} \in_R K$, where the symbol $\in_R$ denotes random selection.

Table 1. Components of Steiner systems formed by *level* 1 nodes

Node	Node-set	Key-set
node 1	$\{1, 8, 9, 10, 11, 12, 13\}$	$\{1, 2, 3, 8, 9, 10, 11\}$
node 2	$\{2, 14, 15, 16, 17, 18, 19\}$	$\{1, 4, 7, 12, 13, 14, 15\}$
node 3	$\{3, 20, 21, 22, 23, 24, 25\}$	$\{1, 5, 6, 16, 17, 18, 19\}$
node 4	$\{4, 26, 27, 28, 29, 30, 31\}$	$\{2, 4, 6, 20, 21, 22, 23\}$
node 5	$\{5, 32, 33, 34, 35, 36, 37\}$	$\{2, 5, 7, 24, 25, 26, 27\}$
node 6	$\{6, 38, 39, 40, 41, 42, 43\}$	$\{3, 4, 5, 28, 29, 30, 31\}$
node 7	$\{7, 44, 45, 46, 47, 48, 49\}$	$\{3, 6, 7, 32, 33, 34, 35\}$

Algorithm : Key Pre-Distribution

$i := 0;$
Node $[1][1] := u_1,$ Node $[1][2] := u_2,$ Node $[1][3] := u_3;$
procedure Key Pre-Distribution (u_1, u_2, u_3)
$X := \{u_1, u_2, u_3\}$;
Choose $\{u_4, u_5, u_6, u_7\} \in_R B$ where $B \subseteq K - X$, B is the set of unused keys
$X := X \cup \{u_4, u_5, u_6, u_7\};$

  $j := 6i + 2;$
    Node $[j][1] := u_1,$ Node $[j][2] := u_4,$ Node $[j][3] := u_7;$
    Node $[j+1][1] := u_1,$ Node $[j+1][2] := u_5,$ Node $[j+1][3] := u_6;$
    Node $[j+2][1] := u_2,$ Node $[j+2][2] := u_4,$ Node $[j+2][3] := u_6;$
    Node $[j+3][1] := u_2,$ Node $[j+3][2] := u_5,$ Node $[j+3][3] := u_7;$
    Node $[j+4][1] := u_3,$ Node $[j+4][2] := u_4,$ Node $[j+4][3] := u_5;$
    Node $[j+5][1] := u_3,$ Node $[j+5][2] := u_6,$ Node $[j+5][3] := u_7;$
$p := 1;$ $r := 1;$ $s := 0;$ $N := r + s$
while $(p < l)$ **do**
    $r := r + 6^p;$ $s := s + 6^{p-1};$
    $p + +;$
    for $i := N$ to $(r + s - 1)$ **do in parallel**
        call Key Pre-Distribution (Node[i][1], Node[i][2], Node[i][3])
    end do
  $N := r + s;$
end do
end Key Pre-Distribution

The detailed hierarchical tree structure (upto *level* 3) has been depicted in Fig.2

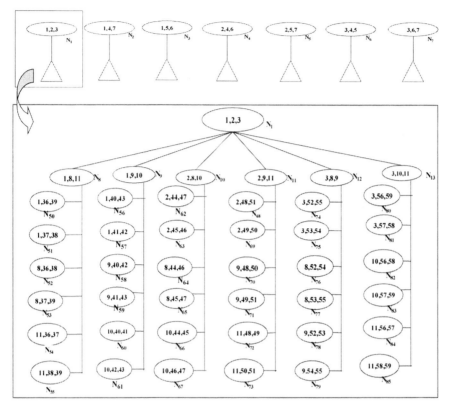

Fig. 2. The nodes, denoted by N_i and corresponding key-chains upto *level* 3

5   Results

Theorem 5.01. *Number of nodes in level j is $n_j = (p^2+p+1)(p^2+p)^{j-1}$, $\forall j \in \{1, \ell\}$.*

Proof: The result holds trivially for $i = 1$.

In *level* 2, each node from *level* 1 forms a projective plane with new $p^2 + p$ *level* 2 nodes. Let us refer to these $p^2 + p$ nodes as the children of that *level* 1 node. Similarly, all *level* 1 nodes have $p^2 + p$ children. Following the same pattern all *level* 2 nodes have $p^2 + p$ children in *level* 3 and this pattern continues. Therefore, we note that the nodes are distributed in the form of $(p^2 + p)$-nary trees corresponding to each of $p^2 + p + 1$ nodes in *level* 1. Thus the nodes form $p^2 + p + 1$ numbers of $(p^2 + p)$-nary trees. Hence the result follows.   □

Corollary 5.01. *Total number of nodes in the network is* $N = \frac{(p^2+p+1)}{(p^2+p-1)}\{$ $(p^2+p)^l - 1\}$

Proof: As the levels of the nodes are exhaustive and disjoint, we have $N = n_1 + n_2 + ... + n_l$, where l represents the total number of levels in the network. Consequently, total number of nodes in the network is $N = \sum_{j=1}^{l}(p^2+p+1)(p^2+p)^{j-1} = \frac{(p^2+p+1)}{(p^2+p-1)}\{(p^2+p)^l - 1\}$. This completes the proof. □

Theorem 5.02. *Number of keys that are used for the first time in level j is* $k_j = p^j(p+1)^{j-2}(p^2+p+1),\ \forall\ j \geq 2\ and\ k_1 = p^2+p+1.$

Proof: There are p^2+p+1 keys in each of the projective planes. As there is only one projective plane is *level* 1, number of keys in *level* 1 is p^2+p+1. We observe that when one node from *level i* forms a projective plane with new nodes from *level* $i+1$, it requires p^2 new nodes to complete the projective plane as $p+1$ keys are already stored in that node. So number of keys required in *level i* is p^2 corresponding to each Steiner system to be formed. If k_j denotes the number of keys in *level j*, then $k_j = p^2 \times n_{j-1} = p^j(p+1)^{j-2}(p^2+p+1)$. □

Corollary 5.02. *Total number of keys in the network is* $K = (p^2+p+1)[1+ \frac{p^2}{p^2+p-1}((p^2+p)^{\ell-1}-1)]$

Proof: As the keys appearing for the first time in a particular *level* are exhaustive and disjoint, we have $K = k_1 + k_2 + ... + k_l$, where l represents the total number of levels in the network. Hence, total number of keys required in the network is $K = (p^2+p+1)\sum_{j=1}^{l}p^j(p+1)^{j-2}$. The result follows on simplification. □

Theorem 5.03. *Number of nodes to which a level i key is assigned to, is given by* $N_i = \frac{p+1}{p-1} \times \{p^{l+1-i}-1\}$, *where l denotes the total number of levels present in the network.*

Proof: The keys that appear for the first time in *level i* is contained in only one Steiner system and hence goes to $p+1$ nodes in *level i*. In the next *level*, i.e. in $(i+1)^{th}$ *level*, that key goes to each of the $p+1$ Steiner systems corresponding to each of the previous *level* nodes and in each system, the key is contained in p new nodes. Thus we observe that the nodes to which a *level i* key is contained, form $(p+1)$ number of p-nary trees with their roots in *level i*. Therefore, the number of nodes to which a *level j* key is assigned to is $\sum_{i=j}^{l}(p+1)p^{i-j}$. Hence the result follows. □

Theorem 5.04. *Number of nodes containing key-chain as (level j, level i,* $\cdots$, *level i) in level i is given by*

$$\begin{cases} (p^2+p+1) \times p^{i-1} \times (p+1)^j\ for\ j = 1; \\ (p^2+p+1) \times p^i \times (p+1)^{j-1}\ \forall\ j = 2,\ 3,\ \cdots,\ (i-1). \end{cases}$$

Proof: We observe that all the nodes in *level* 1 contain $p+1$ *level* 1 keys. In *level* 2, the nodes contain one *level* 1 and p *level* 2 keys. In *level* 3 we get two types of nodes depending on the key distribution. All *level* 3 nodes contain exactly p *level* 3 keys and the remaining key is from *level* 1 or *level* 2, we call the nodes Type 1 and Type 2 accordingly. We also notice that the ratio of Type 1 and Type 2 nodes is $1 : p$ as shown in the Fig. 3.

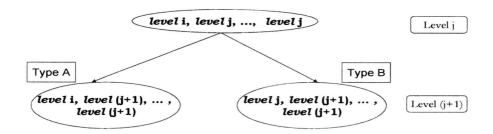

Fig. 3. Type A and Type B nodes in level $j + 1$ are in the ratio $1 : p$

In *level* 4 we get three types of nodes: Type 1 with key chain (*level* 1, *level* 4, $\cdots$, *level* 4); Type 2 with key chain (*level* 2, *level* 4, $\cdots$, *level* 4); Type 3 with key chain (*level* 3, *level* 4, $\cdots$, *level* 4); and they are in the ratio $1 : p : p(p + 1)$. Continuing this process upto *level* i, the nodes are in the ratio $1 : p : p(p + 1) : p(p + 1)^2 : \cdots : p(p + 1)^{i-3}$. Sum of these ratios is $(p + 1)^{i-2}$. Their corresponding proportions are given in Table 2. Now, we know that the number of nodes in *level* i is given by $n_i = (p^2 + p + 1)(p^2 + p)^{i-1}$. Multiplying the proportions of different types of nodes with n_i, we get the individual number of them as provided in Table 2. □

Let us now discuss the effect of adversarial interference. We try to estimate how the network gets disturbed when nodes are captured by the opponent. Since the nodes are deployed in hostile regions, they are likely to be captured frequently. When a node gets captured, all the keys contained in it are also compromised. As a result, the set of links which uses keys from the captured nodes are *destroyed* completely. Moreover, the node which contains any compromised key cannot use it for any further communication, though the other keys stored at them are still secret. We refer to these nodes as (partially) *affected* nodes. We notice that capture of each node reveals only p keys at a time, which is very less portion of the total key-pool. Now we analyse below what portion of the nodes and the links are affected when a single node is captured.

Theorem 5.05. *Let $\phi(i, l)$ be the number of affected nodes when an ith level node is compromised, l being the total number of nodes (and keys) present in the network. Then*

$$\phi(i, l) = \frac{p + 1}{p - 1} \left(p^{l-i+2} - 1 \right) - \frac{p^l}{(p + 1)^{i-3}} - p$$

Table 2. Proportion of different types of nodes

Type	Key-chain	Proportion	Number of Nodes
1	$(level\ 1,\ level\ i,\ \cdots,\ level\ i)$	$1/(p+1)^{i-2}$	$p^{i-1}(p+1)(p^2+p+1)$
2	$(level\ 2,\ level\ i,\ \cdots,\ level\ i)$	$p/(p+1)^{i-2}$	$p^i(p+1)(p^2+p+1)$
3	$(level\ 3,\ level\ i,\ \cdots,\ level\ i)$	$p/(p+1)^{i-3}$	$p^i(p+1)^2(p^2+p+1)$
4	$(level\ 4,\ level\ i,\ \cdots,level\ i)$	$p/(p+1)^{i-4}$	$p^i(p+1)^3(p^2+p+1)$
j	$(level\ j,\ level\ i,\ \cdots,\ level\ i)$	$p/(p+1)^{i-j}$	$p^i(p+1)^{j-1}(p^2+p+1)$
$i-1$	$(level\ i-1,\ level\ i,\ \cdots,\ level\ i)$	$p/(p+1)$	$p^i(p+1)^{i-2}(p^2+p+1)$

Proof : We note that all the *level i* nodes contain p *level i* keys and the remaining key may belong to any of the previous $(i-1)$ levels. Depending on this we divide the nodes into types. Therefore there are $(i-1)$ types of *level i* nodes.

Let n_{ij} denote the number of nodes affected when a *level i* node of Type j, (for $j = 1, 2, ...i - 1$) is compromised. A *level i* node of Type j contains exactly one *level j* key and p *level i* keys. A *level i* node is attached to $\frac{p+1}{p-1} \times \{p^{l+1-i} - 1\}$ nodes. Hence we have, $n_{i1} = \{1 \times (p^l - 1) + p \times \frac{p+1}{p-1}(p^{l+1-i} - 1)\} - p$. Here p is subtracted as a set of $p + 1$ keys is contained in exactly one node (i.e., the compromised node here), which we count once for every key repeating it p extra times. Similarly, we have

$$n_{ij} = \{1 \times (p^{l+1-j} - 1) + p \times \frac{p+1}{p-1}(p^{l+1-i} - 1)\} - p, \quad \forall j \in 1, 2, \cdots, i-1.$$

Simplified expressions for n_{ij} are listed in Table 3.

The proportions of the different types of nodes given in Table. 2. Thus we have $\phi(i, l) = \frac{n_{i1} \times 1}{(p+1)^{i-2}} + \frac{n_{i2} \times p}{(p+1)^{i-2}} + \cdots + \frac{n_{ij} \times p}{(p+1)^{i-j}} + \cdots \frac{n_{i(i-1)} \times p}{(p+1)}$. Substituting the values for n_{ij}, from Table 3, we get the desired expression.   □

Remark 1. If we wish to know the effect of the adversarial attack on the network, $\phi(i, l)$ will provide the average number of the affected nodes (and hence their proportion) when an ith level node is compromised, i.e., $\phi(i, l)$ gives an estimate for resilience involving affected nodes. Resilience involving destroyed links is discussed in the following section.

Table 3. Values of n_{ij}

n_{i1}	$\frac{p+1}{p-1}(p^l - 1) + \frac{p+1}{p-1}(p^{l-i+2} - p) - p$
n_{i2}	$\frac{p+1}{p-1}(p^{l-1} - 1) + \frac{p+1}{p-1}(p^{l-i+2} - p) - p$
n_{i3}	$\frac{p+1}{p-1}(p^{l-2} - 1) + \frac{p+1}{p-1}(p^{l-i+2} - p) - p$
n_{i4}	$\frac{p+1}{p-1}(p^{l-3} - 1) + \frac{p+1}{p-1}(p^{l-i+2} - p) - p$
n_{ij}	$\frac{p+1}{p-1}(p^{l-j+1} - 1) + \frac{p+1}{p-1}(p^{l-i+2} - p) - p$
$n_{i(i-1)}$	$\frac{p+1}{p-1}(p^{l-i+2} - 1) + \frac{p+1}{p-1}(p^{l-i+2} - p) - p$

6   Performance

We determine resilience mathematically by the following formula put forward by Lee-Stinson [8]:

$$fail(s) \; = \; 1 \; - \; \prod_{i=1}^{l}\left(1 \; - \; \frac{N_i - 2}{N - 2}\right)^{s_i}$$

where $fail(s)$ denotes the portion of total link failure when s nodes are compromised, N_i denotes the number of nodes to which a *level i* key is assigned to, s_i is the number of compromised nodes in the ith *level*. Therefore, $\sum_{i=1}^{l} s_i = s$.

Unlike other key pre-distribution schemes based on combinatorial designs, our scheme is heterogeneous, i.e., the nodes are not distributed uniformly. Therefore it is not possible to present the exact value of $fail(s)$. Instead we provide the average value of $fail(s)$.

First, we would like to deduce how the network accomplishes its function when the order of the underlying projective plane is altered (let us consider a network composed of two levels so that for $p = 2$, $T_{nodes} = 49$, for $p = 3$, $T_{nodes} = 169$, for $p = 5$, $T_{nodes} = 961$ and for $p = 7$, $T_{nodes} = 3249$, where T_{nodes} represents total number of nodes occurring in the network). If we wish to estimate their comparative performances by retaining the number of compromised nodes, it would culminate into inadequate consequences. This is due to the evidential information that if we regard only 10 nodes to be compromised then a major portion of the network is interfered for $p = 2$. In contrast to this, for $p = 7$ a very negligible portion of the network is disrupted from normal functioning. To keep up the uniformity on the compromised nodes, instead of a fixed number, we assume that the number of compromised nodes is a certain percentage of the total number of nodes present in the network.

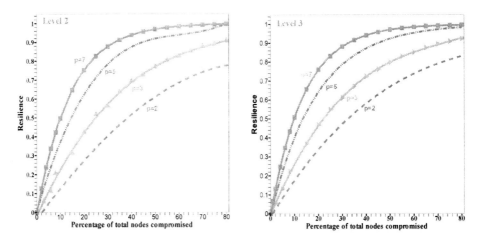

Fig. 4. Networks consisting two levels   **Fig. 5.** Networks consisting three levels

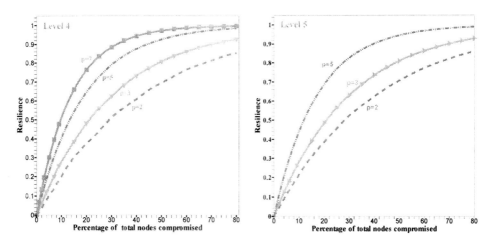

Fig. 6. Networks consisting four levels   **Fig. 7.** Networks consisting five levels

The supportive figures Fig.4 - Fig.7 relate to the comparison between the performance of our scheme making use of different orders of projective planes when the maximum level in the network is predetermined. The four figures Fig.4, Fig.5, Fig.6 and Fig.7 describe and justify the comparison graphically for the networks composed of two, three, four and five levels respectively. In these figures, the percentage of total nodes in the network, which is compromised is plotted against the portion of the destroyed links. From these figures it can be observed that for any network, the resilience gets adversely affected with increasing order of the projective planes, when number of levels is kept unaltered.

Next we shall concentrate on comparing the performance of our scheme with other existing schemes.

In Table 4, we provide the comparison based on the performance of our scheme with Lee-Stinson linear scheme [8], Chakrabarti et al. scheme [3], Ruj-Roy scheme [11] and Lee-Stinson quadratic scheme [10], where T_{nodes} denotes total number of nodes in the network and T_{keys} denotes total number of keys present in each node. To keep up T_{nodes} in our scheme comparable with other schemes, we consider $p = 2$, $level = 4$. The details have been mentioned in the table.

Table 4. Comparison with some of the existing schemes

	[8]	[3]	[11]	[10]	Ours
T_{nodes}	1849	2550	2415	2197	1813
T_{keys}	30	≤ 28	136	30	3
$fail(10)$	0.201070	0.213388	0.0724	0.297077	0.010087

The comparison between the schemes has been represented graphically through figures Fig. 8 and Fig. 9. In Fig. 8 we demonstrate the comparison of our scheme with Lee-Stinson linear scheme [8], Chakrabarti et al. scheme [3], Ruj-Roy scheme [11] and Lee-Stinson quadratic scheme [10] for a handful (i.e., 1 - 10)

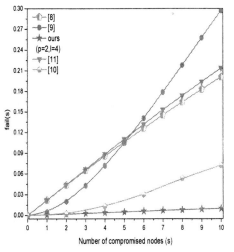

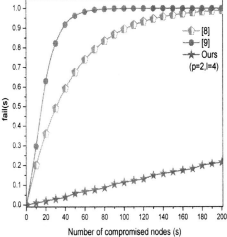

Fig. 8. Comparison of resilience with some of the existing schemes for small number of compromised nodes

Fig. 9. Comparison of resilience with some of the existing schemes for large number of compromised nodes

number of compromised nodes. On the other hand in Fig. 9 we provide the comparison with Lee-Stinson linear scheme [8] and Lee-Stinson quadratic scheme [10] for a large number (i.e., 10 - 200) of compromised nodes. It is very evident from the figures that the networks incorporated on other schemes collapses in no time when compared to ours.

7   Discussion and Conclusion

We have proposed a key pre-distribution scheme by applying combinatorial design. The memory prerequisite in each sensor node is appreciably reduced. Further, we perceive that unlike most of the deterministic and combinatorial design based schemes, the proposed scheme sustains scalability, i.e., a number of nodes could be inserted without interfering the present network set-up. The discussed scheme affords reasonable connectivity: any two nodes are connected either directly or via a key-path. We note that it is advantageous to make use of projective planes of small order as they acquire better resilience. However, comparing with other existing schemes, we come across that our scheme offers enhanced resilience for higher order projective planes. Intuitively, we can also declare that the connectivity gets better with increasing order of the projective plane employed as basic building block to design the whole network.

In the present scheme the lower level nodes are more sensitive compared to the higher level nodes. As a future work, we would like to propose a randomized scheme by merging the more sensitive nodes with less sensitive nodes to achieve uniform sensitivity among the nodes in the network, to continue functioning interactively.

References

1. Çamtepe, S.A., Yener, B.: Combinatorial Design of Key Distribution Mechanisms for Wireless Sensor Networks. In: Samarati, P., Ryan, P.Y.A., Gollmann, D., Molva, R. (eds.) ESORICS 2004. LNCS, vol. 3193, pp. 293–308. Springer, Heidelberg (2004)
2. Camptepe, S.A., Yener, B.: Combinatorial Design of Key Distribution Mechanisms for Wireless Sensor Networks. ACM Trans. Netw. 5(2), 346–358 (2007)
3. Chakrabarti, D., Maitra, S., Roy, B.: A Key Pre-distribution Scheme for Wireless Sensor Networks: Merging Blocks in Combinatorial Design. In: Zhou, J., López, J., Deng, R.H., Bao, F. (eds.) ISC 2005. LNCS, vol. 3650, pp. 89–103. Springer, Heidelberg (2005)
4. Chakrabarti, D., Seberry, J.: Combinatorial Structures for Design of Wireless Sensor Networks. In: Zhou, J., Yung, M., Bao, F. (eds.) ACNS 2006. LNCS, vol. 3989, pp. 365–374. Springer, Heidelberg (2006)
5. Chan, H., Perrig, A., Song, D.X.: Random Key Predistribution Schemes for Sensor Network. In: IEEE Symposium on Security and Privacy, pp. 197–213 (2003)
6. Dong, J., Pei, D., Wang, X.: A Key Predistribution Scheme Based on 3-Designs. In: Pei, D., Yung, M., Lin, D., Wu, C. (eds.) Inscrypt 2007. LNCS, vol. 4990, pp. 81–92. Springer, Heidelberg (2008)

7. Eschenauer, L., Gligor, V.D.: A Key-management Scheme for Distributed Sensor Networks. In: ACM CCS, pp. 41–47. ACM (2002)
8. Lee, J., Stinson, D.R.: A Combinatorial Approach to Key Predistribution for Distributed Sensor Networks. In: IEEE Wireless Communications and Networking Conference, pp. 1200–1205 (2005)
9. Lee, J., Stinson, D.R.: Common Intersection Designs. International Journal of Combinatorial Designs 14, 251–269 (2006)
10. Lee, J., Stinson, D.R.: On The Construction of Practical Key Predistribution Schemes for Distributed Sensor Networks Using Combinatorial Designs. ACM Trans. Inf. Syst. Secur. 11(2) (2008)
11. Ruj, S., Roy, B.: Key Predistribution Using Partially Balanced Designs in Wireless Sensor Networks. In: Stojmenovic, I., Thulasiram, R.K., Yang, L.T., Jia, W., Guo, M., de Mello, R.F. (eds.) ISPA 2007. LNCS, vol. 4742, pp. 431–445. Springer, Heidelberg (2007)

Towards a Complete Multi-layered Framework for IEEE-802.11e Multi-hop Ad Hoc Networks[*]

Rachid El-Azouzi[1], Essaid Sabir[1],
Mohammed Raiss El Fenni[1,2], and Sujit Kumar Samanta[1]

[1] LIA/CERI, University of Avignon, Agroparc BP 1228, Avignon, France
[2] LIMIARF, University of Mohammed V-Agdal, B.P. 1014 RP, Rabat, Morocco
{rachid.elazouzi,essaid.sabir}@univ-avignon.fr,
mohammed.raiss@etd.univ-avignon.fr,
sujitsamanta12@yahoo.com

Abstract. Performance of IEEE 802.11 in multi-hop wireless networks depends on the characteristics of the protocol itself, and on those of the other layers. We are interested in this paper in modeling the IEEE 802.11e Enhanced Distributed Coordination Function. This paper investigates the intricate interactions among PHY, MAC and Network layers. For instance, we jointly incorporate the carrier sense threshold, the transmit power, the contention window size, the retransmissions retry limit, the multi rates, the routing protocols and the network topology. Then, we build a general cross-layered framework to represent multi-hop ad hoc networks with asymmetric topology and asymmetric traffic. We develop an analytical model that predicts the throughput of each connection as well as the stability of forwarding queues at intermediate nodes. To the best of our knowledge, our work is the first to consider general topology and asymmetric parameters setup in PHY/MAC/Network layers. Performance of such a system is also evaluated via simulation. We show that the performance measures of MAC layer are affected by the traffic intensity of flows to be forwarded. More precisely, attempt rate and collision probability are dependent on the traffic flows, topology and routing.

Keywords: Ad hoc network, Performance Evaluation, Cross-layer architecture, Fixed point, Coupled systems.

1 Introduction

In next-generation wireless networks, it is likely that the IEEE 802.11 wireless LAN (WLAN) will play an important role and affect the style of people's daily life. People want voice, audio, and broadband video services through WLAN connections. Unlike traditional best effort data applications, multimedia applications require quality of service (QoS) support such as guaranteed bandwidth and bounded delay/jitter. There was a lot of interest in modeling the behavior

---

[*] This work was partially sponsored by The Indo-French Center for the Promotion of Advanced Research under CEFIPRA Project #4000-IT-1.

D. Simplot-Ryl et al. (Eds.): ADHOCNETS 2011, LNICST 89, pp. 32–48, 2012.
© Institute for Computer Sciences, Social Informatics and Telecommunications Engineering 2012

of the IEEE 802.11 DCF (Distributed Coordination Function) and studying its performances in both the WLAN networks and the multi-hop context. Medium access control protocol has a large impact on the achievable network throughput and stability for wireless ad hoc networks. So far, the ad hoc mode of the IEEE 802.11 standard has been used as the MAC protocols for MANETs. This protocol is based on the CSMA/CA mechanism in DCF.

Related Works and Their Drawbacks. There have been a number of studies on the performance of IEEE 802.11 in ad hoc network. All these studies focus on MAC layer without taking into account the routing and the cooperation level of nodes in ad hoc networks, see e.g. [1, 2, 4, 8, 10–12]. A common point of those efforts was to extend Bianchi's model in saturated or unsaturated ad hoc network. Now, the problems of hidden terminals and the channel asymmetry become real issues. A non rare assumption is to consider implicitly symmetric traffic distribution or nodes randomly distributed on a plane following a Poisson point process. Hence, the collision probability and attempt rate are the same for all users. Yang et al. [12] propose an extension of Bianchi [3] model and characterize the channel activities from the perspective of an individual sender. They studied the impact of carrier sensing range and the transmit power on the sender throughput. The PHY/MAC impact was clearly considered. Basel et al. [1] were also interested in tuning the transmit power relatively to the carrier sense threshold. They provide a detailed comparison performance between the two-way and the four-way handshake. Medepalli et al. [8] propose an interesting framework model for analyzing throughput, delay and fairness characteristics of IEEE 802.11 DCF multi-hop networks. The applicability of the model in terms of network design is also presented.

Aims of the Paper. Our major aim is to build a complete framework to analyze multi-hop ad hoc networks under general and realistic considerations. We present a probabilistic but rigorous model incorporating jointly Network, MAC and PHY layers in a simple cross-layer architecture. This latter one has a potential synergy of information exchange among different layers, instead of the standard OSI non-communicating layers. Moreover, we consider the general case of topological asymmetric ad hoc networks in which the nodes have not the same channel perception and then the attempt rate may not always describe the real channel access. Moreover, this model is extended to the IEEE 802.11e which provides differentiated channel access to packets by allowing different rates and different back-off parameters. In order to handle QoS, several traffic classes are also supported. We also allow that each traffic may have different retry limits after which the packet is dropped. From analyzing the model, we find that the performance measures of MAC layer are affected by routing and the traffic intensity of flows to be forwarded. More precisely, the attempt rate and collision probability are now dependent on the traffic flows, topology and routing. Moreover, end-to-end throughput is independent of cooperation level when all forwarding queues are stable.

Paper Organization. We formulate the problem in Section 2. Then we derive the expression of end-to-end throughput and write a system that determines traffic intensities in the whole network in Section 3. We illustrate our results by some numerical examples in Section 4 and conclude the paper in Section 5. Due to the page limit, many details are omitted, we invite the reader to see our technical report [13].

2   Problem Formulation

2.1   Overview on IEEE 802.11 DCF/EDCF

The distributed coordination function (DCF) of the IEEE 802.11 is based on the CSMA/CA protocol in which a node starts by sensing the channel before attempting any packet. Then, if the channel is idle it waits for an interval of time, called the Distributed Inter-Frame Space (DIFS), before transmitting. But, if the channel is sensed busy the node defers its transmission and waits for an idle channel. In addition, to reduce collisions of simultaneous transmissions, the IEEE 802.11 employs a slotted binary exponential back-off where each packet in a given node has to wait for a random number of time slots, called the back-off time, before attempting the channel. The back-off time is uniformly chosen from the interval $[0, W - 1]$, where W is the contention window that mainly depends on the number of experienced collisions. The contention window W is dynamic and given by $W_i = 2^i W_0$, where i represents the stage number (usually, it is considered as the current retransmission attempt number) of the packet, and W_0 is the initial contention window. The back-off time is decremented by one slot each time when the channel is sensed idle, while it freezes if it is sensed busy. Finally, when the data is transmitted, the sender has to wait for an acknowledgement (ACK) that would arrive after an interval of time, called the Short Inter-Frame Space (SIFS). If the ACK is not received, the packet is considered lost and a retransmission has to be scheduled. When the number of retransmissions expires, the packet is definitively dropped. To consider multimedia applications, the IEEE 802.11e uses an enhanced mode of the DCF called the Enhanced DCF (EDCF) which provides differentiated channel access for different flow priorities. The main idea of EDCF is based on differentiating the back-off parameters of different flows. So, priorities can be distinguished due to different initial contention window, different back-off multiplier or different inter-frame space. An Arbitration IFS (AIFS) is used instead of DIFS. The AIFS can take at least a value of DIFS, then, a high priority flow needs to wait only for DIFS before transmitting to the channel. Whereas a low priority flow waits an AIFS greater than DIFS. In the next paragraph, we used a generalized model of the back-off mechanism.

2.2   Problem Modeling and Cross-Layer Architecture

The network layer of each node i handles two queues, see Figure 1. The forwarding queue F_i carries packets originated from some source nodes and destined to some given destinations. The second one is Q_i which carries own packets of node i itself. We assume that the two queues have an infinite storage capacity. Packets are served with a first in first served fashion. When F_i is not empty, the node chooses to send a packet from F_i with a probability f_i, and it chooses to send from Q_i with probability $1 - f_i$. When one of these queues is empty we choose to send from the non empty queue with probability 1. When node i decides to transmit from the queue Q_i, it sends a packet destined to node d, $d \neq i$, with probability $p_{i,d}$. This parameter characterizes somehow the QoS (Quality of Service) required by the initiated service from upper layers. We consider that each node has always packets to be sent from queue Q_i, whereas F_i maybe empty. Consequently, the network is considered saturated and mainly depends on the channel access mechanism. In ad hoc networks, each node behaves as a router. At each time, it has a packet to be sent to a given destination and starts by finding the next hop neighbor where to transmit the packet. Clearly, each node must carry routing information before sending the packet. Proactive routing protocols as the Optimized Link State Routing construct and maintain a routing table that carries routes to all nodes of the network. To do so, it has to send periodically some control packets. These kind of protocols correspond well with our model, especially since Q_i is non-empty. Here, nodes form a static network where routes between any source s and destination d are invariant. To consider routing in our model, we denote by $R_{s,d}$ the set of nodes between a source s and destination d (s and d not included). Each node in our model can handle many connections on different paths. The traffic flow leaving a node i is determined by the channel allocation using IEEE 802.11 EDCF. However, differentiating the flow leaving F_i and the flow leaving Q_i, allows us to determine the load and the intensity of traffic crossing F_i. We denote here the probability that the forwarding queue F_i is non-empty by π_i. Similarly, we denote the probability that a packet of the path (s, d) is chosen in the beginning of a transmission cycle[1] by $\pi_{i,s,d}$. This quantity is exactly the fraction of traffic related to the path (s, d) crossing F_i, thus $\pi_i = \sum_{s,d:i \neq s} \pi_{i,s,d}$. We analyze in the following each layer separately and show how coupled they are and derive the metrics of interest.

Fig. 1. The interaction among Network, MAC and PHY layers is now clear. Attempting the channel begins by choosing the queue from which a packet must be selected. And then, this packet is moved from the corresponding queue at the network layer to the MAC layer where it will be transmitted according to the IEEE 802.11 DCF protocol. This manner, when a packet is in the MAC layer, it is attempted until it is removed from the node.

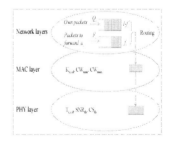

---

[1] A cycle is defined as the number of slots needed to transmit a single packet until its success or drop. It is formed by the four channel events seen by a sender. For instance : idle slots, busy slots, transmissions with collisions and/or a success.

Accumulative Interference and Virtual Node: During a communication between a sender node i and a receiver node j in a given path from s to d (where the source node of a connection is s and the destination node is d), the node i transmits to j with a power $T_{i,s,d}$. The received power on j can be related to the transmitted one by the propagation relation $T_{i,s,d} \cdot h_{i,j}$, where $h_{i,j}$ is the channel gain experienced by j on the link (i, j). In order to decode the received signal correctly, $T_{i,s,d} \cdot h_{i,j}$ should exceeds the receiver sensitivity denoted by RX_{th}, i.e., $T_{i,s,d} \cdot h_{i,j} \geq RX_{th}$. Under symmetry assumption and no accumulative effect of concurrent transmissions, the carrier sense range forms a perfect circle with radius r_1. Even when considering accumulative interference, the carrier sense can be reasonably approached by a circle with radius $r_2 \geq r_1$.

Definition 1. The group $\mathcal{Z}$, composed of nodes that cannot be heard individually by a sender i but their accumulative signal may jam the signal of interest, is called a **virtual node**. This way, the virtual node $\mathcal{Z}$ is equivalent to a **fictive node** being in the carrier sense range of sender i.

We can then formulate the carrier sense set of a node i by the following expression

$$CS_i = \left\{ \mathcal{Z} : \forall s, d, k' \in \mathcal{Z}, \begin{array}{c} \sum_{k \in \mathcal{Z}} T_{k,s,d} \cdot h_{k,i} \geq CS_{th} \\ \sum_{k \in \mathcal{Z} \backslash k'} T_{k,s,d} \cdot h_{k,i} < CS_{th} \end{array} \right\}, \tag{1}$$

where CS_{th} is the carrier sense threshold. One can see CS_i as the set of virtual nodes that may be heard by sender i when it is sensing the channel in order to transmit on the path $R_{s,d}$. In other words, CS_i is the set of all real nodes (if they are neighbors of i) and virtual nodes (due to accumulative interferences) that may interfere with node i. Now, we define $H_{i,s,d}$ as the set of nodes that may sense the channel busy when node i is transmitting on the path (s, d). Then

$$H_{i,s,d} = \{k : T_{i,s,d} \cdot h_{i,k} \geq CS_{th}, \forall s, d\}. \tag{2}$$

For sake of clarity, we are restricted in our formulation to the case of single transmission power. However, our model can be straightforward used for studying power control from nodes individual point of views. An interesting feature is that when the transmission power level is the same for all nodes and accumulative interferences are neglected, we have $CS_i = H_{i,s,d}$. *Later result says that under considered assumptions, the set of nodes node i can hear is exactly the set of nodes that can hear node i when transmitting.* The receiver $j_{i,s,d}$ can correctly decode the signal from sender node i if the Signal to Interference Ratio (SIR) exceeds a certain threshold SIR_{th}. Let the thermal noise variance, experienced on the path (s,d), be denoted by $N_{i,s,d}$, then

$$SIR_{j_{i,s,d}} = \frac{T_{i,s,d} \cdot h_{i,j}}{\sum_{k \neq i} T_{k,s',d'} \cdot h_{k,j} + N_{i,s,d}} \geq SIR_{th}, \ \forall s, d, s', d'. \tag{3}$$

We define now the interference set of a receiver $j_{i,s,d}$ in a path (s,d), denoted by $\mathcal{T}_{j_{i,s,d}}$, as the collection of its virtual nodes, i.e., all combination of nodes whose the accumulative signal may cause collisions at $j_{i,s,d}$. For instance, the virtual node $\mathcal{Z}$ is in the interference set of node $j_{i,s,d}$ iff the received signal from node i is completely jammed when nodes in $\mathcal{Z}$ are transmitting all together. The interference set of node j is then written as

$$
\mathcal{T}_{j_{i,s,d}} = \left\{ \mathcal{Z} : \begin{array}{l} \dfrac{T_{i,s,d}\cdot h_{i,j}}{\sum\limits_{z \in \mathcal{Z}} T_{z,s',d'}\cdot h_{z,j}+N_{i,s,d}} < SIR_{th}, \\[4mm] \dfrac{T_{i,s,d}\cdot h_{i,j}}{\sum\limits_{z \in \mathcal{Z}\setminus z'} T_{z,s',d'}\cdot h_{z,j}+N_{i,s,d}} \geq SIR_{th}, \\[4mm] \forall z', s', d', z' \neq i, s' \neq s, \ d' \neq d. \end{array} \right\}
\tag{4}
$$

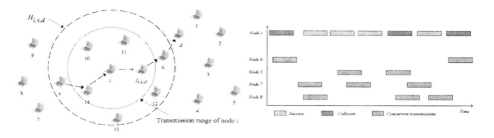

Fig. 2. Those plots show the transmission range of node i and the set of real nodes $H_{i,s,d}$ that can hear i when transmitting to node $j_{i,s,d}$. The carrier sense CS_i of node i and the interference set $\mathcal{T}_{j_{i,s,d}}$ are not plotted because they depend on transmit powers of all nodes in the network as well as the topology and scale of the network. For instance $H_{i,s,d} = \{\{s\}, \{j_{i,s,d}\}, \{6\}, \{10\}, \{11\}, \{12\}, \{13\}, \{14\}, \{7,8,9\}, \{d,4\}, \{1,5,7,8\}, \cdots\}$

Figure 2 shows explicitly two different areas that need to be considered when a couple of nodes are communicating. Here, we distinguish (i) the transmission area where two nodes can send and receive packets mutually, (ii) the set of nodes that may hear ongoing transmissions of node i, and (iii) implicitly the carrier sense area where two nodes may hear each other but cannot decode the transmitted data. In Figure 2, we have situated the communication of i and j on the path (s,d), so we can integrate the impact of the routing in the model. Figure 2 illustrates the effect of accumulative interference on transmission cycles of node i. For illustrative purpose, we consider the following virtual nodes : $\{6\}$ and $\{5,7,8\}$. Node 6 is a neighbor of receiver j which causes collision whenever they both, i.e., nodes i and 6, are transmitting simultaneously. Whereas a failure may only occur when nodes of virtual node $\{5,7,8\}$ are all transmitting altogether with sender i.

Each node uses the IEEE 802.11 DCF to access the channel and each one can use different back-off parameters. Let $K_{i,s,d}$ be the maximum number of transmissions allowed by a node i per packet on the path (s, d). Then after $K_{i,s,d}$ number of transmissions the packet is dropped. Also let p_i be the back-off multiplier of a given node i. The maximum stage number of node i is obtained from $W_{m,i} = p_i^{m_i} W_{0,i}$, where $W_{m,i}$ and $W_{0,i}$ are, respectively, the maximum and initial contention window for node i. If $K_{i,s,d} < m_i$ then m_i takes the value of $K_{i,s,d}$, otherwise $m_i = log_{p_i} \left(\frac{W_{m,i}}{W_{0,i}} \right)$. Using a contention window $W_{k,i}$ for stage k of node i, the average back-off time for this stage is $b_{k,i}$. Remark that back-off parameters of different nodes may be different. Then, the system of nodes are nonhomogeneous as defined by [9].

We consider the modeling problem of the IEEE 802.11 using the perspective of a sender which consists on the channel activity sensed by a sender, or on the state (success or collision) of its transmitted packet. This will facilitate the problem in the ad hoc environment where nodes have an asymmetric vision of the channel. We start by defining the notion of virtual time slot and channel activity, then we write the expression of the attempt probability for the asymmetric topology. Consider that time is slotted with a physical slot duration τ. Nodes transmit in the beginning of each slot and the transmission duration depends on the kind of the transmitted packet. A data packet has a fixed length and takes *Payload* (integer) slots to be transmitted (it includes the header transmission time). While an acknowledgment packet spends ACK slots. In our model we consider the two-way handshaking scheme, but it is easily extended to the four-way handshaking scheme. On one hand, a sender node before transmitting would see the channel either **busy** or **idle**. On the other hand, its transmitted packet may encounter a **success** or a **collision**. These four states define all the possibilities that a sender may observe. Therefore, the average time spent in a given state (seen by this sender) will be referred as the **virtual slot** of this sender. A remarkable feature here is that this virtual time would depend on the receiver, i.e., on the path where the packet is transmitted. In fact, the success or the collision of the transmitted packet is itself function of the actual receiver interferences state. For that, we denote by $\Delta_{i,s,d}$ the virtual slot seen by node i on the path (s, d) that we will derive later on. Considering any asymmetric topology, we will always note the metrics functions of the path chosen for transmission. We recall that when we mention the node $j_{i,s,d}$, it will be clear that this is the receiver of node i on the path (s, d).

At steady state and such as [3], we use the key assumption which states that at each transmission attempts, and regardless of the number of retransmissions suffered, each packet collides with constant and independent probability. However, collisions may depend only on the receiver channel state. For that we denote by $\gamma_{i,s,d}$ the probability that a transmission of a packet of relay i on the path (s, d) fails due to either a corruption of the data or of its acknowledgment. Thus, $(1 - \gamma_{i,s,d})$ is the probability of success in the path (s, d). Henceforth, the attempt probability seen by a sender also depends on the receiver, and the well known formula of [3] can be used in the ad hoc network as confirmed in [12]. However, in the asymmetric network the attempt probability $(P_{i,s,d})$ (in a virtual slot) for a node i will be different for each path (s, d) and can be written as in [6]:

$$P_{i,s,d} = \frac{1 + \gamma_{i,s,d} + \gamma_{i,s,d}^2 + \cdots + \gamma_{i,s,d}^{K_{i,s,d}-1}}{b_{0,i} + \gamma_{i,s,d}b_{1,i} + \gamma_{i,s,d}^2 b_{2,i} + \cdots + \gamma_{i,s,d}^{K_{i,s,d}-1}b_{K_{i,s,d}-1,i}} \tag{5}$$

where $b_{k,i} = (p_i^k W_{0,i} - 1)/2$. In the average, a node i will attempt the channel (for any path (s,d)) with a probability P_i which mainly depends on the traffic and the routing table (here, it is maintained by OLSR protocol). Then

$$P_i = \sum_{s,d:i \in R_{s,d}} \pi_{i,s,d} f_i P_{i,s,d} + \sum_d (1 - \pi_i f_i) p_{i,d} P_{i,i,d}. \tag{6}$$

Similarly, the average virtual slot seen by node i is written

$$\Delta_i = \sum_{s,d:i \in R_{s,d}} \pi_{i,s,d} f_i \Delta_{i,s,d} + \sum_d (1 - \pi_i f_i) p_{i,d} \Delta_{i,i,d}. \tag{7}$$

Remark 1. The attempt probability (or attempt rate) must be differentiated from the transmission probability. This refers to the probability that a node transmits at any slot. Therefore, the transmission probability, if found, can characterize the channel allocation per node. In WLAN, it is sufficient to analyze the back-off rate to determine the channel allocation rate.

Note that $1 - \pi_i f_i$ is the probability to find a packet from Q_i in the MAC layer. It seems important to note that the attempt probability represents the back-off expiration rate. It is the transmission probability in an idle slot (only when the channel is sensed idle). For that, it is convenient to work with MAC protocols that are defined by only an attempt probability, this kind of definition may englobe both slotted Aloha and CSMA type protocols including IEEE 802.11. The problem in ad hoc is that nodes have not the same channel vision (or different back-off parameters) and then the attempt probability may not always describe the real channel access. In [9], the problem of short term unfairness was studied in the context of a WLAN.

Collision Probability and Virtual Slot Expressions. The collision probability of a packet occurs when either the data or the acknowledgment experiences a collision. If we note by $\gamma_{i,s,d}^D$ and $\gamma_{j_{i,s,d},s,d}^A$, respectively, the collision probability of a data packet and its acknowledgement, then we have

$$\gamma_{i,s,d} = 1 - \left(1 - \gamma_{i,s,d}^D\right)\left(1 - \gamma_{j_{i,s,d},s,d}^A\right), \tag{8}$$

The attempt probability of a virtual node $\mathcal{Z}$ is defined by $P_{\mathcal{Z}} = \prod_{z \in \mathcal{Z}} P_z$. Therefore, the virtual slot of a virtual node $\Delta_{\mathcal{Z}}$ can be reasonably estimated using the minimum virtual slot among all nodes in $\mathcal{Z}$, i.e., $\Delta_{\mathcal{Z}} = \min_{j \in \mathcal{Z}} \Delta_j$. Thus the probability that transmitted data collides with other concurrent transmissions can be written as

$$\gamma_{i,s,d}^D = 1 - \prod_{k \in H_{i,s,d} \cap \mathcal{T}_{j_{i,s,d}}} (1 - P_k) \left(1 - \sum_{\mathcal{Z} \in \mathcal{T}_{j_{i,s,d}} \setminus H_{i,s,d}} P_{\mathcal{Z}}^{\frac{Payload}{\Delta_{\mathcal{Z}}}}\right). \tag{9}$$

Indeed, nodes in area $H_{i,s,d} \cap \mathcal{T}_{j_{i,s,d}}$ must be silent at the beginning of node i transmission. While nodes in $\mathcal{T}_{j_{i,s,d}} \setminus H_{i,s,d}$ are hidden to i (they constitute the virtual nodes of i) and needs to be silent during all the data transmission time which is a vulnerable time. The $\frac{Payload}{\Delta_j}$ is the normalized vulnerable time. After the beginning of data transmission, nodes in $H_{i,s,d}$ will defer their transmission to $EIFS$ (Extended Inter-Frame Space) duration, which would insure the good reception of the acknowledgment. In practice, acknowledgement are small packets and less vulnerable to collision, for that it is plausible to consider $\gamma^A_{j_{i,s,d},s,d} \simeq 0$. Then, we can write $\gamma_{i,s,d} = \gamma^D_{i,s,d}$.

Considering the previously defined four states and from node i view, the network stays in a single state a duration equal to $\Delta_{i,s,d}$. It's given by

$$\Delta_{i,s,d} = P^{succ}_{i,s,d}.T_{succ} + P^{col}_{i,s,d}.T_{col} + P^{idle}_i.T_{idle} + P^{busy}_i.T_{busy}, \qquad (10)$$

where $T_{succ} = Payload+ACK+SIFS+DIFS, T_{col} = Payload+ACK+DIFS,$ $T_{idle} = \tau, T_{busy} = Payload+DIFS, P^{succ}_{i,s,d} = P_{i,s,d}(1-\gamma_{i,s,d}), P^{col}_{i,s,d} = P_{i,s,d}\gamma_{i,s,d},$ $P^{idle}_i = \prod_{\mathcal{Z} \in CS_i \cup \{i\}}(1 - P_{\mathcal{Z}})$, and $P^{busy}_i = (1 - P_i)\sum_{\mathcal{Z} \in CS_i} P_{\mathcal{Z}}.$

Finally, let us denote the equations (5), (6), (8) and (10) by *system I*. Normally, it is sufficient to solve the *system I* to derive the fixed points of each node. However, by introducing the traffic metric in equations (6) and (7), these equations cannot be solved without knowing the $\pi_{i,s,d}$ which is defined as the traffic intensity for each path (s, d) crossing node i. Therefore, in Section 3, we proceed in writing the rate balance equations at each node, from which $\pi_{i,s,d}$ can be derived function of P_j and $\gamma_{j,s,d}$, for all j. These rate balance equations that give the traffic intensities. The problem resides in the complexity of the systems and in the computational issue.

3   End-to-End Throughput and Traffic Intensity System

We are interested in this section to derive the end-to-end throughput per connection, function of different layer parameters, including the IEEE 802.11 parameters. It is clear that the average performance of the system is hardly related to the interaction PHY/MAC/NETWORK. We focus now on the traffic crossing the forwarding queues, which may be an issue on the buffers stability. We say that a queue F_i is stable if the departure rate of packets from F_i is equal to the arrival rate into it. This is a simple definition of stability that can be written with a *rate balance equation*. We are going to derive this equation for each node i and each connection (s, d). The system of these equations, for all i and (s, d), will form the traffic intensities system, it will be referred as *system II*. In sum, we are writing a system that determines $\pi_{i,s,d}$ for all i and (s, d). For that, we first derive the average length of a transmission cycle per packet C_i at node i, see [13] for detailed computation. Then we write the departure rate from F_i as well as the arrival rate into it.

Departure Rate: The departure rate from F_i is the probability that a packet is removed from node i (forwarding queue) by either a successful transmission or a drop after successive $K_{i,s,d}$ failures. The departure rate concerning only the packets sent on the path $R_{s,d}$ is denoted by $d_{i,s,d}$. Formally, for any node i, s and d such that $p_{s,d} > 0$ and $i \in R_{s,d}$, the long term departure rate of packets from node i on the route from s to d is given by the following theorem:

Theorem 1. The long term departure rate from node i related to path $R_{s,d}$ is given by

$$d_{i,s,d} = \frac{f_i \pi_{i,s,d}}{C_i}. \tag{11}$$

Proof. The reader is referred to [13] for a detailed proof.

Hence, it is easy to derive the total departure rate d_i on all paths:

$$d_i = \sum_{s',d':i \in R_{s',d'}} d_{i,s',d'} = \frac{\pi_i f_i}{C_i}.$$

Arrival Rate and End-to-End Throughput: The probability that a packet arrives to the queue F_i of the node i is also called the arrival rate, we denote it by a_i. When this rate concerns only packets sent on the path $R_{s,d}$, we denote it by $a_{i,s,d}$. Formally, for any nodes i, s and d such that $p_{s,d} > 0$ and $i \in R_{s,d}$, the long term arrival rate of packets into F_i for $R_{s,d}$ is provided by the following

Theorem 2. The long term arrival rate into node i forwarding queue, related to path $R_{s,d}$, is given by

$$a_{i,s,d} = (1 - \pi_s f_s) \cdot \frac{p_{s,d}}{C_s} \cdot \prod_{k \in R_{s,i} \cup s} \left(1 - \gamma_{k,s,d}^{K_{k,s,d}}\right). \tag{12}$$

Proof. The reader is referred to [13] for a detailed proof.

End-to-End Throughput: The global arrival rate at F_i is $a_i = \sum_{s,d:i \in R_{s,d}} a_{i,s,d}$. Remark that when the node i is the final destination of a path $R_{s,d}$, then $a_{d,s,d}$ represents the end-to-end average throughput of a connection from s to d. Practically, $a_{d,s,d}$ is the number of delivered (to destination) packet per slot. Let ρ be the bit rate in bits/s of the wireless network. Therefore, the throughput in bits/s can be written as follows:

$$thp_{s,d} = a_{d,s,d} \cdot Payload \cdot \rho. \tag{13}$$

Rate Balance Equations/Traffic Intensity System: Finally, in the steady state if all the queues in the network are stable, then for each i, s and d such that $i \in R_{s,d}$ we get $d_{i,s,d} = a_{i,s,d}$, which is the rate balance equation on the path $R_{s,d}$. For all i, s and d we get the traffic intensity system: *system II*. And when we sum the both sides of this last system, we get the global rate balance equation: $d_i = a_i$.

Let $y_i = 1 - \pi_i f_i$ and $z_{i,s,d} = \pi_{i,s,d} f_i$. Thus $y_i = 1 - \sum_{s,d:i \in R_{s,d}} z_{i,s,d}$. Then, the rate balance equation can be written in the following form:

$$\sum_{d:i \in R_{s,d}} z_{i,s,d} = \frac{y_s(\sum_{s',d'} z_{i,s',d'} \hat{C}_{i,s',d'} + \sum_{d''} y_i p_{i,d''} \hat{C}_{i,i,d''}) w_{s,i}}{(\sum_{s',d'} z_{s,s',d'} \hat{C}_{s,s',d'} + \sum_{d''} y_s p_{s,d''} \hat{C}_{s,s,d''})}, \qquad (14)$$

where $w_{s,i} = \sum_{d:i \in R_{s,d}} p_{s,d} \prod_{k \in R_{s,i} \cup s} \left(1 - \gamma_{k,s,d}^{K_{k,s,d}}\right)$.

An interesting interpretation and application of equation (14) are the following : (i) $z_{i,s,d}$ and y_i (can be considered as the stability region of node i) are independent of the choice of f_i. (ii) For some values of f_i the forwarding queue of node i will be stable. Concerning P_i, we notice that it can be written as $P_i = \sum_{s,d:i \in R_{s,d}} z_{i,s,d} P_{i,s,d} + \sum_d y_i p_{i,d} P_{i,i,d}$. Then it depends on $z_{i,s,d}$ and y_i, but it is not affected by f_i. A similar deduction is also observed for the energy consumed when sensing the channel or transmitting data. It turns out to be independent of the choice of cooperation level f_i. Hence, the node can fine-tunes f_i to improve the expected delay without affecting the throughput or the energy consumption. The reader is referred to our technical report [13] for detailed comments and derivation of the average energy. We have also developed an algorithm to jointly solve *System I* and *System II*, see algorithm 1 in our detailed technical report [13].

4   Simulation and Numerical Investigations

We turn in this section to study a typical example of multi-hop ad hoc networks. We consider a simple network formed by 9 nodes, identified using an integer from 1 to 9 as shown in Fig. 3. We establish 9 flows (or connections) labeled by a letter from a to i. Each node is located by its plane Cartesian coordinates expressed in meters. Except contraindication, the main parameters are fixed as follows : $CW_{min} = 32$, $CW_{max} = 1024$, $K_{i,s,d} \equiv K = 5$, $f_i \equiv f = 0.9$ (to insure operating in the stability region of all forwarding queues), $T_{i,s,d} \equiv T = 0.1W$ ($\forall i, s, d$), $CS_{th} = 0$ dBm, $RX_{th} = 0$ dBm, $SIR_{th} = 10$ dB (target SIR), $\rho = 2$ Mbps (bit rate), $\tau = 20\mu s$ (physical slot duration), $DISF = 3\tau$ and $SIFS = \tau$. For sake of illustration, we assume that the signal attenuation is only due to the path-loss phenomenon, i.e., a receiver j experiences a signal power of $c \cdot T_{i,s,d} \cdot d_{i,j}^{-\alpha}$, where $\alpha = 2$ (path-loss exponent) and $c = 6$ dBi (antenna gain).

Model Validation: We first perform extensive numerical and simulation examples to show the accuracy of our model and then study the impact of joint PHY/MAC/NETWORK parameters. For that aim, a discrete time simulator that implements the IEEE 802.11 DCF, integrating the weighted fair queueing over the two buffers previously discussed, is used to simulate the former network. Each simulation is run out during 10^6 physical slots, repeated at least 20 times and then averaged to smooth out the fluctuations caused by random numbers generator of the simulator (back-off counters). We checked the validity of the model by extensively considering different network scenarios (different flows and nodes parameters), several topologies (linear, circular and arbitrary topologies)

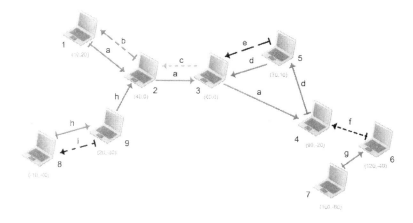

Fig. 3. The multi-hop ad hoc network used for simulations

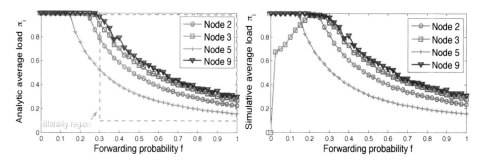

Fig. 4. Average forwarding queues load versus forwarding probability

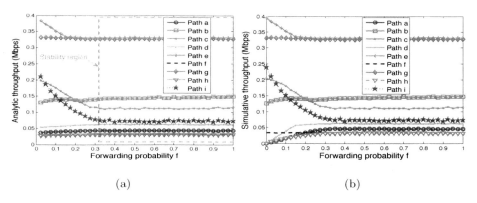

(a)   (b)

Fig. 5. Average e2e throughput versus the forwarding probability

and different network population size. We depict in Fig. 4(a) and Fig. 4(b) the
analytic and the simulated average load π_i of forwarding queues respectively.
Numerical plots show that analytic model match well with simulated results.
Accuracy is particularly high under the stability region which is the main applicability region of our model. We refer to the interval of forwarding probability
that insures a load strictly less than 1 for all queues, as the stability region of the
system. The main difference seen between individual loads is mainly due to the
topology asymmetry. Based on Fig. 5 (a) and (b), we note that our analytic finding, saying that *under the stability condition, the end-to-end throughput does not
depend on the choice of the WFQ weight* (i.e., the cooperation level or also the
forwarding probability f), is confirmed. Therefore, one can *judiciously fine-tune
the cooperation level value to decrease the delay while the average throughput remains almost constant.* This mechanism may play a crucial role in delay sensitive
traffic support over multi-hop networks. One can note that the system stability
region is strongly impacted by the nodes density. Indeed, in regions with relatively high or high nodes density, it is crucial that relay nodes should become
more cooperative to insure their stability. Otherwise, the waiting of packet in
forwarding queues may grow drastically and the network reliability becomes a
hard issue.

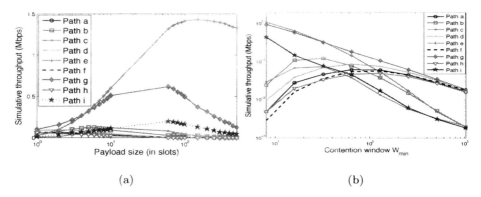

    (a)   (b)

Fig. 6. Average e2e throughput versus payload and contention window

Interested reader is referred to [13] for more details, extensive simulations and
complete performance evaluation in terms of the considered cross-layer architecture. For instance many results on how to set values of CW_{min}, Payload size and
other nodes intrinsic parameters were discussed. We first stipulate that an optimal payload size may not exist, see Fig. 6(a). Indeed, we note that some specific
payload size is providing good performances in term of average throughput over
some paths, but may hurt drastically the throughput on other links and then
the reachability becomes a real issue. *Setting the payload size to a fixed value
over the whole network is, in general, unfair and is not suitable for multi-hop
networks.* However fortunately, locally optimal payload size may exist. This way,
it depends strongly on the topology and the local node densities, i.e., the number

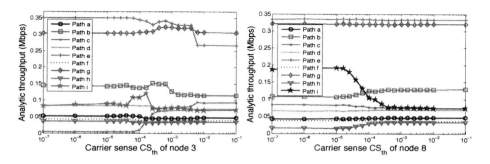

Fig. 7. End-to-end throughput versus carrier sense threshold (in Watt)

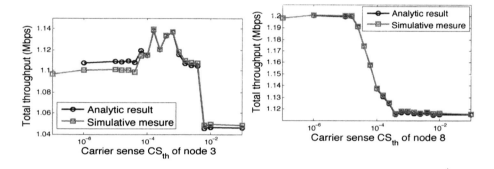

Fig. 8. Total throughput versus carrier sense threshold (in Watt)

of neighbors per m^2, their respective distances with respect to a node and how they are distributed in the network. In terms of the minimum contention window CW_{min}, see Fig. 6(b), the throughput has two different behaviors. Indeed, when the nodes density is low, the throughput is maximized for short backlog duration. Here, nodes tend to transmit more *aggressively*, having a relatively low collision probability due to low number of competitors. We also note that contention windows tends to increase as the nodes density becomes high. This statement is quite intuitive and due to the competitions that becomes colossal. In terms of queues load (equivalently delay), it is clear that when the contention windows increases it implies the increase of queues load, thus node may suffer from huge delay.

Per Path Power and Carrier Sense Control: We can reconsider here the Spanning tree-based algorithm proposed in [7] to compute the optimal transmit power for each path. *Each node sets its transmit power to a level that allows reaching the farthest neighbor*, i.e., the received power is at least equal to the receiver sensitivity. Consequently, this per path power control may improve the spatial reuse. In order to analyze the impact of carrier sense threshold on network performances, we vary CS_{th} for some node and fix it to the default value

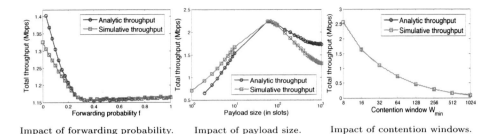

Impact of forwarding probability.   Impact of payload size.   Impact of contention windows.

Fig. 9. The system total throughput under different parameters variation

for remaining nodes, i.e., $CS_{th} = 0$ dBm. We plot in Fig. 7 the average through-put on all paths when tuning the carrier sense threshold of node 3 which is located in a relatively dense zone. The throughput of all connections continues to decrease (in particular connections crossing node 3 or its immediate neighbors) with CS_{th} except connections originated from node 3. Now we analyze the interplay of node 8 (in a low dense zone) carrier sense on network throughput. We note that the only negatively impacted connection is the connection i originated from node 9 (immediate neighbor of node 8). When carrier sense of node 8 is increasing, it becomes more nose-tolerant which implies high transmission aggressiveness. Which explains the throughput decrease of connection i. Thus connections crossing neighbors of node 9 take benefit from the low attempt rate of node 9 to improve their throughput, for instance connections a, b and h.

Aggregate Throughput: In terms of total capacity, see Fig. 8, and depending on the local nodes density, the carrier sense control may increase the network capacity. Indeed, when a node in a dense zone fine-tunes its carrier sense threshold, we note existence of a region where the total capacity is maximized. This region correspond to a CS_{th} interval where node benefits from relatively high throughput and other nodes don't suffer much. Whereas, it seems that tuning carrier sense by nodes in low dense parts of the network may cause a through-put decrease. To sum up, we can say that on one hand, a higher carrier sense threshold encourages more concurrent transmissions but at the cost of more collisions. On the other hand, a lower carrier sense threshold reduces the collision probability but it requires a larger spatial footprint and prevents simultaneous transmissions from occurring, which may result in limiting the system capacity. Analyzing Fig. 9 where the behavior of the total capacity is depicted as a function of nodes intrinsic parameters (f_i, $Payload_i$ and CW_{min}) we note the following : As expected from equation (14), the total capacity is insensitive for all cooperation level in the stability region. However, the cooperation is crucial to maintain the network connectivity. In terms of minimum contention window is seems that a as the CW_{min} increases as the total capacity decreases, and an optimal payload length that maximizes the total capacity may exist. More discussions are available in the full version [13].

5   Conclusion

In multi-hop ad hoc networking, a stack of protocols would interact with each other to accomplish a successful packet transfer. In this context, we have developed a cross-layered model built on the IEEE 802.11e EDCF standard. We studied the effect of forwarding on end-to-end performances. We have discovered that the modeling of the IEEE 802.11 in this context is not yet mature in the literature and to the best of our knowledge, there is no study done that considers jointly the PHY/MAC/NETWORK interaction in a non-uniform traffic and a general network topology. This has led us to build a general framework using the perspective of individual senders. The attempt and collision probabilities are now functions of the traffic intensity, on topology and on routing decision. The fixed point *system I* is indeed related to the traffic intensity *system II*. This paper opens many interesting directions to study in future such as power control and delay-based admission control with guaranteed throughput. Moreover, we will deal with the issue of cooperation between node in a game theoretical perspective.

References

1. Alawieh, B., Assi, C., Mouftah, H.T.: Investigation of Power-Aware IEEE 802. 11 Performance in Multi-hop Ad Hoc Networks. In: Zhang, H., Olariu, S., Cao, J., Johnson, D.B. (eds.) MSN 2007. LNCS, vol. 4864, pp. 409–420. Springer, Heidelberg (2007)
2. Barowski, Y., Biaz, S., Agrawal, P.: Towards the performance analysis of IEEE 802.11 in multi-hop ad-hoc networks. In: Proceedings of IEEE Wireless Communications and Networking Conference (WCNC), pp. 100–106 (March 2005)
3. Bianchi, G.: Performance analysis of the IEEE 802.11 distributed coordination function. IEEE Journal on Selected Areas in Communications 18(3), 535–547 (2000)
4. Camp, J., Aryafar, E., Knightly, E.: Coupled 802.11 Flows in Urban Channels: Model and Experimental Evaluation. In: INFOCOM, San Diego, CA (March 2010)
5. Kherani, A., El-Khoury, R., El-Azouzi, R., Altman, E.: Stability-throughput trade-off and routing in multi-hop wireless ad-hoc networks. Computer Networks 52(7), 1365–1389 (2008)
6. Kumar, A., Altman, E., Miorandi, D., Goyal, M.: New insights from a fixed point analysis of single cell IEEE 802.11WLANs. In: INFOCOM, pp. 1550–1561 (2005)
7. Li, N., Hou, J.C., Sha, L.: Design and analysis of a MST-based distributed topology control algorithm for wireless ad-hoc networks. IEEE Transactions on Wireless Communications 4(3), 1195–1207 (2005)
8. Medepalli, K., Tobagi, F.A.: Towards performance modeling of IEEE 802.11 based wireless networks: A unified framework and its applications. In: Proceedings of IEEE INFOCOM (2006)
9. Ramaiyan, V., Kumar, A., Altman, E.: Fixed point analysis of single cell IEEE 802.11e WLANs: uniqueness, multistability and throughput differentiation. SIGMETRICS Performance Evaluation Review 33(1), 109–120 (2005)

10. Sakurai, T., Vu, H.L.: Mac access delay of IEEE 802.11 DCF. IEEE Transactions on Wireless Communications 6(5), 1702–1710 (2007)
11. Vassis, D., Kormentzas, G.: Performance analysis of IEEE 802.11 ad hoc networks in the presence of exposed terminals. Ad Hoc Networks 6(3), 474–482 (2008)
12. Yang, Y., Hou, J.C., Kung, L.C.: Modeling the effect of transmit power and physical carrier sense in multi-hop wireless networks. In: Proceedings of IEEE INFOCOM (2007)
13. El-Azouzi, R., Sabir, E., Raiss-El-Fenni, M., Samanta, S.K.: A Complete Multi-layered Framework for IEEE 802.11e Multi-hop Ad hoc Networks, http://lia.univ-avignon.fr/fileadmin/documents/Users/Intranet/chercheurs/sabir/802eTechReport.pdf

Towards Realistic and Credible
Wireless Sensor Network Evaluation

Kamini Garg, Anna Förster, Daniele Puccinelli, and Silvia Giordano

Networking Lab
University of Applied Sciences of Southern Switzerland
{kamini.garg,anna.foerster,daniele.puccinelli,
silvia.giordano}@supsi.ch

Abstract. This position paper explores the problem of realistically evaluating wireless sensor network (WSN) applications, algorithms and protocols. It surveys the currently available techniques, such as simulators, testbeds and real world deployments and compares their properties and challenges. While we underline the significance of simulation tools, we also observe that the state of the art simulation models at all levels (from physical to application) still lack realistic behavior. To demonstrate this gap we performed a broad study of simulation models and real world behavior of wireless links and compared those in various settings, including outdoor environments and battery-based deployments. Based on the provided survey and wireless link case study, we outline a strategy of how to enable realistic, efficient, low-cost and repeatable WSN evaluation scenarios.

Keywords: WSN, Simulation Models, Real Deployment, Wireless Propagation.

1 Introduction

This position paper presents our vision and ongoing work on the credible evaluation of Wireless Sensor Networks (WSN) using the three basic evaluation environments available in this field: real-world deployments, testbeds, and simulators. We offer two main contributions: (1) an extensive overview of the state of the art evaluation environments for WSNs and (2) a thorough comparative study of wireless link properties across different environments.

We begin by defining general credibility and usability requirements for WSN evaluation in Section 2. Section 3 presents a detailed overview of the state of the art: we explore the three basic evaluation environments in terms of wireless propagation, energy consumption and battery behavior, as well as application-level events. In Section 4 we dive deeper into one of these dimensions, namely wireless propagation, and present a comparative study between various real-world environments (indoor and outdoor), energy sources (wall power and battery power), as well as different simulation models. The main goal of this study is to highlight the huge differences between those models. Finally, based on the survey and the case study, we define our credible WSN evaluation strategy and present our ongoing work in Section 5.

D. Simplot-Ryl et al. (Eds.): ADHOCNETS 2011, LNICST 89, pp. 49–64, 2012.
© Institute for Computer Sciences, Social Informatics and Telecommunications Engineering 2012

2   Evaluation Requirements for Sensor Networks

The driving motivation of this work is to enable credible and convenient evaluations for WSNs. First of all, we abstract away from any specific evaluation methodologies, approaches, and models, and we identify the key properties of WSN evaluation environments and studies:

Scalability: The evaluation environment needs to support any number of network nodes and node density.

Flexibility: The environment needs to support various parameters and scenarios, such as indoor and outdoor wireless propagation, node mobility, or different hardware platforms.

Accuracy: The environment must reproduce the real-world behavior of WSN deployments.

Repeatability: Each experiment must be 100% repeatable.

Visibility: The distributed network state must be visible to the user at any given time.

Cross-Environment Validity: Studies in one environment must be comparable to studies in another environment.

Re-Usability: Implementations targeted for a given environment must be re-usable in others.

This list is clearly idealistic and very hard to achieve in practice. However, it provides us with a solid basis of the goals and requirements for any evaluation scenario or environment and allows us to compare different evaluation environments to each other, such as simulation against testbeds.

The above requirements are not new and have been defined many times before [11,18]. However, as we will show in the next section, there is still no standardized evaluation environment, nor is there a consensus on which ones should be uses. The main goal of this paper is to demonstrate the gap between real world deployments and current evaluation environments and to propose a new evaluation suite, which covers most of the above requirements and enables credible and usable techniques for the evaluation of WSNs.

3   State of the Art of Evaluation Approaches

In this section, we turn our attention to existing WSN evaluation models and environments. We concentrate on three key approaches: simulators, testbeds and real-world deployments. Our approach is top-down: first, Table 1 presents a general comparison between those three environments in terms of the WSN evaluation requirements we defined in the last section. Then, we dive into each of them and break them down into their components to discuss their individual properties.

Table 1. High-level comparison of different WSN evaluation environments

WSN Evaluation Requirements	Real world deployments	Indoor testbeds	Network Simulators
Scalability	Scalable, but very costly (money, time, effort)	Scalable, but costly	Unlimited scalability
Flexibility	Medium/Rigid	Rigid	Flexible
Accuracy	Accurate	Less accurate	Inaccurate
Repeatability	Medium	Good	Perfect
Visibility	Low	Medium	Perfect
Cross-environment validity	High	High	Low
Re-usability	Medium/high	Medium/high	Low

Looking at Table 1, real world deployments clearly offer the most realistic evaluation environment, but are also very hard to manage, are costly, require a lot of effort and time, are typically not flexible, and are generally not conducive to repeatability. Testbeds offer a great alternative and offer better repeatability; however, even if the nodes are stationary, the environment can still change quickly and unpredictably [16]. Visibility is generally good because testbeds typically come with a dedicated infrastructure (backchannel). However, testbeds are usually wall-powered, thus lacking the complexity and the unreliable behavior of battery-deployed sensor nodes.

Simulation can offer great repeatability, visibility, unlimited scalability and flexibility. Unfortunately it suffers heavily from the poor accuracy of implemented simulation models and protocols, has very low reusability in general (especially general use network simulators) and the results gathered on one simulator are hardly comparable to results from others.

In the next paragraphs we explore the individual components of testbeds and simulators and compare them to real world deployments, which we identify as the ground truth. We argue that simulation is a currently underestimated and underused tool in the WSN community, whose problems and drawbacks could be solved by implementing cross-platform valid simulation models. The provided survey in the next paragraphs is the key to finding the right models.

The components we explore are wireless propagation, battery consumption, energy expenditure, and application-level events. We step through each of them in the next paragraphs.

3.1   Wireless Propagation

Wireless propagation in real world WSN deployments is extremely complex and depends on the radio hardware, its physical layer calibration, the orientation of the antenna, the inter-node distance (large-scale path loss), the presence of obstacles that block off the line of sight (shadowing), the presence of radio interference, the geometry of the surrounding environment (responsible for multipath fading), and the general conditions (temperature, humidity, sunlight, wind,...).

Small changes in the deployment area can change dramatically the properties of the wireless medium and lead to fundamentally different results. This complexity makes wireless links inherently unreliable and results in phenomena such as transitional links [31], asymmetric links, and burstiness. WSN testbeds are built with real hardware. They are typically deployed indoors, in office buildings that generally provide rich scattering conditions, thus accentuating the impact of multipath fading over the large-scale path loss and providing propagation conditions that are extremely different from the ones of outdoor deployments. Another key difference between real deployments and testbeds in terms of wireless propagation is the impact of the energy source. While real world deployments typically rely on off-the-shelf batteries, testbeds are wall-powered. We have shown in [13] that the vagaries of commercial batteries have a significant impact on the performance of low-power transceivers, and this observation should be taken into account in WSN evaluation and modeling.

Simulation models rely either on real wireless traces replay or on mathematical models. Well-known mathematical models [19] such as the unit disk model, the free-space propagation model, the two ray ground model, or the log-normal shadowing model fail to reproduce the real world behavior of WSNs. Much better alternatives have been also proposed, such as the Radio Irregularity Model [30], but are rarely used in practice, mostly because of their implementation complexity.

Playback of real world wireless traces has recently become a preferred simulation strategy, as it recreates the behavior of real world wireless propagation. Several variations of this model exist. One of the first trace-based models was implemented in TOSSIM [8,9,21], the standard TinyOS simulator, using real link traces to compute the empirical delivery probability and the statistical distribution of RSSI values on the individual links. Such a model accurately reproduces key properties of wireless channels, such as asymmetric links and link quality fluctuation, but it fails to represent link burstiness and the usage of a random number generator (RNG) hinders repeatability, especially across different simulators.

The problem of including burstiness in trace-based simulations has been tackled in WSNSimPy [11], a WSN simulator written in Python. It uses real-world traces by storing the real link qualities individually. When a node needs to transmit, it randomly selects one of the entries in the trace library. If the next transmission of the node is conducted soon thereafter, the next entry form the trace file is used instead of a random one. This captures relatively well the real burstiness of links. However, it does not allow perfect re-play of the experiment, again because a random number generator is used.

The work in [6] presents an algorithm called Multi-level Markov Model (M&M) to produce synthetic traces with the same statistical properties as some real trace and thus to simplify the process of gathering traces and "stretching" them. However, to the best of our knowledge, there is no fully deterministic implementation of wireless trace usage.

An inherent advantage of trace-driven simulation over model-based approaches is that model implementations change over time, while traces do not. When new model implementations become available, the old ones become obsolete. When new traces becomes available, the old ones still represent valid benchmarks.

In the next Section 4 we present an experimental study of the accuracy of various mathematical and trace-based models, compared to indoor and outdoor real world deployments.

3.2   Power Consumption Models

Power consumption refers to the current draw at the sensor node and its individual components (micro-controller, sensors, flash memory, external memory, LEDs, radio transceiver, etc). Some testbeds (e.g. MoteLab [25]) have limited support for measuring of the actual power draw, but typically the on-time of various components is used as the best proxy for energy consumption. Simulation provides finer-grained information.

Generally, simulators employ simple power consumption models, which differentiate between components and their current state and assign a current draw to each of those. Coarse grained models, such as the EnergyFramework of OMNeT++/MiXiM [4] consider only the radio and its main states sleep, receive and transmit. Finer grained models, such as in Cooja [3] or PowerTOSSIM [23], also consider sensors, micro-controller, and LEDs. In [13] we have shown that the most power hungry components on a system are usually the radio transmitter and the on-board flash. This is of course true for the specific sensor node hardware used for the experiments (TelosB); other platforms may behave differently.

3.3   Battery Models

Battery models are different from energy expenditure models, as they measure what is the remaining energy in the batteries over time. Relevant studies include [12] and [13], which focuses on the battery discharge behavior.

While no existing testbed employs batteries, there exist several simulation models. The most widely used model is linear and assumes that the battery is a bucket of energy units that are used up over time. A much more sophisticated non-linear model is proposed by Rakhmatov and Vrudhula [17], and captures the discharge and the recovery effects of batteries.

3.4   Application-Level Events

Application-level traces are rare in practice, both for testbeds and for simulation. Cooja is such a rare example, which use the WiseML [10] format for replaying application traces from real-world environments. The basic idea is that the application trace is a sequence of events at the application level with local timestamps. These traces should be preferably recorded at real world deployments, but can also be artificially created. Application-level traces build a basis for structured testing and evaluation, as they provide the lower communication protocols with traffic, which they need to manage.

Table 2. List of state of the art simulation models and their availability for various simulators

Simulation Model	Cooja	ns-3	OMNeT++ / MiXiM	Shawn	TOSSIM	Qualnet
Deterministic wireless link traces [6]	Trace-based, median based	Yes for ns-2, own format [14]	In progress (WiseML format)	No [22]	Non-deterministic median-based	No information
Fine-grained energy expenditure model	Yes [3]	Yes [29]	Yes, radio only [4]	No	Yes, PowerTOSSIM [23]	No information
Non-linear battery model of Rakhmatov-Vrudhula [17]	No Information	Yes	No	Yes	Own Non-linear model PowerTOSSIMz [15]	Yes
Application-level traces [1]	Yes, WiseML	No Information	Yes, own format	Yes, WiseML	No	No Information
General credibility	**medium**	**medium**	**low/medium**	**low/med**	**medium**	**low**
User friendliness, support, documentation	Strong	Weak	Strong	Medium	Medium	Strong
Supported real operating systems	Contiki	TinyOS in progress [20]	In progress (TinyOS, Scatterweb) [5]	Implicitly, through WiseLib [1]	TinyOS	No

3.5 Summary

Table 2 offers an overview of all described sophisticated evaluation/simulation models for some of the most popular simulation environments for WSNs. We point out that individual network simulators rarely offer a complete suite of sophisticated simulation models and model suites of different simulators are never the same. This lowers the credibility of individual simulators but also makes cross-platform comparison of simulation results impossible. The credibility grade we gave for each simulator is valid only if the most sophisticated models suite available is used. This is a crucial requirement to achieve credibility, as all simulators also offer simplified models, such as the unit disk model for wireless propagation.

Next, we present a detailed study of wireless propagation from real world deployments, testbeds and simulation models and demonstrate once again the gap between them.

4   Case Study on Wireless Links Properties

We have studied the properties of wireless links with lengths ranging from 2 to 6 meters in several different environments with various parameters: battery-powered indoor and outdoor real deployments, wall-powered indoor and outdoor testbeds, wireless trace based simulation with various noise addition under TOSSIM [9] and various mathematical models in OMNeT++/MiXiM [26]. While the main purpose of this study is to show the clear discrepancies between simulation models and reality and even between different environments (indoor and outdoor), we note that, to the best of our knowledge, a comparison between a wall-powered and a battery-powered deployment has never been carried out before.

We consider standard link metrics such as delivery rate and RSSI. In addition to the mean values, we present broad statistical values such as lower and higher quartiles, outliers, etc. We claim that the low accuracy of most simulation models is due to the fact that they are unable to completely capture the significant fluctuation of the individual metrics.

4.1 Experimental Setup

For our real world and testbed deployments, we use a basic star topology with 2 or 3m distance from the center, see Figure 1. We use TelosB nodes with minimum transmission power setting (-25dBm). The application is based on TinyOS and is taken from [6]: one node in the network is assigned the role of the sender, while all others are receivers. The sender sends packets with an inter-packet interval (IPI) of 20 ms and the receivers log the received packets with packet id, RSSI and LQI level. After some time (2-10 minutes), we switch to a different sender. The logged data is either forwarded to the testbed base station via the serial interface or is logged locally. Note that this approach avoids any kind of inter-node interference and only external interference is present.

A typical example of a code-level WSN simulator is TOSSIM, a part of the standard TinyOS [9]. TOSSIM is a discrete event simulator, where simulation events represent hardware interrupts, high-level system events and posted tasks. The basic TOSSIM wireless channel model is based on defining the large-scale path loss for each pair of nodes in both directions. Loss values can be obtained from real world traces or based on a radio propagation model. RF noise and interference from other nodes and outside sources are also simulated [8]. The Closest Pattern Matching (CPM) algorithm is used to analyze real noise trace and create a statistical model from it [21]. We map our experimental data for

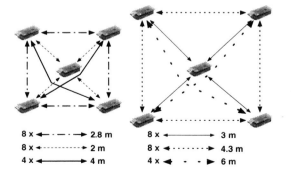

Fig. 1. Used topologies with all unidirectional links and their distances

both wall-powered and battery-powered nodes by giving the network topology information and the average directional RSSI between all node pairs. In addition to that, we also gathered noise traces around each node by using the standard *RssiSample* [8] program. Similarly to our real experimental setup, we use the same 5-node topologies with IPI of 20 ms.

We also investigate the performance of a typical general-use event-based network simulator OMNeT++ with its mobile ad hoc extension MiXiM [7]. We developed a simple communication stack, consisting of a simple CSMA MAC protocol and an application. The application is the same as our TinyOS implementation and the same topologies are reproduced. However, in contrast to TOSSIM, MiXiM implements mathematical models for the simulation of wireless propagation. The currently available models are LogNormalShadowing, SimplePathLoss and JakesFading. One immediate disadvantage of these models is the possibility to freely combine them. This makes it possible, for example, to use Jakes Fading alone (that should be used only in combination with path-loss). We employed the parameters from the real world deployments (radio frequency, transmission power, topology, etc.) as closely as possible.

4.2   Delivery Rate

Figure 2 presents the obtained results in terms of delivery rate. The top row of graphs corresponds to our hardware experiments with battery-powered and wall-powered nodes in outdoor and indoor environments. To the best of our knowledge, this study is the first to methodologically explore the differences in link quality between battery-powered and wall-powered nodes. As it can be seen from the top graphs, the indoor links exhibit a remarkably stable behavior even over different distances and there is no major difference between wall- and battery-powered deployments. However, outdoor links are completely different in their statistical values: the median of the delivery rate falls significantly with increasing distance between the nodes, and, most importantly, the battery-powered experiments almost fail to deliver any data. The consequence of this observation is clear and important:

Observation 1. *Battery-powered indoor testbeds do not mimic the behavior of outdoor battery-powered deployments.*

Next, we compare the above real world experimental data with ones obtained from TOSSIM simulations. Note that we used the real-world trace data from each of the above described deployments to mimic its behavior in TOSSIM. We present two TOSSIM settings: one with constant noise for all nodes, taken from noise measurements of the central node in the topologies, and one with individual noise traces for each node. It is interesting to note that it seems TOSSIM with individual noise traces is able to pretty well mimic the behavior of real-world links for wall-powered links, and less for battery-powered ones. The difference becomes extreme for outdoor battery-powered nodes, even if this particular data sets was used for the trace-based simulation.

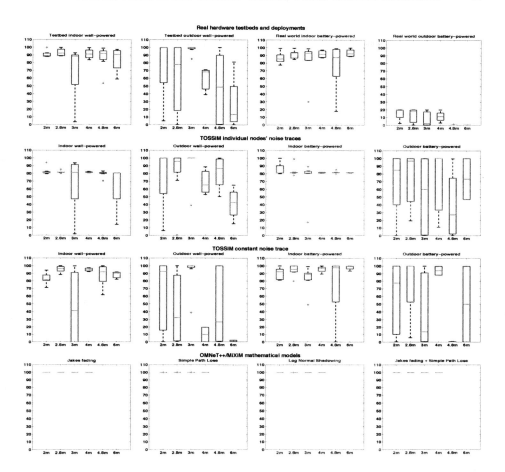

Fig. 2. Delivery rate over various environments. The box has lines at the lower quartile, median, and upper quartile values. Whiskers extend from each end of the box to the adjacent values in the data within 1.5 times the interquartile range from the ends of the box. Outliers are displayed with a + sign.

TOSSIM simulations with constant noise traces for all nodes seem to be less accurate, compared to TOSSIM with individual noise traces. The difference between simulation and reality for outdoor battery-powered links is significant.

We also ran TOSSIM experiments without any noise data, but failed to exchange even a single packet. The reason for this is the receiving threshold of TOSSIM, which is set to -72 dBm and is derived from experimental data collected using two MicaZ nodes, RF shielding, and a variable attenuator [24]. Obviously, this threshold is not very realistic for our deployments and needs to be carefully re-validated.

For OMNeT++/MiXiM and its mathematical models, only one conclusion can be drawn: even if the implemented models are considered more sophisticated and realistic than the the simple unit disk model, they completely fail to simulate the lossy nature of links and produce almost binary links.

4.3   Received Signal Strength Indicator

Figure 3 presents the data of our case study in terms of logged/calculated RSSI values for individual packets. Real-world deployments and testbed tend to have very fluctuating values even in short time intervals, as it has been shown many times before, e.g. [16,31]. However, new results present the difference between battery-powered and wall-powered links and between indoor and outdoor links. The observation is the same as for delivery rate: outdoor links have different properties than indoor ones and are generally less reliable. Some of the reasons behind *Observation 1* might be temperature [2], humidity, wind etc. Overheating of sensor nodes (due to sunlight), specially affected battery-powered nodes and reduced their PDR and RSSI.

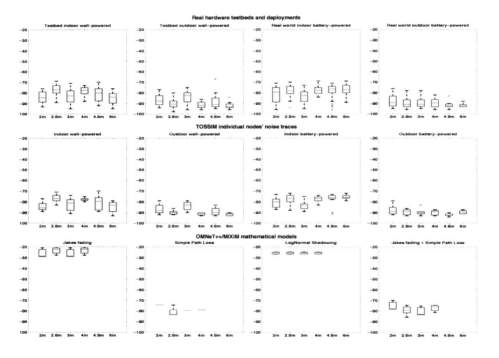

Fig. 3. RSSI values over various evaluation environments. The box has lines at the lower quartile, median, and upper quartile values. Whiskers extend from each end of the box to the adjacent values in the data within 1.5 times the interquartile range from the ends of the box. Outliers are displayed with a + sign.

TOSSIM simulations seem to mimic the real-world quite well, although the fluctuations of the values are lower. OMNeT++/MiXiM presents completely different results for the different simulation models. For example, Jakes Fading and LogNormal Shadowing produce unrealistically good RSSI values, far away of any real-world observations. On the other hand, Simple Pathloss, the simplest of the here presented models, produces much more realistic data, which almost fall in the same interval as real-world observations. The best performing combination of these models was identified to be Jakes fading and simple pathloss, which in combination produce a realistic data interval with some fluctuations. Given the discussions about delivery rate and RSSI values, it can be also generalized that parametrization and usage of simulation models is tricky and requires expertise.

Observation 2. *Parametrization of simulation models is a major challenge towards credible, realistic evaluation.*

5   Enabling Credible WSN Evaluation

This paper has presented an extensive study and comparison of WSN evaluation models and environments. We explored several important properties of WSNs, such as wireless propagation, energy expenditure, etc. in real world deployments, testbeds, and simulation. As expected, real-world deployments naturally provide the most realistic environment, simulation still leaves a lot to be desired, and testbeds lie somewhere in between (see Table 1). In the next paragraphs, we outline our vision for streamlining the evaluation process of WSNs in all environments and mainly in simulation and discuss related efforts in this area, including our own ongoing work.

5.1   Credible WSN Simulations

The main drawback of WSN simulations is their low credibility because of over-simplified simulation models. As our case study on wireless propagation in Section 4 has shown, there are great discrepancies between simulation models and reality. Furthermore, another significant challenge is the parametrization and usage of these models. TOSSIM's trace-based simulation of wireless links presents a credible environment, but TOSSIM users need to be aware of all possible additional models, such as add-on noise traces or the sensitivity threshold, in order to achieve maximum credibility. A novice or non-expert can easily miss some details and use unconsciously a simplified, less-credible environment. We claim that full and safe simulation credibility can be achieved only by implementing deterministic, parameter-free simulation models. This approach will not only simplify the work with simulators and make them credible, but also enable cross-platform comparison of simulation results. The most important models to be implemented are:

Wireless Propagation Model. The most deterministic and realistic model is the playback of real wireless traces. This model has two main requirements: implementing the model itself and building a wireless trace database with sufficient number of traces from different environments and different topologies. The important implementation challenges of trace driven wireless propagation model include inter-node interference model, interference from distant nodes, spatial and temporal extension of available traces etc. To the best of our knowledge, there is no deterministic playback model implemented yet for any simulator (see Section 3). Our own work in progress includes such a model for OMNeT++/MiXiM and TOSSIM. In terms of data format for the captured wireless traces, WiseML [10] is a perfect candidate, since a small database of traces in this format is already available [28].

Fine-Grained Energy Expenditure Model. Energy expenditure is a vital metric of WSNs and thus needs to be monitored carefully. Simulation is a great tool for this, as it offers fine-grained state observation of individual components. A credible energy expenditure model will include at least the radio transceiver, sensors, and processing. It must capture at least their main states, e.g. sleep, receive, transmit for the radio. A significant component of this model are realistic, fine-grained energy expenditure measurements from real platforms, such as PowerTOSSIMz [15]. The remaining challenge is to perform fine-grained real-world experiments of energy consumption of individual components on a wide range of sensor platforms.

Non-Linear Battery Model. Battery models are closely related to energy expenditure models and enable predictions about the lifetime of sensor nodes. Credible models capture the non-linear behavior of batteries like self-discharge, fluctuating output voltage, etc. However, even sophisticated battery models like Rakhmatov-Vrudhula [17] remain to be validated for a complete battery lifetime on real sensor nodes.

Application Model. This is probably the least complex model, which we require for credible simulations. However, this upper layer dictates when events occur in the network and how they are disseminated. Thus, we also dictate the data traffic in the whole network, which can be periodic, bursty, event-based, etc. Such models exist for OMNeT++, Cooja and Shawn. The last two support WiseML for reading application events, OMNeT++ supports its own simple table format.

5.2 Optimized WSN Testbeds

WSN testbeds have proved to be a handy tool for evaluating WSNs. One of their main advantages is the direct portability of code between a testbed and a real environment. However, as we discussed in Section 3, there exists a gap between a testbed and a real world deployment, because testbeds are wall-powered, deployed indoors, and typically completely stationary. In order to counteract these challenges, we propose the following further optimizations of existing testbeds:

Wireless Propagation Model. There is a clear need to reproduce the vagaries and features of outdoor deployments. Deploying testbeds outdoors is generally not practical. We propose the implementation of a trace-based simulation wireless channel, identical to the above described deterministic wireless propagation model for simulations, enabled through the backchannel infrastructure of the testbed. This will allow two important novelties: perfect repeatability of experiments and cross-platform comparison between simulation and testbeds. Of course, the main goal is to be able to playback real world wireless traces from any environment. Note that this model does not eliminate the other hard challenges of testbeds, such as real hardware, clock drift, processing time, etc.

Energy Consumption Model. An energy consumption model needs to monitor the work of individual hardware components and to estimate on-line their individual energy consumption. Such a functionality is already provided by the embedded operating system Contiki [3]; TinyOS implementations are not readily available, but trivial to add.

Battery Model. Using real batteries on remote testbeds is very inconvenient and does not mimic outdoor battery-powered deployments, see Section 4. We propose the adoption of a battery simulation model, as described for simulations above. This can be easily combined with the energy consumption model, where the testbed server monitors the energy consumption of all nodes and automatically shuts down the ones whose simulated battery dies. To the best of our knowledge, this simple idea has not been considered so far.

5.3   Real World Deployments

The main disadvantage of real-world deployments is their restricted visibility that makes debugging very challenging. Furthermore, energy consumption measurements are typically out of scope. Much effort has been already invested in improving the visibility and debugging tools for real world deployments, for example Marionette [27] for TinyOS, which enables remote function call invocation on sensor nodes. Our own efforts in developing FLEXOR [5] also target more visibility and control over remote sensor nodes.

5.4   Summary

A generalized view of our implementation and research strategy towards credible WSN evaluation is depicted as a work flow graph in Figure 4. The center of the graph build the three evaluation environments: real world, testbeds and simulation. They are surrounded by cross-platform operating systems, programming languages, and software architectures in order to enable portability and re-usability of code across different environments. The rest of the graph consists of the four models described above: non-linear batteries, energy consumption, wireless propagation and application events. For each of them the necessary steps are depicted, with input coming mostly from real world deployments (the bold lines). The grey vertices underline future work, while white vertices represent already available tools and methodologies, which might need some extensions only.

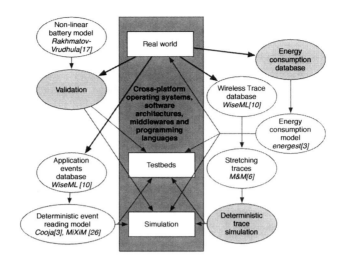

Fig. 4. Future directions for enabling credible WSN evaluation. See inline for detailed explanation.

6   Conclusion

In this paper, we presented our vision and strategy towards enabling credible, realistic and convenient WSN evaluation. We presented the basis of our strategy, consisting of broad state of the art survey of evaluation approaches and models and a rigorous case study to identify and demonstrate the gaps between real world deployments and current evaluation and simulation models. Our immediate future plans include the implementations of deterministic wireless trace based simulation model for OMNeT++/MiXiM and TOSSIM and WiseML-support to those two simulators. Discussions and collaborations are highly welcome.

References

1. Baumgartner, T., Chatzigiannakis, I., Fekete, S., Koninis, C., Kröller, A., Pyrgelis, A.: Wiselib: A Generic Algorithm Library for Heterogeneous Sensor Networks. In: Silva, J.S., Krishnamachari, B., Boavida, F. (eds.) EWSN 2010. LNCS, vol. 5970, pp. 162–177. Springer, Heidelberg (2010)
2. Boano, C.A., Brown, J., He, Z., Roedig, U., Voigt, T.: Low-Power Radio Communication in Industrial Outdoor Deployments: The Impact of Weather Conditions and ATEX-Compliance. In: Komninos, N. (ed.) SENSAPPEAL 2009. LNICST, vol. 29, pp. 159–176. Springer, Heidelberg (2010)

3. Dunkels, A., Osterlind, F., Tsiftes, N., He, Z.: Software-based on-line energy estimation for sensor nodes. In: Proceedings of the 4th Workshop on Embedded Networked Sensors (EmNets), Cork, Ireland (2007)

4. Feeney, L.M., Willkomm, D.: Energy framework: an extensible framework for simulating battery consumption in wireless networks. In: Proceedings of the 3rd International ICST Conference on Simulation Tools and Techniques, Torremolinos, Malaga, Spain (2010)

5. Förster, A., Förster, A., Leidi, T., Garg, K., Puccinelli, D., Ducatelle, F., Giordano, S., Gambardella, L.: Poster abstract: Motel: Towards flexible mobile wireless sensor network testbeds. In: Proceedings of the 8th European Conference on Wireless Sensor Networks (EWSN), Bonn, Germany (February 2011)

6. Kamthe, A., Carreira-Perpiñán, M.A., Cerpa, A.E.: M&M: multi-level Markov model for wireless link simulations. In: Proceedings of the 7th ACM Conference on Embedded Networked Sensor Systems, SenSys 2009, pp. 57–70. ACM, Berkeley (2009)

7. Köpke, A., Swigulski, M., Wessel, K., Willkomm, D., Haneveld, P.T.K., Parker, T.E.V., Visser, O.W., Lichte, H.S., Valentin, S.: Simulating wireless and mobile networks in omnet++ the mixim vision. In: Proceedings of the 1st International Conference on Simulation Tools and Techniques, Marseille, France (2008)

8. Lee, H., Cerpa, A., Levis, P.: Improving wireless simulation through noise modeling. In: Proceedings of the 6th International Conference on Information Processing in Sensor Networks, IPSN 2007, Cambridge, Massachusetts, USA, pp. 21–30 (2007)

9. Levis, P., Lee, N., Welsh, M., Culler, D.: Tossim: accurate and scalable simulation of entire tinyos applications. In: Proceedings of the 1st International Conference on Embedded Networked Sensor Systems (SenSys), Los Angeles, CA, USA, pp. 126–137 (2003)

10. Li, Q., Österlind, F., Voigt, T., Fischer, S., Pfisterer, D.: Making wireless sensor network simulators cooperate. In: Proceedings of the 7th ACM Workshop on Performance Evaluation of Wireless Ad Hoc, Sensor, and Ubiquitous Networks (PeWASUN), Bodrum, Turkey (2010)

11. Marchiori, A., Guo, L., Thomas, J., Han, Q.: Realistic performance analysis of wsn protocols through trace based simulation. In: Proceedings of the 7th ACM Workshop on Performance Evaluation of Wireless Ad Hoc, Sensor, and Ubiquitous Networks, PE-WASUN 2010, pp. 87–94. ACM, Bodrum (2010)

12. Menzel, T., Willkomm, D., Wolisz, A.: Improving battery-efficiency of embedded devices by favorably discharging only towards end-of-life. In: Proceedings of the CONET 2011 Workshop in Conjunction with CPSWeek 2011, Chicago, USA (April 2011)

13. Nguyen, H.A., Förster, A., Puccinelli, D., Giordano, S.: An experimental study of sensor node lifetime. In: Proceedings of the 7th IEEE International Workshop on Sensor Networks and Systems for Pervasive Computing (PerSens). Seattle, WA, USA (2011)

14. NS-2 (May 2011), http://nsnam.isi.edu/nsnam/index.php

15. Perla, E., Catháin, A., Carbajo, R.S., Huggard, M., Mc Goldrick, C.: Powertossim z: realistic energy modelling for wireless sensor network environments. In: Proceedings of the 3nd ACM Workshop on Performance Monitoring and Measurement of Heterogeneous Wireless and Wired Networks, Vancouver, British Columbia, Canada (2008)

16. Puccinelli, D., Gnawali, O., Yoon, S., Santini, S., Colesanti, U., Giordano, S., Guibas, L.: The Impact of Network Topology on Collection Performance. In: Marrón, P.J., Whitehouse, K. (eds.) EWSN 2011. LNCS, vol. 6567, pp. 17–32. Springer, Heidelberg (2011)

17. Rakhmatov, D., Vrudhula, S.: Energy management for battery-powered embedded systems. ACM Transactions on Embedded Computing Systems 2, 277–324 (2003)
18. Raman, B., Chebrolu, K.: Censor networks: A critique of "sensor networks" from a systems perspective. ACM SIGCOMM Computer Communication Review 38(3), 75–78 (2008)
19. Rapapport, T.: Wireless Communications: Principles and Practice. Prentice Hall (2001)
20. Riliskis, L., Osipov, E., Maróti, M.: Tos-ns3: a framework for emulating wireless sensor networks in the ns3 network simulator. In: Proceedings of the 3rd International Workshop on NS3, in Conjunction with SimuTOOLS, Malaga, Spain (2010)
21. Rusak, T., Levis, P.A.: Investigating a physically-based signal power model for robust low power wireless link simulation. In: Proceedings of the 11th International Symposium on Modeling, Analysis and Simulation of Wireless and Mobile Systems, pp. 37–46 (2008)
22. Shawn: https://www.itm.uni-luebeck.de/shawnwiki
23. Shnayder, V., Hempstead, M., Chen, B.R., Allen, G.W., Welsh, M.: Simulating the power consumption of large-scale sensor network applications. In: Proceedings of the 2nd International Conference on Embedded Networked Sensor Systems, SenSys 2004, Baltimore, MD, USA, pp. 188–200 (2004)
24. TOSSIM: Simulating TinyOS Networks: http://www.cs.berkeley.edu/~pal/research/tossim.html
25. Werner-Allen, G., Swieskowski, P., Welsh, M.: Motelab: a wireless sensor network testbed. In: Proceedings of the 4th International Symposium on Information Processing in Sensor Networks (IPSN), pp. 483–488 (April 2005)
26. Wessel, K., Swigulski, M., Köpke, A., Willkomm, D.: Mixim: the physical layer an architecture overview. In: Proceedings of the 2nd International Workshop on OMNeT++, Rome, Italy, pp. 1–8 (2009)
27. Whitehouse, K., Tolle, G., Taneja, J., Sharp, C., Kim, S., Jeong, J., Hui, J., Dutta, P., Culler, D.: Marionette: using rpc for interactive development and debugging of wireless embedded networks. In: The Proceedings of the 5th International Conference on Information Processing in Sensor Networks, IPSN 2006, pp. 416–423 (2006)
28. Wisebed (2011), http://www.wisebed.eu
29. Wu, H., Nabar, S., Poovendran, R.: An energy framework for the network simulator 3 (ns-3). In: Proceedings of the 4th International Conference on Simulation Tools and Techniques (SimuTOOLS), Barcelona, Spain (2011)
30. Zhou, G., He, T., Krishnamurthy, S., Stankovic, J.A.: Models and solutions for radio irregularity in wireless sensor networks. ACM Transactions on Sensor Networks 2(2), 221–262 (2006)
31. Zuniga, M., Krishnamachari, B.: An analysis of unreliability and asymmetry in low-power wireless links. ACM Transactions on Sensor Networks 3 (June 2007)

Adaptive Hierarchical Network Structures for Wireless Sensor Networks[*]

Dimitrios Amaxilatis[1,2], Ioannis Chatzigiannakis[1,2], Shlomi Dolev[3],
Christos Koninis[1,2], Apostolos Pyrgelis[1,2], and Paul G. Spirakis[1,2]

[1] Computer Technology Institute & Press (CTI), Patras, Greece
[2] Computer Engineering and Informatics Department, University of Patras, Greece
[3] Department of Computer Science, Ben-Gurion University of the Negev, Israel
{amaxilat,ichatz,koninis,pyrgelis,spirakis}@cti.gr, dolev@cs.bgu.ac.il

Abstract. Clustering is a crucial network design approach to enable large-scale wireless sensor networks (WSNs) deployments. A large variety of clustering approaches has been presented focusing on various aspect such as minimizing communication overhead, controlling the network topology etc. Simulations on such protocols are performed using theoretical models that are based on unrealistic assumptions like ideal wireless communication channels and perfect energy consumption estimations. With these assumptions taken for granted, theoretical models claim various performance milestones that cannot be achieved in realistic conditions. In this paper, we design a new clustering protocol that adapts to the changes in the environment and the needs and goals of the user applications. We provide a protocol that is deployable protocol in real WSNs. We apply our protocol in multiple indoors wireless sensor testbeds with multiple experimental scenarios to showcase scalability and trade-offs between network properties and configurable protocol parameters. By analysis of the real world experimental output, we present results that depict a more realistic view of the clustering problem, regarding adapting to environmental conditions and the quality of topology control. Our study clearly demonstrates the applicability of our approach and the benefits it offers to both research & development communities.

Keywords: Algorithm Engineering, Clustering, Self-Stabilization, Implementation, Protocols, Software Design, Cross-layer, Cross-platform.

1 Introduction

During the last decade, *wireless sensor networks* (WSNs) gained the interest of computer science, industries and academia, not only from theoretical but also from practical perspectives [22]. Consisting of spatially distributed autonomous sensor-equipped devices, WSNs allow the cooperative monitoring of physical or environmental conditions (e.g., temperature, light, pollutants, etc.), enabling a multitude of applications in both urban and rural contexts.

---

[*] This work has been partially supported by the European Union under contract numbers ICT-2008-215270 (**FRONTS**) and ICT-2010-258885 (**SPITFIRE**).

D. Simplot-Ryl et al. (Eds.): ADHOCNETS 2011, LNICST 89, pp. 65–80, 2012.

Current WSN technologies used by the vast majority of off-the-shelf sensor nodes allow short range message exchanges. They employ flat network organization structures for message exchanges, data aggregation and actuators operation. Thus, they typically allow the operation of a few dozens of nodes.

Many of the proposed applications assume large node populations densely deployed over sizable areas. Although thus far, we have only a few examples of large-scale deployments of such systems, we are currently seeing great advances, as signified by research projects such as CitySense [12] and SmartSantander [29].

It is therefore important that future WSN have scalable network structures that achieve appropriate levels of organization and integration. This organization and integration needs to be achieved seamlessly and with appropriate levels of flexibility, in order to be able to accomplish their global goals and objectives. And it needs to be done in a proactive way to meet the current or anticipated needs of their "users". For this reason, they need to adapt to the changes in their environment and change their internal organization by communicating, cooperating and forming goal-driven sub-organizations.

Since [4], grouping sensor nodes into clusters has been widely pursued by the research community in order to achieve network scalability and fault-tolerance. A large variety of approaches has been presented focusing on different performance metrics. Some have been proposed as stand alone methods (e.g., [19]), others incorporated as sub protocols in larger solutions designed to solve more specific problems such as query execution, aggregation, localization etc. (e.g., [20,32]).

Unfortunately, even though all of them have many potential applications, extremely few software implementations for real sensor nodes is available to the community [33,20,19]. Furthermore, none of them has been widely adopted by the community. This is partially because cluster formations remain static throughout the execution of the network. Thus, it is difficult to react to "external changes" that affect the topology of the network (e.g., due to node failures) or to "internal changes" requested by the application (e.g., to reduce cluster sizes). Sudden variations of service requests or environmental physical conditions or of motion of nodes disrupts the system from serving its goals.

Clearly, technology expects future WSN to be dependable and adaptive to: the user needs, sudden changes of the environment and specific applications characteristics. This means that the system continues to operate in a set of desired states with maintained, or gracefully degraded or even improved quality of service. In order to design such systems we adopt the concept of [3] for self-organization that has been widely mentioned in the scope of distributed computing and peer to peer networks. We consider self-stabilizing distributed algorithms for cluster definition in communication graphs of bounded degree processors as well as for hierarchical distributed snapshots. We observe that as far as dynamic changes are limited within a cluster they do not affect the rest of the network.

We implement our solution by following a component-based design. We totally avoid implementing our algorithm as a monolithic, stand-alone piece of code. Thus, our code promotes **exchangeability** of different modules that interact using well-defined interfaces. The modules can be easily integrated as sub-protocols in other problems such as energy conservation, routing, role assignment, security etc.. Furthermore, we use the Wiselib [8]: a code library, that allows implementations to be OS-independent. It is implemented based on C++ and templates, but without virtual inheritance and exceptions. All implemented algorithms are **platform independent** as they can be compiled on a number of different hardware platforms (e.g., TelosB, iSense, ScatterWeb) and **OS independent** as they can be automatically used in systems implemented using C (Contiki), C++ (iSense), and nesC (TinyOS).

We conduct a thorough evaluation using an experimental testbed environment. For all cases, our results indicate that our approach adapts to the external and internal changes. The results of the evaluation also indicate that our implemented code achieves high **scalability** and **efficiency**. To the best of our knowledge, this work is among the very few that conducts experiments and assess the practicality of a clustering approach in real WSN.

2   Previous Work

A large variety of clustering algorithms has been presented during the past years. In the relevant bibliography there exist several surveys and tutorials (e.g., [1,25,21,11]) that attempt to categorize and classify the various protocols based on the design choices and the mode of operation.

In terms of *Cluster-head selection* in some algorithms, like [18,6] each node is assigned a probability p of becoming a cluster-head. In algorithms like [27,5,32], some deterministic criteria like node connectivity, node identity and energy are respectively used for electing cluster-heads. Finally, algorithms like [9,14] are based on the combination of criteria in order to assign weights to nodes and decide the cluster-heads based on those.

In terms of *Node Grouping*, when a node is elected as cluster-head, it advertises itself to neighboring nodes in order for them to join its cluster. A node can decide to join a cluster based on various criteria. In most algorithms, e.g., [18,34,7], the main criterion for a node to join a cluster is the distance to the cluster-head. In other algorithms, like [31,28,9] the nodes decide to join a cluster-head based on some cluster-head attribute like remaining energy, time to live, etc..

In recent years, the concept of self-organization has been widely mentioned in the scope of distributed computing and peer to peer networks. Many works have claimed being self-organizing, but a mere fraction of these works also tries to give a specific definition of what self-organization really is. In [3] a framework for self-organization is proposed, including formal definitions of the self-organization concept and complementary proof techniques which can be used to prove that algorithms are indeed self-organizing.

Self-stabilizing and self-healing constructions of hierarchies, in the domain of sensor networks, appear in [35]. The authors divide the plane into hexagonal cells. In each cell, a head that corresponds with a cluster leader is elected. In [26], Wattenhofer and Moscibroda present an algorithm for computing a maximal independent set in radio networks where processors can broadcast their messages asynchronously, but no collision detection mechanism is provided. Snapshot algorithms are used for recording a consistent global state of a distributed asynchronous system. A self-stabilizing snapshot algorithm was first introduced in [23], where repeated invocations of snapshots are used to ensure stabilization of a non-stabilizing algorithm. Following [23], several works have studied ways of achieving efficient snapshots in different models e.g., message passing, bounded links message passing and shared memory ([30,2,13]).

The initial point of our work is [15]. We are inspired by this protocol due to its inherent simplicity, ease of deployment, scalability and self-stabilizing properties. In this work, we move beyond this protocol's ([15]) abstract design. We provide a solution that resolves crucial issues such as bidirectionality and reliability of channel communication between the nodes, adaptive detection of changes to the network topology and the efficient usage of communication mechanisms. We propose specific algorithmic solutions and provide software components fine tuned for real WSN hardware. In contrast to [15] and to the majority of the previous related work, we evaluate the system in real testbeds to measure the performance of the resulting adaptive clustering protocol.

3   An Adaptive Hierarchical Network Structure

The main idea of the algorithm is to partition the nodes of the network into small clusters that are then merged to form bigger clusters and so on. Nodes continuously monitor the local topology. Based on this information, if they do not detect any cluster, they take the initiative to create a new one. If one or more clusters exist, they join one of these using some very simple criteria.

The clustering algorithm maintains the self-stabilizing properties analysed in [15]. It uses the network parameter k for controlling the size of the clusters. The value of k is set by the network operator during the deployment phase of the system and can be modified during the execution of the protocol. Essentially, the protocol adapts to the external requests by properly adjusting the cluster size so that they have a diameter of $2 \times k$. The adaptation to the new size requires $O(k)$ execution rounds (in [15] in order to measure the communication complexity they assume the existence of a global clock, however for the actual execution of the algorithm in real networks no such global clock is required).

3.1   Initialization Phase

Our algorithm follows the self-stabilization approach, so we do not assume any initialization phase. Hence, it is capable of starting from any configuration where the nodes of the network are set to any arbitrary state. Thus, some nodes may consider themselves as cluster heads, others may consider as members of non-existing clusters, etc.. Regardless of this initial arbitrary state, within a bounded number of steps, our algorithms converges to a stable configuration, i.e., a configuration where all nodes of the network participate in a valid cluster of $k -$ *hop* diameter. This is done regardless of the way that the devices are positioned in the network area. In fact, as explained in the following section our algorithm will suitably adapt its operation to the physical topology of the network.

We do not assume any kind of global clock synchronization among the nodes of the network. Yet we assume that clocks of all nodes have similar (if not identical) drift rates. Thus they are capable of measuring the same amount of time for a given period.

In the sequel, for simplicity we assume that nodes are provided with unique identities. Still, in large-scale deployments this may not be guaranteed by the technical personnel involved during the network installation. Note that this problem can be easily solved by a very simple extension provided in [15] that uses random choice used to break symmetry between nodes (for further motivation, see the asynchronous version of the algorithm in [15]).

3.2 Neighbor Discovery

An important aspect of the algorithm is the ability to detect the current topology of the network. The purpose for detecting the topology is twofold. First, to discover the target nodes as they change their position within the network area. Second, to detect changes to the local connectivity so that the spreading of the traces is properly adjusted to frequent and/or significant topology changes.

A simple approach would be for each node to periodically broadcast beacon messages that include their unique id. For each received message beacon the algorithm considers the sender node as a neighbor. Similarly, if a node stops receiving beacons from a neighbor, it removes the node from the list of neighbors.

This simple approach has to deal with the fact that communication is carried out via a wireless channel. Naturally, the quality of the wireless channel is subject to a number of environmental effects and thus its quality varies over time. This means that some beacons from neighboring nodes may not be received, while the topology has not changed. The algorithm falsely translates this as if the topology has changed. Accordingly, the perceived neighborhood of the node is changed. Then, when the temporary degradation of channel quality is restored, the beacons are received again, and the nodes are reinstated in the neighborhood. Hence, the perceived neighborhood of the node is changed once again. This series of events is temporary, does not reflect the actual state of the neighborhood and forces the algorithm to take unnecessary actions for adaptation.

Our approach is to take into account the Link Quality Indicators (LQI) provided by the MAC layer for each received message beacon. The goal is to filter out the neighbors that have poor communication channel quality. The nodes will consider the broadcaster as a neighboring node only if it receives a number of consecutive beacon messages with LQI above a certain threshold. In order to prevent the occasional short channel degradation from negatively impacting the above strategy, we allow a node to miss a number of beacons within a given period of time before removing it (called the *timeout period*). We also set a second LQI threshold; message beacons with LQI below this threshold are dropped (and therefore count towards the number of beacons that are missed). In Sec. 5.1, we report a preliminary set of experiments we conducted in order to fine tune these LQI thresholds and the timeout period.

Another crucial aspect of the neighbor discovery operations of the algorithm is the periodicity of the broadcast beacons. One would expect that there exists a linear correlation between the time required for the neighbor discovery to stabilize (i.e., correctly detect passing by nodes) and the beacon interval. Reducing the beacon interval period (i.e., increasing the rate of transmission) should lead to a quicker response to changes in the topology (i.e., shorter delays in detecting a mobile node and potential changes to the neighboring nodes). Interestingly, the experiments reported in Sec. 5.1 indicate that there is a lower bound in the beacon interval period beyond which the network is congested with messages leading to instability in the operation of the algorithm. The experiments indicate a suitable value around $1000ms$ and $2000ms$. Our experiments indicate that these values are very suitable for the proper operation of the algorithm. However, in some cases we may wish to have faster response times. For this reason we allow the mobile nodes to have a different beacon interval period than the rest of the static nodes. This way, we can set the beacon interval to be as low as $100ms$. This essentially allows us to have a very low response time without creating a large overhead on the wireless channel. In fact, the response time achieved is much lower than other RF technologies, like, e.g., Bluetooth devices that has an interval period of about 12sec [17].

3.3   Leader Election Phase

Each node u maintains an internal list with all the leader nodes that are within $k - hop$ distance. This list is continuously broadcast to all neighboring nodes by piggy packing it in the periodic beacons of the neighbor discovery module.

A node u that has an empty list decides to nominate itself as a local leader and insert in the list the entry $\{id_u, dist_u = 0, null\}$.

When a node v that receives a list from a neighboring node u, it processes it as follows: for each entry $\{id_u, dist_u = 0, null\}$ it adds $\{id_u, dist_u = 1, v\}$; for each entry $\{id_x, dist_x, u\}$ it adds $\{id_x, dist_x + 1, v\}$. After processing the incoming list, it drops duplication entries and merges the conflicting entries (in which the id is the same) as follows: the node chooses the entry with the minimum id with the minimal dist (further ties are broken using the parent value).

Remark that the above update algorithm is a simplification of the one presented in [15]. Each node v maintains an internal array which consists of the most recent topology list received from each neighboring node u. The computation of v's topology list is done on the basis of this list. Furthermore, in the validation phase we also delete entries with $dist > k$. Consequently, v's list will reflect its neighborhood up to distance $k - hops$ from u. The correctness of the revised update algorithm is trivially preserved, and the convergence time is $O(k)$ rounds.

3.4   Clusters Construction Phase

As soon as a node nominates itself as a local leader it enters a waiting period of $O(k)$ period of time. Then it waits for the self-stabilizing update algorithm to collect the other identifiers and notify for the leader identity all nearby nodes within at most $O(k)$ rounds. If there does not exist a node u with distance less than k from v, with lower id than v, then v is a stable leader and initiates the cluster construction phase. If another node u is identified (With lower id) then v exits the waiting period and becomes passive.

Next, each active local leader starts a breadth-first search to identify all nearby nodes and invite them in its cluster. Nodes receiving the search message of local leader u respond by joining the cluster of the leader. The leaders define the cluster structure and since each node v may follow a different local leader in its neighborhood, if v decides to join the cluster formed by node u it sends back to u a response message. This process requires an additional $O(k)$ rounds.

The above algorithm is self-organizing based on the arguments used in [15] and the convergence time is $O(k)$ rounds.

4   Component-Based Implementation

4.1   Generic Implementation Using Wiselib

More often than not, in Theoretical Computer Science, researchers tend to design an algorithm in an abstract way. This happens because an algorithm should be able to be used in many different situations and it is up to the developer to decide the way it should be turned into code for a real system. Algorithm Engineering requires the algorithm developer to actually implement algorithms. This step from theory into practice is often considered hard and requires programming skills in addition to knowledge in algorithm theory. Almost every time the developer finds many limitations in the ways she can operate within the given hardware and software specifications. These problems are further augmented when implementing algorithms for wireless sensor networks due to the extremely limited resources and also due to the heterogeneous nature (both in terms of hardware and software). This also explains why many theorists, having only little Software Engineering experience, never engage in Algorithm Engineering. This situation is particularly alarming in distributed embedded systems.

We decided to implement our algorithm using Wiselib [8]: a code library, that allows implementations to be OS-independent. It is implemented based on C++ and templates, but without virtual inheritance and exceptions. Algorithm implementations can be recompiled for several platforms and firmwares, and even for simulators without the need to change the code. In its current version Wiselib can interface with systems implemented using C (Contiki), C++ (iSense), nesC (TinyOS), Android (via the C/C++ NDK) and iPhone OS.

An important feature of Wiselib are the already implemented algorithms and data structures. Since different kind of hardware uses different ways to store data (due to memory alignment, inability to support dynamic memory, etc.), it is important to use these safe types as much as possible since they have been tested before on most hardware platforms. In its current version, Wiselib includes about 60 Open Source implementations of standard algorithms including Localization algorithms, Cryptographic schemes, Distributed data structures etc..

Wiselib also runs on the simulator Shawn [16] and TOSSIM [24], hereby easing the transition from simulation to actual devices. This feature allows us to validate the faithfulness of our implementation and also get results concerning the quality of our algorithms without time consuming deployment procedures and harsh debugging environments. Furthermore, apart from ordinary sensor node targets or simulation environments, it is also possible to run Wiselib code directly on a PC. The PC therefore acts as a sensor node, but without any code space or execution speed limitations. On the one hand, there is basic OS functionality provided, such as a timer for event registration, or a clock providing the current time. On the other hand, it is possible to connect an IEEE 802.15.4 device to the PC, so that the PC can directly communicate with other sensor nodes.

4.2 Components Description

The component-based design that we propose is depicted in Fig. 1. We partition the logic of the clustering algorithm into three pieces with clear boundaries in terms of functionality provided. Each partition is designed so that it can progress its work in a relatively independent manner while ensuring the correct functionality of the algorithm. Clean interfaces are provided so that the partitions can easily communicate, fast and without heavy information exchange.

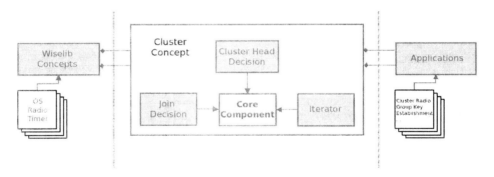

Fig. 1. Basic components and relation with Wiselib

Cluster-Head Decision (CHD). The first partition that we propose is related to the cluster-head selection process. We wish to implement the leader election mechanism as a single, stand-alone, software component. The component uses *call-backs* to the NEIGHBORHOOD DISCOVERY component so that it is re-executed whenever a change is detected in the node's neighborhood.

Join Decision (JD). The second partition is related to the methodology by which nodes decide to join cluster-heads. This component constructs the necessary payloads for the JOINREQUEST/JOINDENY/JOINACCEPT messages and it determines if a node will join a cluster when a JOINREQUEST message is received. The decision is based on the distance of the leader node and the ID of the node as described in Sec. 3.4.

Iterator (IT). The third partition is related to the organization of the nodes while clustering decisions are made by each node. This component is responsible for categorizing and storing neighbors into nodes that have already joined the cluster, nodes that have not joined the cluster yet and nodes that have joined another cluster. Collected information is maintained in *membership tables* by the IT component. These tables are of crucial importance for the algorithms that will be executed on top of the clustering – they are necessary to ensure cross-layering. This component also monitors the node's neighborhood and updates the *membership tables* based on observed changes to the network. This information can be used from the other components. For example, changes in the neighborhood that indicate that a node has left a cluster can trigger a new join decision process from the JD component.

The above three components are used by the main component which we call the **Core Component (CC).** It is the kernel of our architecture that controls and coordinates all other components so that clusters are properly formed and maintained. The CC provides a public interface for other algorithms to take advantage of the resulting network organization. In the following we present the life-cycle of CC when forming a new cluster.

1. CHD is invoked to determine if the node will become a cluster head or not.
2. If the node is a cluster-head: JD is invoked to send JOINREQUEST messages to nearby nodes and invite them to the cluster. The JOINREQUEST messages can be sent to all available nodes using Broadcast messages or to selected nodes using the selected nodes ids.
3. Upon receiving a *Join Request* message, CC isolates the message's payload and passes it to JD.
   If JD decides to join, a JOINACCEPT message is sent to the originator of the JOINREQUEST message, IT is notified of the address so for it to be saved as the node's *Cluster-head.*
   If JD decides not to join, a JOINDENY message is generated along with a payload from JD and passed to the originator of the JOINREQUEST message.
4. If a JOINDENY message is received, its payload is passed to JD to be examined, in case the neighborhood's conditions are of interest and the IT is notified in order to keep track of which neighbors have joined the cluster and which have not.
5. When all nodes have been examined the membership tables are generated by the IT and the process of cluster formation completes.

4.3 Implementation Details

In the following, we present a Wiselib concept for each one of four basic components. The design goal of the concept is provide clear interfaces so that the implementation can be easily used by other algorithms with minimum effort.

Core Component (CC) Concept. The CC concept takes as template parameters a set of components types such as RADIO, TIMER and DEBUG that are needed for sending messages, registering events and optionally printing debug messages. The most important parameters are the types for the CHD, JD and IT which the CC will use for the clustering algorithm. The first method that initializes the module also provides instances of the components that the module will use. Then we have two methods for enabling and disabling the module, which is useful when it should only be run in certain points in time. After the module is enabled, the FIND_HEAD() method is called and starts the cluster formation. Next, we have a method for setting the parameters of the algorithm, which also sets the parameters for every other component. Then, we have a method for registering a callback in order to get notifications upon events. Finally, CC provides a set of functions to access useful information such as the cluster id, the parent node(if any) etc.

The CC components also provides a public interface *that implements the Wiselib concept of Clustering* and thus provides the cluster's ID, the ID of the cluster-head, and also allows to register a function callback in order to be able to deliver events to external components whenever an change to the cluster occurs, e.g., when the node joined a new cluster, or a neighbor from different cluster was discovered, or a new cluster was formed etc..

Cluster Head Decision (CHD) Concept. In the CHD concept we have a method for setting the parameters (e.g., the probability value that the module will use). Additionally, there is the method for calculating if the current node is a cluster-head and a method to get this result.

Join Decision (JD) Concept. In the JD concept we have a method that gives the hop count from the cluster-head, after the node has joined a cluster. It also provides methods that set the payload for specific types of messages. The minimum requirement is three methods, for the JOINREQUEST, the JOINACCEPT and the JOINDENY messages. Finally, we have the method JOIN that is called with a new JOINREQUEST payload, and decides if it is going to join the cluster.

Iterator (IT) Concept. For IT, we provide methods for getting the cluster id and the parent of the node. Moreover, the NEXT_NEIGHBOR() method allows iterating through the neighborhood of the node. If the neighborhood information is not available, we can register a callback function that the Iterator will call to inform us about changes in the neighborhood.

5 Real Experiments

Recently, experimentally-driven research has become an instrumental tool in designing and optimizing novel networking applications. While simulations are still important tools, they suffer from several imperfections as they make artificial assumptions on radio propagation, traffic, failure patterns and topologies. Especially in the domain of wireless sensor networks, which are embedded into the environment, applications strongly depend on real-world processes that are often a result of complex interactions and are extremely difficult to model accurately. In order to design robust applications, developers need appropriate tools and methods for testing and managing their applications on real hardware in large-scale deployments. However, testbeds are expensive to set up and to maintain, hard to reconfigure for a different experiment and usually feature a fixed number of nodes. A possible approach to deal with these issues is to federate smaller-scale testbeds to form a virtual unified laboratory. WISEBED[1] [10] provides such a federation of testbeds consisting of heterogeneous sensor nodes (such as TelosB, Mica2, iSense or Sun Spot equipped with different sensors) and a collections of tools and methods to cope with implementing protocols and applications for heterogeneous networks.

We ended up using the WISEBED testbeds at UNIGE, CTI and UZL that are comprised of iSense nodes. An iSense node provides an IEEE 802.15.4 compliant radio, a 32-bit RISC controller running at 16MHz, 96kbytes of memory, a highly accurate clock and a switchable power regulator. We used 26 iSense nodes in UNIGE, 20 iSense nodes in CTI and 20 iSense nodes in UZL. In all experiments we set the transmission power set at $-6dB$ to enforce one-hop neighborhoods in room resolution. Data samples are collected every one second via the USB connectivity. The debugging was encoded out-of-band and it did not affect the experiments.

Due to space limitations we here report the results from the UNIGE experiment. Similar results hold for the other testbeds.

5.1 Assessing Channel Quality and Its Effect on the Performance of the Neighborhood Discovery Module

We conduct some preliminary experiments in order to fine tune the neighbor discovery operation of the algorithm. This essentially includes the appropriate adjustment of the two LQI threshold pairs (see Sec. 3.2) and the periodicity of the broadcast beacon. As expected the stricter the LQI thresholds, the smaller and more stable the neighborhood sizes will be. While when relaxing the LQI thresholds, the neighborhood sizes increase but also the system become prone to channel quality fluctuations. We tested two different pairs of LQI thresholds: $(35, 75)$ and $(55, 95)$. The resulting neighborhood sizes are depicted in Fig. 2. We conclude that the LQI threshold pair $(55, 95)$ is more suitable for the experimental testbed used. For this range the algorithm generates stable neighborhoods within a short period of time and the resulting topology is dense enough to allow the proper spreading of the traces (as it shall be reported in the sequel).

---

[1] http://www.wisebed.eu

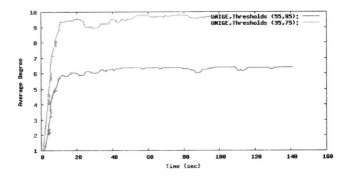

Fig. 2. Average neighborhood size with different LQI thresholds

We also examine the impact of beacon interval period and the neighbor timeout period in the detection of neighboring nodes. In Fig. 3 we test four different sets of beacon intervals. We measure the number of changes in the detected neighborhoods (i.e., the events) as the experiment evolves. It is evident that as the beacon interval increases, the neighbor discovery experiences fewer fluctuations. We believe that a beacon interval of $2000ms$ and above is a good trade-off between adaptivity and responsiveness to topology changes and induced overhead on the wireless medium.

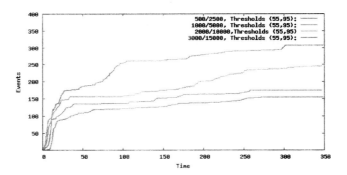

Fig. 3. Neighbor discovery for various beacon interval and timeout periods

5.2   Assessing the Speed and Quality of Adaptation

One would expect there exists a linear correlation between the time required for the module to stabilize (i.e., correctly detect the neighboring nodes) and the beacon interval. Reducing the beacon interval period (i.e., increasing the rate of transmission) should lead to a quicker response to changes in the topology (i.e., shorter delays in detecting changes to the neighboring nodes). Surprisingly, the results show that our intuition was wrong, the experiments reveal that for small beaconing values (less than $1000ms$) the time the Neighbor discovery module needs to stabilize is longer. This leads to a larger number of events generated. This is caused by the excess traffic generated due to the short beacon interval, which itself creates interference that leads to losses of message beacons. Thus, many neighbors are falsely removed and then re-added to the neighborhoods. Compared to the $1000ms/5000ms$, the $500ms/2500ms$ Beacon Interval/Neighbor Timeout needs about 30% more time to stabilize and generates almost double more events.

In order to assess how this *period of stabilization* affects the performance of the other modules of the network layer. Essentially, we wish to investigate if a high rate of events prevents the other algorithms from stabilizing and thus functioning properly. We run 30 minute experiments using short beacon interval periods of $500ms/2500ms$ and long beacon interval periods of $3000ms/150000ms$. As observed in Fig. 4, for the case of $500ms$ period, we observe that the total number of events. The Neighbor discovery module wrongfully reports changes in the topology for such sort beacon interval and this leads the Clustering module to constantly attempt to adapt to the new state. However, when using $3000ms$ beacon interval, the communication channels reported by the Neighbor discovery module seems to be stable as the number of generated events is very limited.

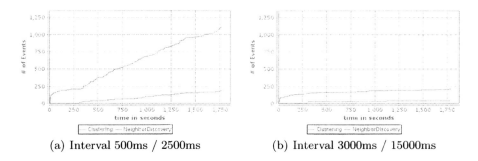

(a) Interval 500ms / 2500ms   (b) Interval 3000ms / 15000ms

Fig. 4. Events generated by the Clustering mod. while reacting to events generaged by the Neighborhood discovery module

5.3 Assessing the Ability to Adapt to Channel Failures

Channel failures refer to a situation where a node is unable to successfully send most of its outgoing messages due to temporary noise on the wireless communication medium. We emulate such a behavior by introducing a node called "the Jammer" that continuously broadcasts big messages in order to create collisions, reduce link quality and in general reduce the message delivery rate. The Jammer has normal communication range, identical to all other nodes. We position it in such a way to disrupt almost 50% of the network.

The experiments conducted consisted of 3 stages. Firstly, the Adaptation and Clustering modules worked for 10 minutes to reach a stable state, then the Jammer was turned on for 10 minutes and finally the Jammer was turned off and the network was left to stabilize again. As we can see in Fig. 5 the function of the Jammer heavily disrupts the smooth operation of both modules. During the channel disruption the Adaptation module continuously produces events and so does the Clustering module. Essentially, it creates the need to send more control messages in order to adapt to the new network state increasing the network traffic. When the disruption is over, network stabilizes and new events are rare.

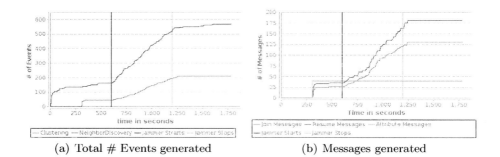

(a) Total # Events generated   (b) Messages generated

Fig. 5. Effect of channel failures on the performance of the Neighborhood discovery and Clustering modules

6   Conclusions

In this paper we have designed, implemented and extensively evaluated a clustering scheme for establishing adaptive hierarchical network structures for wireless sensor networks. We follow an experimental-driven research approach so that our system can be executed in real sensor networks. The extended experimental evaluation indicates that with proper fine tuning of the various algorithm's parameters, the resulting system can adapt to various internal and external events. In testbeds located in single-floor office spaces, stabilization was always reached within a very short period of time. In all cases the system returned to a stable state where all nodes participated in one of the formed clusters.

We believe that our experimental driven approach can be further optimized and for this we plan to conduct further experiments. We wish to examine mechanisms to adapt the protocol parameters as the system evolves dynamically. We wish to examine mechanisms that can adapt to concurrent events with heterogeneous performance parameters and in some cases conflicting goals. We also wish to combine our algorithm with specific application environments by exploiting the rich set of algorithm implementation provided by WISELIB pool of algorithms. One such application domain is the tracking of mobile assets in large-scale deployments. We believe that the hierarchical structure proposed here can be exploited to improve the scalability of the tracking process.

References

1. Abbasi, A.A., Younis, M.: A survey on clustering algorithms for wireless sensor networks. Comput. Commun. 30(14-15), 2826–2841 (2007)
2. Afek, Y., Dolev, S.: Local stabilizer. Journal of Parallel and Distributed Computing, Special Issue on Self-Stabilizing Distributed Systems 62(5), 745–765 (1997)
3. Anceaume, E., Défago, X., Gradinariu, M., Roy, M.: Towards a Theory of Self-organization. In: Anderson, J.H., Prencipe, G., Wattenhofer, R. (eds.) OPODIS 2005. LNCS, vol. 3974, pp. 191–205. Springer, Heidelberg (2006)
4. Baker, D., Ephremides, A.: The architectural organization of a mobile radio network via a distributed algorithm. IEEE Transactions on Communications 29(11), 1694–1701 (1981)
5. Baker, D.J., Ephremides, A.: A distributed algorithm for organizing mobile radio telecommunication networks. In: ICDCS, pp. 476–483. IEEE Computer Society (1981)
6. Bandyopadhyay, S., Coyle, E.J.: An energy efficient hierarchical clustering algorithm for wireless sensor networks. In: INFOCOM (2003)
7. Banerjee, S., Khuller, S.: A clustering scheme for hierarchical control in multi-hop wireless networks. In: INFOCOM, pp. 1028–1037 (2001)
8. Baumgartner, T., Chatzigiannakis, I., Fekete, S.P., Koninis, C., Kröller, A., Pyrgelis, A.: Wiselib: A Generic Algorithm Library for Heterogeneous Sensor Networks. In: Silva, J.S., Krishnamachari, B., Boavida, F. (eds.) EWSN 2010. LNCS, vol. 5970, pp. 162–177. Springer, Heidelberg (2010)
9. Chatterjee, M., Das, S.K., Turgut, D.: Wca: A weighted clustering algorithm for mobile ad hoc networks. Cluster Computing 5(2), 193–204 (2002)
10. Chatzigiannakis, I., Fischer, S., Koninis, C., Mylonas, G., Pfisterer, D.: WISEBED: An Open Large-Scale Wireless Sensor Network Testbed. In: Komninos, N. (ed.) SENSAPPEAL 2009. LNICST, vol. 29, pp. 68–87. Springer, Heidelberg (2010)
11. Chen, Y.P., Liestman, A., Liu, J.: Clustering algorithms for ad hoc wireless networks. Ad Hoc and Sensor Networks 30, 2826–2841 (2007)
12. Citysense - An Open, Urban-Scale Sensor Network Testbed, http://www.citysense.net/
13. Cournier, A., Datta, A., Petit, F., Villain, V.: Enabling snap-stabilization. In: Proc. of the 23rd International Conference on Distributed Computing Systems, pp. 12–19 (2003)
14. Ding, P., Holliday, J., Celik, A.: Distributed Energy-Efficient Hierarchical Clustering for Wireless Sensor Networks. In: Prasanna, V.K., Iyengar, S.S., Spirakis, P.G., Welsh, M. (eds.) DCOSS 2005. LNCS, vol. 3560, pp. 322–339. Springer, Heidelberg (2005)
15. Dolev, S., Tzachar, N.: Empire of colonies: Self-stabilizing and self-organizing distributed algorithm. Theoretical Computer Science 410, 514–532 (2008); FRONTS-TR-2008-22
16. Fekete, S.P., Kröller, A., Fischer, S., Pfisterer, D.: Shawn: The fast, highly customizable sensor network simulator. In: Proceedings of the Fourth International Conference on Networked Sensing Systems, INSS 2007 (2007)
17. Hay, S., Harle, R.: Bluetooth Tracking without Discoverability. In: Choudhury, T., Quigley, A., Strang, T., Suginuma, K. (eds.) LoCA 2009. LNCS, vol. 5561, pp. 120–137. Springer, Heidelberg (2009)
18. Heinzelman, W.R., Chandrakasan, A.P., Balakrishnan, H.: Energy-efficient communication protocol for wireless microsensor networks. In: 33rd IEEE Hawaii International Conference on System Sciences (HICSS 2000), p. 8020 (2000)

19. Iwanicki, K., van Steen, M.: Multi-hop Cluster Hierarchy Maintenance in Wireless Sensor Networks: A Case for Gossip-Based Protocols. In: Roedig, U., Sreenan, C.J. (eds.) EWSN 2009. LNCS, vol. 5432, pp. 102–117. Springer, Heidelberg (2009)
20. Iwanicki, K., van Steen, M.: On hierarchical routing in wireless sensor networks. In: Proceedings of the Eighth ACM/IEEE International Conference on Information Processing in Sensor Networks (IPSN 2009), IP Track, San Francisco, CA, USA, pp. 133–144 (April 2009)
21. Jiang, C., Yuan, D., Zhao, Y.: Towards clustering algorithms in wireless sensor networks: a survey. In: WCNC 2009: Proceedings of the 2009 IEEE Conference on Wireless Communications & Networking Conference, pp. 2009–2014. IEEE Press, Piscataway (2009)
22. Karl, H., Willig, A.: Protocols and Architectures for Wireless Sensor Networks. John Wiley & Sons (2005)
23. Katz, S., Perry, K.: Self-stabilizing extensions for message-passing systems. In: Proceedings of the Ninth Annual ACM Symposium on Principles of Distributed Computing, pp. 91–101 (1990)
24. Levis, P., Lee, N., Welsh, M., Culler, D.: TOSSIM: Accurate and scalable simulation of entire tinyos applications. In: 1st ACM International Conference on Embedded Networked Sensor Systems (SENSYS 2003), pp. 126–137 (2003)
25. Mamalis, B., Gavalas, D., Konstantopoulos, C., Pantziou, G.: RFID and Sensor Networks: Architectures, Protocols, Security and Integrations. In: Clustering in Wireless Sensor Networks. Taylor & Francis Group (2009)
26. Moscibroda, T., Wattenhofer, R.: Maximal independent sets in radio networks. In: PODC 2005: Proceedings of the Twenty-Fourth Annual ACM Symposium on Principles of Distributed Computing, pp. 148–157. ACM, New York (2005)
27. Parekh, A.: Selecting routers in ad hoc wireless networks. In: Proccedings of ITS, Rio-de-Janeiro, Brazil, pp. 420–424 (1994)
28. Selvakennedy, S., Sinnappan, S.: An adaptive data dissemination strategy for wireless sensor networks. IJDSN 3(1), 23–40 (2007)
29. SmartSantander - A unique in the world city-scale experimental research facility, http://www.smartsantander.eu/
30. Varghese, G.: Self-stabilization by counter flushing. SIAM Journal on Computing 30(2), 486–510 (2000)
31. Ye, M., Li, C., Chen, G., Wu, J.: An energy efficient clustering scheme in wireless sensor networks. Ad Hoc & Sensor Wireless Networks 3(2-3), 99–119 (2007)
32. Younis, O., Fahmy, S.: Heed: A hybrid, energy-efficient, distributed clustering approach for ad hoc sensor networks. IEEE Trans. Mob. Comput. 3(4), 366–379 (2004)
33. Younis, O., Fahmy, S.: An experimental study of routing and data aggregation in sensor networks. In: Proceedings of the IEEE International Workshop on Localized Communication and Topology Protocols for Ad Hoc Networks (IEEE LOCAN), pp. 50–57 (2005)
34. Youssef, A.M., Younis, M.F., Youssef, M., Agrawala, A.K.: Distributed formation of overlapping multi-hop clusters in wireless sensor networks. In: GLOBECOM. IEEE (2006)
35. Zhang, H., Arora, A.: Gs3: Scalable self-configuration and self-healing in wireless networks. In: Symposium on Principles of Distributed Computing, pp. 58–67 (2002)

Algorithms on Improving
End-to-End Connectivity and Barrier Coverage
in Stochastic Network Deployments

Zhilbert Tafa

Department of Computer Science
Belgrade University, Serbia
tafaul@t-com.me

Abstract. When a wireless network is randomly deployed on a region, there is only a certain degree of probability that the connectivity and/or barrier coverage between two sites will be provided. Therefore, it is important to develop mechanisms that will assure the high probability for these two QoS parameters to be provided when the gaps appear in the network. This paper involves the mobile nodes in order for the connectivity and/or barrier coverage gaps to be filled. The simulation results aim to evaluate the network deployment parameters (i.e., density of stationary and mobile nodes with respect to the communication or sensing radii, the size of the deployment area, and the deployment manner) in order the end-to-end (EE) connectivity (and, in similar manner, barrier coverage) to be provided with the probability close to one. By finding the most appropriate paths between two sites, two algorithms presented in this paper provide the directions on using mobile nodes for the EE connectivity and the barrier coverage to be improved in stochastically deployed networks.

Keywords: Algorithms, Barrier coverage, Connectivity, Wireless Sensor Networks.

1   Introduction

One of the most demanding implementations of the wireless sensor networks (WSNs) is related to military surveillance of the large inaccessible regions. When these networks are needed to be installed in order to detect the events, it is expected that their nodes wake up, organize themselves as a network, and start sensing the area for a phenomenon. There are many parameters that define the deployment quality. But, the main issue regarding the QoS is related to the ability of the network to cover the area of interest (i.e., sense the events) and transmit the information between the two accessible sites by either using single-hop or multi-hop communications. On top of these issues, other challenges are considered, such as: energy-efficiency of the media access and routing protocols, redundancy, security, etc. When dealing with deterministic network implementations, all of these issues can be more or less optimized. But, in practical stochastic deployments, there is no way for the connectivity and barrier coverage between a specific node of the network and the

D. Simplot-Ryl et al. (Eds.): ADHOCNETS 2011, LNICST 89, pp. 81–92, 2012.
© Institute for Computer Sciences, Social Informatics and Telecommunications Engineering 2012

accessible sites to be assured. Instead, regarding the connectivity, by using the theoretical observations such as the one given in [1], as well as the practical experiments such as the ones given in [2] and [3], by increasing the number of nodes and the communication radius, the connectivity can be improved to the probability near 1. But, due to the energy constraints, the communication radius is a very limited value, while the increase in the number of nodes is constrained by practicality. In addition to the application cost and the impracticality of placing the number of nodes (n) where n→ ∞, it has been observed in practice that a sensor network cannot be too dense because of spatial reuse; specifically, when a particular node is transmitting, all other nodes within its transmission radius must remain silent to avoid collision and corruption of data [4]. Therefore, other mechanisms on improving the connectivity should be explored.

In this work, we refer to the EE connectivity as the network ability to transfer the information from one site (end) to another in multi-hop manner using at least one path. Similarly, a belt region is considered to be barrier covered if there is at least one chain-like structure (formed by sensors) along the length of the belt that assures no object can cross the width of the belt without being detected by the network. Unlike the EE connectivity, where two sensors are considered to be connected if their distance is smaller than the smaller communication radius among them; when dealing with the barrier coverage, two nodes (u and v) are considered to be connected if their sensing ranges intersect, i.e., if the distance between them is smaller than the sum of their sensing radii. Building this structure between two parallel edges of the rectangle makes impossible for the object to remain undetected while crossing the region between two other perpendicular edges of the rectangle.

This paper covers the possibility of using robot-nodes (i.e., the nodes with incorporated mobility) for the lengthwise EE connectivity or barrier coverage to be improved across the rectangular area.

The main contributions of this paper are as follows. We design two algorithms namely: greedy path construction algorithm (GPCA), and run-based path construction algorithm (RBPCA). Using GPCA, we evaluate the influence the network density and the nodes' transmitting ranges on the ability of the network to transfer data from one site to another or to create the barrier in the same direction. We experimentally derive the values of the deployment parameters (the number of stationary nodes and the sensing/communication radii) that assure the barrier coverage and/or lengthwise EE connectivity between two sites and we additionally estimate the number of the mobile sensor nodes (and their positions) that would fill the EE connectivity and barrier coverage gaps when the network parameters deviate from these values. These results can also help in assessing the economical feasibility in implementations where the addition of few mobile nodes is economically comparable with deploying the much greater number of stationary nodes in order for the higher degree of the deployment quality to be provided.

The reminder of this paper is organized as follows. Section 2 reviews previous work on topic. The analysis framework with the basic definitions and problem formulation is given in section 3. In section 4 the designed algorithms are described. Section 5 contains the simulation results derived using GPCA algorithm. Conclusions and discussions, and future work are contained in section 6.

2   Related Work

In literature, connectivity issue is often treated together with the coverage. This is due to the fact that the models for the sensing and communication ranges are similar.

Critical conditions for the existence of barrier coverage along with an algorithm to construct sensor barriers are presented in [5]. Authors of [6] estimate the density needed to achieve coverage and connectivity in thin strips of finite length for four models of coverage, using the uniform deployment manner. A network model for barrier coverage, along with an algorithm to construct barriers is proposed in [7]. The authors compare line-based normal distributed vs. uniformly distributed networks in terms of barrier coverage. Similar work is presented in [8], where a probability analysis of barrier coverage is additionally conducted.

The methodology of relocating the mobile sensors with limited moving range, with the aim to minimize the variance in the number of sensors among the regions is presented in [9]. The construction of the maximum number of barriers with minimum sensor moving distance along with the effects of the number of mobile nodes on the barrier coverage are also covered in [10]. An algorithm similar to the one used in this paper was presented in [11]. However, this algorithm is designed specifically for finding and mending gaps in a network where there is a high probability for the next neighbor node toward the destination to be the one which also leads to the connected graph with the largest carry towards the destination. This is not the case in uniformly distributed network neither in some specific situations that we address in this paper.

3   The Analysis Framework

In this work, we experimentally evaluate the gap filling process in order for the EE connectivity and the barrier coverage to be improved. These two issues are treated together because the process of gap filling is the same for the both issues. Here, only the definition of a connection link differs depending on context being used.

In context of connectivity, we consider two nodes u and w to be in each other communication range (i.e., connected) if the distance between them is smaller than communication radius, that is $d(u,v)<Rc$. Generally, two nodes have different communication radii (because of various environmental factors). In that case, the upper inequality involves the smaller communication radius. In our analysis, we will consider the sensors have the same communication radii.

In the context of barrier coverage, the aim is for the sensor nodes to create the barrier, i.e., to be connected in the sense that their sensing ranges intersects. If a number of sensors create a barrier while connected this way, they provide the barrier coverage.

Given the above reasons, we will refer to the Rc as the connection radius. This parameter has different meaning depending on the context. It represents the communication radius (that is used for the connectivity issue) between two nodes u and w, with the nodes considered connected if $d(u,v){\leq}Rc$. In context of barrier coverage, it presents the sensing radius with the nodes considered "connected" if $d(u,v){\leq}2Rc$. Therefore, even though the proceeding analysis is related to the EE connectivity, the gap filling algorithm works in the same manner for the case of the barrier coverage, with the only difference in the way the two nodes are considered to be connected.

In Fig. 1 we consider the left vertical edge of the rectangle to be the source (S) and the right edge to be the destination (D). The aim is for the most efficient connection path from S to D to be provided. The path is considered to be efficient if it involves the smaller number of gaps and the smaller number of mobile nodes that would be necessary to fill these gaps. The nodes that are in certain proximity to the S are the only candidates to construct the paths. In Fig. 1 two connection paths from source to destination are provided: S1-D and S2-D. These paths are constructed by using stationary and mobile nodes. Among them, path S1-D is more efficient since it needs a smaller number of additional mobile nodes for the EE connectivity to be provided. Red lines present the connection links among stationary nodes that are in each others' communication radius, while black lines (also marked with X) show the possible position of the gaps (i.e., virtual connections).

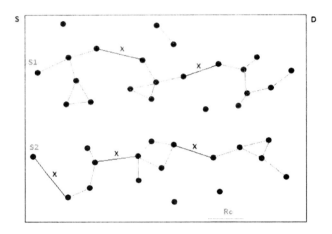

Fig. 1. Finding and mending connectivity or barrier gaps using mobile nodes

Description: In this example, GPCA algorithm is used. It is obvious that the path S1-D is more efficient than S2-D because it involves the smaller number of mobile nodes.

In the case when the density and the communication/sensing radius are constant values, we propose GPCA algorithm. The framework includes networks that are randomly distributed across the square region where starting and ending nodes have to be on the parallel edges of the square. We consider two deployment styles on the area, namely uniform and line-based.

First case refers to the network deployed across the square region randomly with the density $\rho = \frac{n}{A}$, where n is the number of nodes and A is the area of the region. The starting point of the analysis (S) is the proximity (smaller than Rc) to one edge of the square, while the ending point is the proximity (smaller than Rc) to another parallel edge.

The process of dropping the nodes out of a plane is often approximated using so-called line based deployment. It is defined as a combination of the uniform distribution along one axis and the normal distribution along other. Depending on the variance σ^2, the deployment can be wider or narrower in width, which corresponds to the deployment occasions (such as the influence of the wind, the height of the flight, the influence of the terrain, etc.). Both uniform and line based distributions are simulated using GPCA algorithm. This algorithm begins from the points of the accessible site, constructs communication paths (or builds the barriers) by using the stationary nodes, and proposes the positions of the mobile nodes until the created chain-like structures reach the destination site.

Our third scenario is (only theoretically) covered by using a designed RBPCA algorithm. This algorithm aims to overcome the observed weakness of the GPCA algorithm in situations where the density of the network and the communication/sensing radius vary on two-dimensional space. For example, the expected range of the transmitting radii for the free-space environment is different comparing to the range of the devices when the network is deployed in a forest. The examples of analysis regarding the differences in propagation patterns due to the type of the environment can be found in [12] and [13]. This means that, in a region, when designing the coverage and connectivity issues, the environment factor should be included. Therefore, the critical network density for achieving the connectivity and coverage varies over the same region. Furthermore, for example, in the case of airdropped sensors on the small hill, a greater number of sensor nodes are expected to be positioned on the bottom of the hill. These sensors now are more likely to get connected in a non-uniform manner resulting in some sub-graphs having the greater reach to the destination. Consequently, there is a higher probability that the connectivity and barrier coverage will be more efficiently addressed using the designed RBPCA algorithm.

4   The Algorithm Description

4.1   The Greedy Path Construction Algorithm (GPCA)

Let's denote the coordinates of the node i with Xi and Yi, *respectively*. The left and the right edges of the region (i.e., square) will generally be denoted by S and D, respectively. This algorithm firstly finds the nodes that can be accessed from an accessible site. These nodes communicate with other nodes in their radii and the connecting process continues until the graph created that way reaches the destination or maximum run on the direction of the destination. The node of the created graph that is closest to the destination now virtually connects to the nearest node toward the destination. This is registered as a gap, and the needed number of mobile nodes to mend this gap is calculated. The algorithm continues till the connection path reaches the destination.

The GPCA now works as follows:

1) Initialize the minimum number of gaps g=0 and the minimum number of needed mobile nodes m=0.
2) Find the nodes that are connected to the leftmost edge. If there are no such nodes, the network is deployed unsuccessfully. In simulation, the deployment is repeated.
3) Perform a routine that constructs a connectivity graph for each of these nodes, i.e., find the nodes that are situated in radius r, add them to the

appropriate sub-graph, and continue searching for their neighbors. Repeat the searching routine for each newly included neighbor until there are no more neighbors to be added. The output from this routine will be a number of connected or trivial graphs G1 (V1, E1), G2 (V2, E2)... Gn (Vn, En). Each of these graphs have at least one node reaching the S edge.

4) If any of the nodes that belong to G1, G2,..Gn has reached the distance Rc from the right edge, than the EE connectivity is considered to be provided and the program terminates returning minimum number of gaps g = 0 and minimum number of needed mobile nodes m = 0.

5) If not, find the rightmost node i from graph G1.

6) From the rest of the nodes (that do not belong to any of the graphs) find the node j which is closest to i and where $Xj > Xi$. This node will be positioned at a distance larger than r from node i, otherwise it would be reached by some of the graphs. Now connect i and j (in GUI depicted by black line). Increment g, and find the parameter m

If: $(d_{ij} - r) \bmod(r) = 0$

$$m = \frac{d_{ij} - r}{r} + m \ . \tag{1}$$

else:

$$m = \frac{d_{ij} - r}{r} + 1 + m \ . \tag{2}$$

In equation (2), the whole number part of the quotient (d_{ij} -r)/r is returned. Then 1 is added along with the previous value of the parameter m. In simulation program, the distance d_{ij} is approximated to the integer value.

7) Perform the routine (such as one in step 3) to construct the connected graph starting from the point j.

8) If the new rightmost node i (of the new graph) has not reached the distance smaller than r from D, then repeat from step 6. Otherwise return the values $g1$ and $m1$.

9) Repeat from step 5 for the graphs G2,...Gn.

10) Return $g = MIN (g1, g1,...,gn)$ and $m = MIN (m1, m2,.., mn)$.

When the algorithm terminates, only one of the graphs G1, G2,... Gn will be selected to provide the full barrier coverage from S to D (Fig. 7). It will contain the additional links created from the potentially added mobile nodes.

In analyzing the barrier coverage, only instead of using r (which in the above algorithm refers to the communication radius), the *2r* value is used, with *r* representing the sensing radius.

4.2   The Run-Based Path Construction Algorithm (RBPCA)

The RBPCA algorithm differs from the previous one in fact that, in the process of finding and mending the gaps, instead of looking for the next closest node (in the direction of D), it observes the trivial graphs and connected sub-graphs as a whole, while the main criterion in making the decision on which of them to use is the balance between their distance from a given graph and the run they provide toward the destination.

A simplified situation that describes the way the RBPCA functions is depicted in Fig. 2.

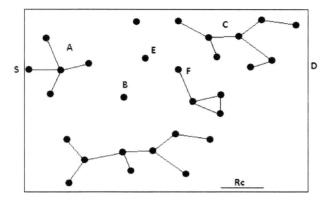

Fig. 2. An example when RBPCA over performs the GPCA

Description: In order to bridge the gap, GPCA would first choose the node B. In proceeding, according to GPCA, nodes E and graph F would be chosen successively. In the end, one of the nodes of graph F will bridge the gap with the graph C. This results in at least four additional mobile nodes. Using RBPCA, graph A directly bridge the gap with graph C, by using only two mobile nodes.

The decision (on which virtual link to use) is made based on maximum value among the ratios that satisfy:

$$\frac{RUN\ (Gi) - RUN(G_0)}{d_{ij} - Rc} > 1. \tag{3}$$

$$\text{While, } d_{ij} \leq 3Rc \ . \tag{4}$$

Where, RUN (G_i) and RUN (G_0) present the closest points the graphs G_i and G_0 can provide toward destination, respectively, while d_{ij} is the distance between the closest nodes of the graphs G_i and G_0. We refer to the node u that belongs to the sub-graph G_k , and that is closest to the D as RUN-node. This construction should overcome the problem of great number of small runs that can appear in GPCA algorithm. Great number of small runs can be expensive in the sense that they involve the greater number of mobile nodes. On the other hand this algorithm obviously introduces an extra communication and computation operations (because it does not search for only the nearest node in the direction of destination), which makes it more resource-hungry compared to the GPCA.

We have chosen maximum two mobile nodes for the depth of this algorithm, since we consider that a higher degree would degrade the performance, especially when the nodes are uniformly scattered, hence they would need more energy to cross the paths in order to mend larger barriers. For the case of $d_{ij}>3Rc$, the GPCA subroutine (i.e., finding the closest node toward the D) is simply performed.

The RBPCA works as follows: Initialize the minimum number of gaps g=0 and the minimum number of needed mobile nodes m=0.

1) Perform a routine that constructs connectivity graphs by connecting the neighbor nodes of each of the deployed nodes, i.e., find the nodes that are situated in radius Rc, and continue searching for their neighbors. Repeat the searching routine for each newly included neighbor until there are no more neighbors to be added. Group the nodes that can reach each other (in multi-hop communication) into sub-graphs and identify them by the sub-graph number. We choose for the sub-graph number to be the lowest ID of the node. The output from this routine will be a number of connected or trivial graphs G1 (V1, E1), G2 (V2, E2)... Gn (Vn, En).

2) Calculate the RUNs for each of the sub-graph (i.e., calculate the closest point to the D each sub-graph can reach to). At this point, besides its ID and the absolute position, each node knows the number of sub-graph it belongs to as well as the common RUN for that sub-graph.

3) Find all the sub-graphs Gsi that have at least one node situated in the proximity Rc from the S. If there is no such a sub-graph or trivial graph, the algorithm is terminated.

4) Given a Gsi (starting from i=0), from all the graphs Gj find the one that satisfies the condition given by inequality (4) and afterward calculate:

$$Max \ \{\frac{RUN \ (Gj)-RUN(Gsi)}{d_{ij}-Rc} > 1\} \ . \tag{5}$$

5) IF there is no such a sub-graph, find the RUN-node of the Gsi and treat the path between that node and the closest node toward D (ni) as the optimal one, i.e., perform a routine of the GPCA algorithm. Now let let Gj=Gsi.
ELSE Gj=Gsi.

6) Increment g and find the parameter m:
If: $(d_{ij} - r) \mod(r) = 0$

Then use equation (1), else use equation (2).
Here d_{ij} is the distance between the RUN-node of the sub-graph i and graph Gj

7) IF the RUN-node of the sub-graph Gj did not reach the destination, repeat from step 4.
ELSE: i++, repeat from step 4.

8) Return g = MIN (gs1, gs2,....,gsn) and m = MIN (ms1, ms2,.., msn).

5   Simulation Results

In order to generalize the observations, we deploy a number of stationary nodes on the square areas. By running the GPCA, we derive the number of additional mobile nodes needed for the EE connectivity to be provided with the probability close to one. The simulation results are shown in Figure 3. Here, the number of robots needed to mend the network gaps is presented with respect to the number of the stationary nodes and the ratio a/r, where a is the length of the edge, while r is the communication radius.

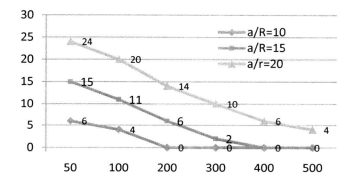

Fig. 3. The minimum number of additionally needed robots for the EE connectivity to be achieved with high probability (near one)

Description: Given the communication radii, one can determine the minimum number of mobile nodes needed to mend the connectivity gaps. The results can also be applied for the strip-like regions when the length of the region is an integer multiple of the region width. In the case of barrier coverage, the 2Rs parameter is used instead of Rc. As can be noted, the communication or sensing radius, greatly impacts the issues of EE connectivity and barrier coverage, respectively.

An important conclusion from the simulation is that, for a given number of stationary nodes deployed on a square region, numbers g and m depend only on ratio a/R. For typical communication radii of 10m, 20m, and 50m, our simulations now include the square regions 100x100, 150x150, 200x200, 300x300, 400x400, 500x500, 750x750, and 1000x1000. Another important conclusion is that these results can also be applicable for the strip-like regions where the area is $S=a \times (ka)$, precisely, if the length of the region is a k (integer) multiple of the area width, the number of additionally needed robots is $k \times m$, where m is the number of additional robots in the case of a square with dimensions $a \times a$. If the number of stationary nodes is p for the axa region, than this parameter would be xp for the area S. For example, from the Fig 3, one can conclude that, in a region of dimensions 600x300 = 2x300x300, when 400=2x200 stationary nodes are uniformly deployed across the region, with the communication range of 20 m (i.e., a/r=15), on average, 12 robot nodes will be necessary to mend the connectivity gaps with high probability.

Line-based deployment relies on uniform distribution along one axis and the normal distribution along other axis. In our case, sensors are uniformly distributed along the horizontal axis and normally along the vertical axis. According to the 68-95-99.7 rule for the Gaussian distribution, 99.7% of number of nodes is expected to fall within the distance $\pm3\sigma$ from the mean value, i.e., the horizontal line. Hence, the width of the region is not important as long as it is greater than 6σ. In this implementation, the network density cannot be expressed a constant value. Therefore, we find more appropriate to evaluate the minimum number of mobile nodes that can assure connectivity for different communication radii. In Fig. 4, the results are obtained using following values: $\sigma=10$, $\sigma = 20$, r=10, and r=20. The dimensions of the region are 400x400.

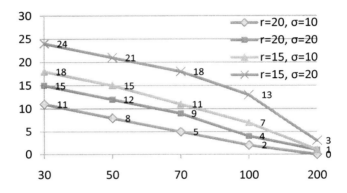

Fig. 4. Number of additionally needed mobile nodes versus number of stationary nodes in a line-based deployment across the 400x400 m2 area

Description: The dependence of value m (for two different radii and two different variances) on the number of stationary nodes across a 400x400 m² region where the network is deployed based on normal distribution along vertical axe.

It is important to note that these results can be generalized for distances shorter or longer than 400m. For example, for the area length of 1200=3x400 m, where r=20 and $\sigma=20$, if the network is deployed using 300=3x100 stationary nodes, the number of additionally needed robot nodes would be 12=3x4.

By relying on results in Fig. 4, we notice that the greatest impact on the EE connectivity and the barrier coverage in a line-based deployed network has the communication and sensing radius, respectively. The second parameter ordered by the influence on these issues is the variance, while the last important parameter is the number of stationary deployed nodes. In realistic implementations, the communication and sensing radii cannot be adjusted (primarily due to the energy and the environment constraints). Therefore, the designer should aim to improve the variance by making the width of the deployment area as narrower as possible. Afterward, by using results from Fig. 4, the number of additionally needed robots can be estimated.

6   Conclusions Discussions and Future Work

Stochastic deployment of the WSNs presents the most challenging design space for the network designer. In this environment, all layers of the protocol stack should be carefully planned. In addition, the cross-layer design is the only appropriate approach, especially when the large-scale, long-term WSN applications are meant to be installed on the inaccessible regions.

Connectivity and coverage are two of the basic issues that are to be evaluated at the very beginning of the network implementation. Shortly, without good coverage, network cannot sense the area properly while without network connectivity, it cannot transmit the sensed data. Therefore, these two issues give the meaning of using the WSNs for a given purpose.

The scope of analysis in this paper is limited to the barrier coverage and the EE connectivity issues.

We present two algorithms. GPCA algorithm is simpler and is appropriate when there is no information about the deployment environment. When the deployment is uniform over the region, there is the same probability for the sub-graphs with the same distance between the closest and the farthest position in one direction to be situated in proximity of any of the nodes. Therefore, the choice of the node that belongs to the sub-graph with the higher reach to the destination increases the probability for the most efficient path to be chosen. However, the situation that makes RBPCA more efficient is naturally unlikely to happen in a line-based deployed network, especially if the σ parameter is smaller. On the other hand, if the sensing or communication radii can be estimated, and if the deployment environment is known leading to the creation of the irregular sub-graphs, the presented RBPCA algorithm can perform better than the GPCA.

Since the difference between GPCA and RBPCA has its meaning only in specific situations, we present only the construction of the RBPCA and the situations where the routines of this algorithm can be used. On the other hand, in order to derive the experimental results and generalize them for the situations where environment factors cannot be predicted, a simulation process based on GPCA algorithm is conducted.

The results provide the minimum number of mobile nodes that would be necessary in the gap mending process of a randomly deployed network in a specific region. The results show that the main factor in constructing the EE connectivity and barrier coverage is the communication and sensing range, respectively. When these radii are large enough comparing to the area width (e.g., larger than 1/10), then the number of created gaps becomes similar or equal to the number of the needed mobile nodes to mend these gaps. Another important conclusion is derived on the fact that given the same number of stationary nodes and the same value of the ratio a/r, the number of mobile nodes remains the same.

The simulation results provide values for the various and the most typical WSN's implementations. Relying on these results, the designer can predict network parameters when planning to combine the stationary and mobile nodes in a specific deployment.

Our future work will be focused on building the simulation framework based on the RBPCA. A comparison of the results based on GPCA versus those based on RBPCA will also be the object of follow-up.

References

1. Gupta, P., Kumar, P.R.: Critical Connectivity Phenomena in Multi-hop Radio Models. IEEE Trans. Communication 37, 770–777 (1989)
2. X-Gang, Q., Li-Fang, L., San-Yang, L.: Experimental Study on Connectivity for Wireless Sensor Networks. JDCTA: International Journal of Digital Content Technology and its Applications 4(3), 184–189 (2010)
3. Maity, C., Gupta, A.: Critical Communication Radius Prediction with Random Distributed Nodes in WSN. In: Proc. of ASCNT, CDAC, India, pp. 31–38 (2010)
4. Ghosh, A., Das, S.K.: Coverage and Connectivity Issues in Wireless Sensor Networks. In: Shorey, R., Ananda, A.L., Chan, M.C., Ooi, W.T. (eds.) Mobile, Wireless, and Sensor Networks: Technology, Applications, and Future Directions, pp. 221–256. John Wiley & Sons (2006)
5. Dousse, O., Liu, B., Wang, J., Saipulla, A.: Strong Barrier Coverage of Wireless Sensor Networks. In: Proc. of the ACM International Symposium on Mobile Ad Hoc Networking and Computing, pp. 411–419 (2008)
6. Balister, P., Bollobas, B., Sarkar, A., Kumar, S.: Reliable Density Estimates for Coverage and Connectivity in Thin Strips of Finite Length. In: Proc. of the ACM on Mobile Computing and Networking, pp. 75–86 (2007)
7. Saipulla, A., Liu, B., Wang, J.: Barrier Coverage with Airdropped Wireless Sensors. In: Proc. of IEEE MILCOM 2008, pp. 1–7 (2008)
8. Saipulla, A., Westphal, C., Liu, B., Wang, J.: Barrier Coverage of Line-based Deployed Sensor Networks. In: Proc. of the INFOCOM 2009, pp. 127–135 (2009)
9. Chellappan, S., Gu, W., Bai, X., Xuan, D., Ma, B., Zhang, K.: Deploying Wireless Sensor Networks Under Limited Mobility Constraints. IEEE Transactions on Mobile Computing 6(10), 1141–1157 (2007)
10. Saipulla, A., Liu, B., Xing, G., Fu, X., Wang, J.: Barrier Coverage with Sensors of Limited Mobility. In: Proc. of the ACM on Mobile Ad Hoc Networking and Computing, pp. 201–210 (2010)
11. Saipulla, A., Liu, B., Wang, J.: Finding and Mending Barrier Gaps in Wireless Sensor Network. In: GLOBECOM, pp. 1–5 (2010)
12. Gay-Fernandez, J.A., Sanchez, M.G., Cuinas, I., Sanchez, J.G., Miranda-Sierra, J.L.: Propagation Analysis and Deployment of a Wireless Sensor Network in a Forest. Progress in Electromagnetic Research 106, 121–145 (2010)
13. Thelen, J., Goense, D., Langendoen, K.: Radio Wawe Propagation in Potato Fields. In: Proc. of the 1st Workshop on Wireless Network Measurements, Venice, Italy (February 2005)

Collaborative Spectrum Sensing Scheme: Quantized Weighting with Censoring

Valentina Pavlovska and Liljana Gavrilovska

Faculty of Electrical Engineering and Information Technologies, Skopje, Macedonia
{valenpav,liljana}@feit.ukim.edu.mk

Abstract. Spectrum vacancies that stem from current non-usage of the spectrum band by legacy primary users can be detected using various spectrum sensing techniques. These techniques depend on the actual knowledge of the radio environment being inspected, i.e. signal characteristics, noise levels etc. The simplest and most common spectrum sensing technique is energy based detection that needs no a priori knowledge about the monitored spectrum, but may lead to imprecision when assessing the possible presence (or absence) of a primary user. Therefore, possible collaboration among the nodes performing the energy based spectrum sensing (in terms of sensing reports exchanges) improves the reliability and avoids the hidden terminal problem caused by the shadowing from large obstacles. This paper introduces a novel collaborative spectrum sensing scheme with light communication overhead called Quantized Weighting with Censoring (QWC). The scheme includes censoring of the unreliable sensing reports in some range of uncertainty and introduces weighting coefficients for different quantization levels. The performances of the QWC scheme are compared with the Majority Voting (MV) and Equal Gain Combining (EGC) schemes. The results show that the QWC scheme outperforms the well known EGC scheme.

Keywords: collaborative spectrum sensing, quantized decision combining, data fusion, and cognitive radio networks.

1   Introduction

Wireless technologies and services lately experience tremendous growth making the available spectrum a scarce resource. Traditionally, the problem of spectrum insufficiency in wireless networks is tackled by fostering additional spectrum portions. Recently, several measurement campaigns showed that the current spectrum is underutilized [1] as a result of the currently static spectrum access policies that allow only legacy licensed users (termed as primary users) to use the spectrum. However, allowing so called unlicensed users (i.e. non-legacy users, secondary users etc.) to use the vacancies of the licensed spectrum (when the primary users do not use it) leads to significant improvements in the overall spectrum usage. This opens the possibilities for *dynamic spectrum access* and *cognitive radio networks* as its enablers.

The cognitive radio networks cope with the problem of spectrum scarcity by introducing secondary cognitive users, which are able to sense the spectrum and

D. Simplot-Ryl et al. (Eds.): ADHOCNETS 2011, LNICST 89, pp. 93–105, 2012.
© Institute for Computer Sciences, Social Informatics and Telecommunications Engineering 2012

detect temporary unused spectrum parts i.e. spectrum holes [2]. The secondary users communicate over the available spectrum holes left vacant by the primary users. The system of secondary (i.e. cognitive) users operates inconspicuously from the primary users. As a result, the secondary users must ensure reliable primary user detection by exploiting some spectrum sensing technique.

The simplest and most common spectrum sensing technique is *energy detection* [3]. It requires no a priori knowledge about the inspected spectrum. However, unexpected channel conditions may significantly degrade the performances since, due to fading or shadowing, a secondary user may infer absence of primary user even when it is present. The *collaborative spectrum sensing* overcomes this issue by using spectrum sensing data from more nodes in the final decision about the presence of the primary user (i.e. introduces a form of spatial diversity) [4, 5].

Collaborative spectrum sensing usually operates in two phases, i.e. *sensing* and *reporting*. In the sensing phase, each node senses the spectrum individually. In the reporting phase, the nodes report the sensing observations to common receiver/s (e.g. fusion centre/s) that reach the final decision about the presence of a primary user.

Collaborative spectrum sensing schemes can operate in various network topologies:

- centralized,
- decentralized and
- cluster based.

In *centralized* network structures, the nodes send the sensing observation to a common fusion centre that makes the final sensing decision and announces it to the nodes [6, 7]. In *decentralized* solutions, each node senses the spectrum locally and distributes its observation to all one-hop neighboring nodes. Afterwards, each node reaches the final decision based on its own and the received sensing observations [8]. The *cluster-based* solution applies a two level hierarchical approach. The nodes first contribute to the spectrum sensing decision process into the cluster. The cluster-heads then report the sensing decision to a common receiver that gives the sensing result [9, 10]. Generally, the collaboration is reduced to collecting the sensing reports and combining them in the decision making process.

The collaboration among network nodes can eminently improve the sensing performance because of the introduced spatial diversity. On the other hand, the collaboration gain causes additional control overhead [11]. Based on the way that the common receiver combines (i.e. fuses) the sensing reports, the following types of collaborative spectrum sensing schemes exist:

- Hard Decision Combining (HDC),
- Soft Decision Combining (SDC) or
- Quantized Decision Combining (QDC).

HDC schemes use one bit decisions of local nodes that are sent to the common receiver. The receiver combines the collected decisions with some specific fusion rule, e.g. AND, OR, Majority Voting etc. [12]. The SDC schemes combine the locally measured soft sensing results and operate better than HDC, but include higher control overhead compared with the one bit decisions in HDC [13]. The QDC schemes use quantization of the measurement reports in order to reduce the control overhead. These schemes are based on combining the quantized measured observation and usually operate better than HDC and worse than SDC [14]. Additionally, the censoring schemes exclude the nodes with unreliable observations from the collaboration, thus reducing the control overhead [8, 15].

This paper introduces a novel, bandwidth efficient, scheme for collaborative spectrum sensing, called Quantized Weighting with Censoring (QWC). In the QWC scheme, local node observations obtained with energy detectors are censored when they belong in the uncertainty area. Otherwise, the observations are quantized to one of four possible quantization levels. Additionally, a node calculates a weighting coefficient based on the amount of observed energy and forms a three bit local sensing report. These sensing reports are then linearly combined at the common receiver. The paper also introduces a novel method for optimal threshold selection for the quantized decision combining schemes. Furthermore, the Receiver Operating Characteristics (ROCs) of the newly introduced QWC scheme are elaborated in a comparison with the well known Equal Gain Combining (EGC) [13] and Majority Voting (MV) [12] combining rules. The results show that the QWC scheme outperforms both rules.

The QWC model for collaborative spectrum sensing performs the quantization differently from the existing models. The model proposed in [14] bases on uniform quantization method taken from the classical quantization approaches, while the QWC takes the PDF of the received signal when the primary user is present as a base for quantization. Furthermore, the QWC includes weighting coefficients, while the already known methods for collaborative spectrum sensing do not take weighting coefficients when performing quantization [14, 16]. Another novelty introduced in this paper is a method for decision thresholds calculation in a quantized decision combining model for collaborative spectrum sensing, based on the source definition for thresholds selection.

This paper is organized as follows. Section 2 describes the basic system model. Section 3 elaborates the collaborative quantized weighting with censoring strategy. Section 4 gives performance analysis of the proposed scheme. Finally, section 5 concludes the paper.

2   Analytical Background

This section explains the analytical background of the newly proposed QWC scheme. The targeted scenario of interest assumes one common receiver, several collaborating nodes and one primary user. However, the analysis is general enough, since the QWC scheme can be easily adapted to operate in decentralized scenarios as well as larger scenarios.

The secondary users sense a single path Rayleigh fading channel (i.e. narrowband flat fading channel). They use energy detectors to get an initial sensing observation and the received signal at the local nodes is:

$$y(t) = \begin{cases} h \cdot x(t) + n(t) & H_1 \\ n(t) & H_0 \end{cases} \tag{1}$$

where the received signal is given for the two possible hypotheses: H_1 when a primary user exists and H_0 when a primary user does not exist, $x(t)$ is a QPSK modulated primary user signal, $n(t)$ is a zero mean complex Gaussian noise and h represents the channel gain.

The energy detector calculates the sum of the squared samples of the received signal:

$$E_y = \sum_{n=1}^{N} |y[n]|^2 \tag{2}$$

where N is the number of sampling points.

The Probability Density Function (PDF) of the received signal with the energy detector under both hypotheses is [17]:

$$f_Y(y) = \begin{cases} \dfrac{1}{2^u \, \Gamma(u)} \, y^{u-1} e^{-\frac{y}{2}} & H_0 \\[2ex] \dfrac{1}{2}\left(\dfrac{y}{2\gamma}\right)^{\frac{u-1}{2}} e^{-\frac{2\gamma+y}{2}} I_{u-1}\left(\sqrt{2\gamma y}\right) & H_1 \end{cases} \tag{3}$$

where $\Gamma(u)$ is a gamma function, $I_n(.)$ is the nth order modified Bessel function of the first kind, $u = TW$ is the time bandwidth product and γ is the received Signal to Noise Ratio (SNR). The PDF of the received signal $f_Y(y)$, given with eq. (3) is chi-quadrate with $2u$ degrees of freedom under the hypothesis H_0 and non central chi-quadrate under the hypothesis H_1 with $2u$ degrees of freedom and parameter of non centrality 2γ. For large u ($u > 100$) these distributions become Gaussian.

The analysis in this paper assumes that the collaborating nodes exchange the sensing reports over an already established and error-free control channel because of the spatial proximity of the collaborating nodes. Generally, the establishment of the control channel and its impact on the sensing reports must be considered. The RAC^{2}E protocol, introduced in [18], can be used in a distributed network of cognitive users. It operates successfully and overcomes the problem of synchronization among secondary nodes.

3   Collaborative Spectrum Sensing Scheme

This section concentrates on a novel bandwidth efficient scheme for collaborative spectrum sensing, named Quantized Weighting with Censoring (QWC). QWC operates in a bandwidth efficient manner because the control channel relays only the quantized measurement reports and the scheme censors the nodes with unreliable observations. This scheme achieves better performances than the schemes with higher control overhead. The QWC scheme functions through the following phases: *quantization*, *weighting coefficients* selection, *thresholds determination* and *decision making* procedure.

3.1   Quantization

The main idea behind the quantization levels and thresholds selection is to divide the critical range of received energies in several segments (the QWC in this paper considers four segments). For this purpose, the Cumulative Density Function (CDF) of the received signal under H_1 is used. This CDF represents the probability for a primary user to be present over the range of received energies and it is used for quantization thresholds selections.

Each node determines the CDF under H_1 for the appropriate received SNR γ, by means of eq. (3). However, in some real implementation scenario the CDF should be predicted using one of the methods for PDF estimation elaborated in [19].

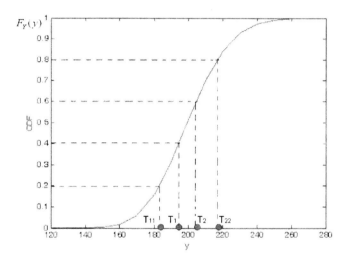

Fig. 1. Quantization threshold selection

Fig. 1 depicts the CDF of chi-quadrate distribution, $F_Y(y)$ for primary user presence under H_1 with $2u$ degrees of freedom and $\gamma = 0$. The quantization thresholds and levels are determined as follows.

• If $Ey \leq T_{11}$ then the quantization level is:

$$q_1 = T_{11} - (T_{11} - T_{11}')/2 \qquad (4)$$

where Ey is the amount of the received energy of a sensing node and T_{11} is the threshold for which the probability for primary user presence is 0.2

($F_Y(T_{11}) = 0.2$, Fig. 1). The threshold T_{11}' for which $F_Y(T_{11}') = 0.01$ is introduced because the quantization must be in some finite set of values.

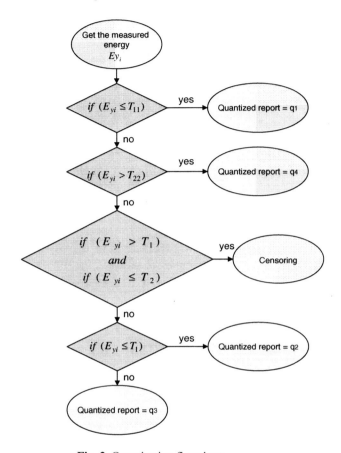

Fig. 2. Quantization flowchart

- If $T_{11} < Ey \leq T_1$ then the quantization level is:

$$q_2 = T_{11} + (T_1 - T_{11})/2 \qquad (5)$$

where, T_1 is chosen so that $F_Y(T_1) = 0.4$.

- If $T_1 < Ey \leq T_2$, then the QWC scheme censors the node.

The T_2 threshold is chosen so that $F_Y(T_2) = 0.6$. Thus, when Ey falls in an interval of $[T_1 - T_2]$, the probability for a primary user to be present (or absent) has the largest uncertainty (i.e. $0.4 < F_Y(E_y) < 0.6$) and therefore the node remains *censored*. Only nodes with reliable observations (i.e. lower uncertainty in terms of $F_Y(y)$) contribute to the decision making process for the presence of the primary user.

- If $T_2 < Ey \le T_{22}$ then the quantization level is:

$$q_3 = T_{22} - (T_{22} - T_2)/2 \tag{6}$$

where T_{22} is chosen so that $F_Y(T_2) = 0.8$.

- If $T_{22} < Ey \le T'_{22}$ then the level of quantization is:

$$q_4 = T_{22} + (T'_{22} - T_{22})/2 \tag{7}$$

where the QWC scheme introduces the threshold T'_{22} for which $F_Y(T'_{22}) = 0.99$, because the quantization thresholds must be fixed when determining the quantization level.

Fig. 2. depicts the quantization procedure with a flowchart for getting the quantized report from the measured energy observation E_{yi}, for the ith node.

3.2   Weighting Coefficients

The main idea behind the *weighting coefficients* selection is to assign an appropriate weighting coefficient for each measured E_y. The weighting coefficients emphasize the importance (i.e. reliability) of each local observation. This will result in intensifying the best sensing results for primary user presence and weakening the impact of the unimpressive ones.

The scheme chooses the weighting coefficients according to the CDF for primary user presence $F_Y(y)$, and they are calculated by each node locally using:

$$w_i = P(\gamma = E_{yi} / H_1) = F_Y(E_{yi}) \tag{8}$$

In order to avoid additional overhead, (because w_i should be also sent to the fusion centre) the number of coefficients is limited to eight. The calculated w_i-s are rounded to the closest coefficient from the set of determined eight coefficients.

The weigthing coefficients procedure uses only two coefficients per quantization level and this results in a total number of eight quantization levels. The final sensing report (quantized and weighted) from the ith node is given with:

$$\hat{E}_i = w_i q_i \tag{9}$$

The existence of only eight sensing report combinations reduces the control overhead to only three bits of information.

In general case, more than two coefficients per quantization level can be used. However, this increases the control overhead and imposes higher computation complexity calculating the decision thresholds.

3.3   Threshold Determination

The QWC scheme combines the quantized and weighted sensing reports from all nodes at the common receiver as a simple sum of individual sensing reports. The result of the combining is:

$$\hat{Y} = \sum_{i=1}^{Nu} \hat{E}_i = \sum_{i=1}^{Nu} w_i * q_i \tag{10}$$

where N_u is the number of collaborating users. The common receiver has to compare $\hat{Y}$ with a *threshold* in order to decide about the presence (or absence) of the primary user.

In general, the threshold for comparison is selected for a fixed false alarm probability, eq. (11):

$$P_{fa} = P(\hat{y} > Thr./H_0) = \int_{Thr.}^{\infty} f_{\hat{Y}/H_0}(y)dy = 1 - F_{\hat{Y}/H_0}(Thr.) \tag{11}$$

Adapted to the QWC scheme, $f_{\hat{Y}/H_0}(y)$ in eq. (11) represents the PDF of the quantized weighted and censored received signal under H_0 hypothesis. Then, $F_{\hat{Y}/H_0}(y)$ in eq. (11) is the appropriate CDF for $f_{\hat{Y}/H_0}(y)$.

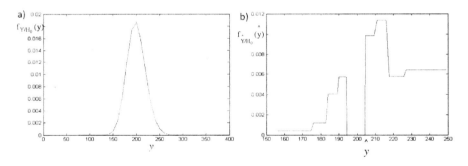

Fig. 3. PDF of the received signal with energy detector under H_0 a) without quantization, weighting and censoring, b) QWC case

The $f_{\hat{Y}/H_0}(y)$ needs to be calculated in order to find the optimal decision thresholds for QWC, following eq. (11). Fig. 3a represents the PDF of the received signal at a sensing node with energy detector under H_0, $f_{Y/H_0}(y)$ without quantization, censoring and weighting. The PDF at Fig. 3a is used for obtaining the PDF at a sensing node with QWC method, $f_{\hat{Y}/H_0}(y)$, where quantization, censoring and weighting are applied. Fig. 3b shows the PDF of the received signal under H_0 calculated for a sensing node that applies QWC, $f_{\hat{Y}/H_0}(\hat{y})$.

The $f_{\hat{Y}/H_0}(\hat{y})$, at Fig. 3b calculated from $f_{Y/H_0}(y)$ at Fig. 3a, uses the same quantization procedure (the same quantization thresholds and levels introduced in subsection 3.1).

The optimal thresholds determination when more than one node is implemented in the QWC scheme requires calculation of the joint distribution of the combined QWC sensing reports under H_0. The joint PDF is calculated as a convolution of the PDFs of quantized weighted and censored noise samples, $f_{\hat{Y}/H_0}(\hat{y})$ (depicted in Fig. 3b), since the QWC sensing reports are simply summed at the common receiver. Fig. 4 demonstrates these PDFs for different number of collaborating nodes.

The QWC scheme calculates the optimal decision thresholds for the appropriate number of collaborating nodes in accordance to eq. (11), integrating the PDFs on Fig. 4. Each value assigned to the P_{fa} results in a different decision threshold. This model for thresholds calculation assumes that noise PDF can be estimated at the common receiver through the methods for PDF estimation (elaborated in [19]). It should be noticed that the thresholds are simply the margin of noise for the collected sensing reports, above which the primary user signal is proclaimed as present.

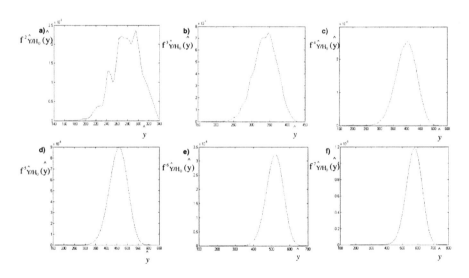

Fig. 4. The PDFs of the combined signal with QWC under H_0 for a) 2 nodes, b) 3 nodes, c) 4 nodes, d) 5 nodes, e) 6 nodes and f) 7 nodes

The common receiver computes the thresholds depending on the number of collaborating nodes after the initial establishment of collaboration group based on the measured noise statistics. For further operation the thresholds are already calculated and may be periodically refreshed based on updates of noise statistic estimations.

3.4   Decision Making Process

The decision making process results in the final collaborative sensing decision regarding primary user presence. The common receiver decides about the presence of the primary user comparing the combined sensing report with a threshold. The decision $d(\hat{Y})$ is either 1, when $\hat{Y}$ is larger than a predicted *threshold* (i.e. a primary user is found), or 0, when $\hat{Y}$ is lower than a predicted *threshold* (i.e. a primary user is not found):

$$d(\hat{Y}) = \begin{cases} 1, & if \quad \hat{Y} > Threshold \\ 0, & if \quad \hat{Y} \leq Threshold \end{cases} \tag{12}$$

4   Performance Analysis

This section elaborates the performances of the QWC collaborative spectrum sensing scheme. It compares the ROC curves of the QWC scheme for different number of collaborating nodes with the MV decision rule as the most common representatives of the HDC [12] and EGC schemes respectively [13]. Additionally, the section observes the detection probability dependence from the received SNR at the nodes.

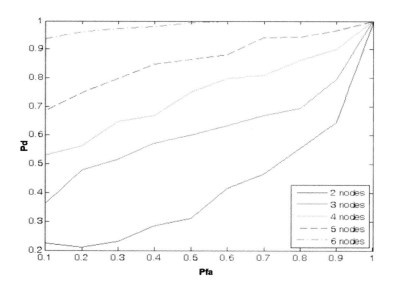

Fig. 5. ROC curves for different number of nodes in QWC scheme

The ROC curves for various numbers of collaborating nodes for QWC are depicted on Fig. 5. It is obvious that collaboration leads to significant collaboration gain as the number of collaborating nodes increases. Fig. 6 demonstrates the comparison between the QWC, MV and EGC for different number of collaborating nodes. The collaboration gain of QWC exceeds those of the MV and EGC for the case of six collaborating nodes (Fig. 6a). When the number of collaborating nodes decreases, the collaboration gain for QWC also decreases (Fig. 6b and 6c). For two collaborating nodes (Fig. 6c), the detection probability of QWC is smaller than EGC, but still higher than MV. The tendency of the QWC scheme to perform better than the EGC is due to the changed noise and signal statistics. As a result, the ROC curves of QWC have tendencies to increase faster with increased number of nodes and vice versa. The considered sampling frequency for the results on Fig. 5 and 6 is 10 KHz, the time bandwidth product u is 100, which means the number of sampling points is $N = 2*u$ and the received SNR γ at the nodes is 0 dBm. The results are obtained by Monte Carlo simulations done in MATLAB [20] based on centralized scenario with several collaborating nodes, one primary user and one common receiver, as supposed in section 2.

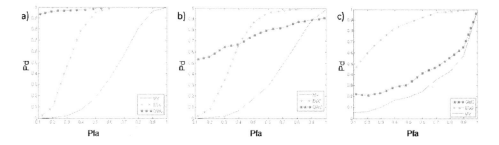

Fig. 6. Comparison of MV, EGC and QWC, for: a) 6 nodes, b) 4 nodes and c) 2 nodes

It is evident that the minimal required number of nodes for justifiable QWC usage in the targeted scenario is six. As the number of collaborating nodes decreases, the detection probability also decreases faster than in the EGC and MV cases. Additionally, it is recommended to use more than six nodes in collaborating groups since the censoring scheme itself yields frequent operation of various nodes in the censored fashion. This will avoid the collaboration gain reduction.

Fig. 7 shows the detection probability versus SNR for a fixed value of false alarm probability of 0.5. It can be concluded that all schemes operate well when the received SNR is higher than 0 dBm. For six collaborating nodes the QWC scheme achieves better detection probability than the EGC and MV schemes for the same value of SNR (Fig. 7a). For two nodes (Fig. 7c), the QWC operates worse than EGC and slightly better from MV as expected.

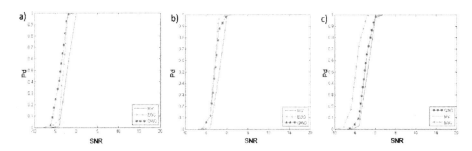

Fig. 7. Detection probability versus SNR, for Pfa=0.5 for: a) 6 nodes, b) 4 nodes, c) 2 nodes

5   Conclusion

This paper introduced a novel method (i.e. QWC) for combining the quantized measurement reports from the individual nodes that participate in collaborative spectrum sensing. The QWC is a bandwidth and energy efficient method that censors the unreliable nodes, while the remaining ones are allowed to send only three bits of quantized sensing report to the common receiver. The QWC outperforms the EGC, even with smaller overhead, because the quantization and weighting coefficients modify the test statistics of the received signal and the optimal decision thresholds are calculated, accordingly.

Future work will be concentrated on expanding the QWC scheme to joint multiband collaborative spectrum sensing.

Acknowledgements. Parts of this work were funded by the EC through the FP7 projects QUASAR (ICT-248303) [21] and inspired by ACROPOLIS (FP7-257626) [22]. The authors would like to thank everyone involved.

References

1. Federal Communications Commission. Spectrum policy task force report, FCC 02-155 (November 2002)
2. Akyildiz, I.F., Lee, W.-Y., Vuran, M.C., Mohanty, S.: NeXt Generation / Dynamic Spectrum Access / Cognitive Radio Wireless Networks: A Survey. Computer Networks Journal (Elsevier) 50, 2127–2159 (2006)
3. Digham, F.F., Alouini, M.S., Simon, M.K.: On the energy detection of unknown signals over fading channels. In: IEEE International Conference on Communications, ICC 2003, vol. 5 (2003)
4. Letaief, K.B., Zhang, W.: Cooperative Communications for Cognitive Radio Networks. Proceedings of the IEEE 97(5) (May 2009)
5. Akyildiz, I.F., Lo, B.F., Balakrishnan, R.: Cooperative Spectrum Sensing in Cognitive Radio Networks: A Survey. Physical Communication (Elsevier) Journal 4(1), 40–62 (2011)
6. Zhang, W., Mallik, R.K., Letaief, K.B.: Cooperative Spectrum Sensing Optimization in Cognitive Radio Networks. In: Proc. IEEE ICC 2008 (2008)

7. Li, J., Liu, J., Long, K.: Reliable Cooperative Spectrum Sensing Algorithm Based on Dempster-Shafer Theory. In: Proceedings of IEEE Globecom (December 2010)
8. Kaewprapha, P., Li, J., Yu, Y.: Cooperative Spectrum Sensing with Tri-State Probabilistic Inference. In: Proceedings of MILCOM 2010 (November 2010)
9. Kim, W., Jeon, H., Im, S., Lee, H.: Optimization of Multi-Cluster Multi-Group based Cooperative Sensing in Cognitive Radio Networks. In: Proceedings of MILCOM 2010 (November 2010)
10. Haas, Z.J., Chen, T.-C.: Cluster-based Cooperative Communication with Network Coding in Wireless Networks. In: Proceedings of MILCOM 2010 (November 2010)
11. Ghasemi, A., Sousa, E.S.: Spectrum sensing in cognitive radio networks: the cooperation-processing tradeoff. Wireless Communications & Mobile Computing 7(9), 1049–1060 (2007)
12. Armi, N., Saad, N.M., Arshad, M.: Hard Decision Fusion based Cooperative Spectrum Sensing in cognitive Radio System. ITB Journal of Information and Communication Technology 3(2), 109–122 (2009)
13. Ghasemi, A., Sousa, E.S.: Opportunistic Spectrum Access in Fading Channels Through Collaborative Sensing. Journal of Communications 2(2), 71–82 (2007)
14. Birkan Yilmaz, H., Tugcu, T., Alagoz, F.: Uniform Quantizer for Cooperative Sensing in Cognitive Radio Networks. In: Proceedings of 21st Annual IEEE International Symposium on Personal, Indoor and Mobile Radio Communications (September 2010)
15. Sun, C., Zhang, W., Letaief, K.B.: Cooperative Spectrum Sensing for Cognitive Radios under Bandwidth Constraints. In: Proceedings of IEEE WCN (March 2007)
16. van den Biggelaar, O., Dricot, J.M., De Doncker, P., Horlin, F.: Quantization and Transmission of the Energy Measures for Cooperative Spectrum Sensing. In: Proceedings of VTC Spring (2011)
17. Atapattu, S., Tellambura, C., Jiang, H.: Relay Based Cooperative Spectrum Sensing. In: Proceedings of IEEE Globecom (December 2009)
18. Pavlovska, V., Denkovski, D., Atanasovski, V., Gavrilovska, L.: RAC2E: Novel Rendezvous Protocol for Asynchronous Cognitive Radios in Cooperative Environments. In: Proceedings of 21st Annual IEEE International Symposium on Personal, Indoor and Mobile Radio Communications (September 2010)
19. Raykar, V.C.: Probability Density Function Estimation by different Method, report for ENEE 739Q, part of the course project (Spring 2002)
20. MATLAB. Information, http://www.matlab.com
21. EC FP7 project QUASAR, Information, http://www.quasarspectrum.eu
22. EC FP7 project ACROPOLIS, Information, http://ict-acropolis.eu

Performance Analysis of Multichannel Radio Link Control in MIMO Systems

Jun Li[1], Yifeng Zhou[1], Yuanyuan Liu[2,*], and Louise Lamont[1]

[1] Communications Research Centre Canada, Ottawa, ON, Canada K2H 8S2
{jun.li,yifeng.zhou,louise.lamont}@crc.gc.ca
[2] School of Mathematics, Central South University, Changsha, China 410075
liuyy@csu.edu.cn

Abstract. With rapid advances in wireless communications, multiple-input multiple-output (MIMO) antennas technology has been integrated into next-generation wireless communication standards. In this paper, we introduce a MIMO system model, propose a multichannel radio link control protocol and a dynamic channel scheduling policy. We then conduct a performance study on the multichannel link control protocol with two different scheduling policies (*i.e.*, dynamic and static scheduling) using simulations. Simulation results show that the dynamic scheduling outperforms the static scheduling. It is observed that the average packet delay with the dynamic scheduling increases with the average error rate of parallel channels, but decreases with the variance in the error rates of parallel channels. More interestingly, the number of parallel channels has only an insignificant impact on the average packet delay, when the dynamic scheduling is applied in MIMO systems, from which we confirm that the use of parallel channels is a favorable option for packet data networking in the point of view of the link-layer performance.

Keywords: Mobile communications, MIMO techniques, flow and error control, resource allocation and management, performance modeling and analysis, packet delay.

1 Introduction

With rapid advances in wireless communications, multiple-input multiple-output antennas (MIMO) technology [19] has been adopted for next-generation (*i.e.*, 4G) wireless or mobile communication standards, such as high-speed downlink packet access (HSDPA) [2], IEEE 802.16 (WiMax) [1], and 3GPP Long Term Evolution (LTE) [3], to increase data transmission rate. Since an automatic-repeat-request (ARQ) scheme (*i.e.*, one of the following three classical ARQ schemes: stop-and-wait ARQ (SW-ARQ), go-back-N ARQ (GBN-ARQ), and selective-repeat ARQ (SR-ARQ) achieves reliable transmission of packets over intrinsically unreliable wireless links, ARQ-based radio link control has been

---

* Corresponding author.

D. Simplot-Ryl et al. (Eds.): ADHOCNETS 2011, LNICST 89, pp. 106–116, 2012.
© Institute for Computer Sciences, Social Informatics and Telecommunications Engineering 2012

extensively used in current-generation (*i.e.*, 3G) wireless networks, such as Universal Mobile Telecommunications System (UMTS) [4] and CDMA2000, with the aim at the provisioning of data services. Moreover, it has been reported that these traditional ARQ protocols, which have been developed for single-channel communications, can be generalized to achieve reliable packet transmission over multiple channels [10,13,17,21]. As a result, multichannel ARQ has become an integral part in the radio link control sub-layer of 4G wireless communication standards for high-speed multimedia services [8,11].

Several studies on multichannel ARQ protocols have been reported in the literature. System throughput performance in multichannel ARQ protocols was studied in [7,12,20], which are not directly related to the performance metric studied in this paper. Chang and Yang [5] analyzed the average packet delay for the three classical ARQ protocols over multiple identical channels (*i.e.*, all channels have the same transmission rate and the same error rate). Fujii and Hayashida and Komatu [9] derived the probability distribution function of the packet delay for GBN-ARQ over multiple channels that have the same transmission rate but possibly different error rates. Ding [6] considered ARQ protocols for parallel channels that possibly have both different transmission rates and different error rates, and derived approximate expressions of the mean packet delay for them. Unfortunately, it was reported that these approximation results can substantially deviate from the true values as the error rates become relatively large [6]. The resequencing issue in multichannel ARQ protocols was addressed by Shacham and Chin [18], and recently by Li and Zhao [14], who also studied the packet delay distribution function for SW-ARQ over multiple channels by using an end-to-end analytical approach [15].

Thanks to studies (*e.g.*, [5,7,20]) on the system throughput, multichannel SR-ARQ has been shown to be the most efficient in terms of the throughput performance among these multichannel ARQ protocols. In comparison, we have a lack of understanding of the packet delay performance of multichannel SR-ARQ. In this paper, we propose a SR-ARQ based link control protocol for MIMO and systematically evaluate the average packet delay performance of the multichannel radio link control protocol with either dynamic or static channel scheduling. We first introduce a MIMO system model, where a transmitter-receiver pair connected by a generic number of forward channels is considered. The multichannel radio link control sub-layer of the MIMO system is composed of two components: the SR-ARQ based protocol for MIMO (SABP) and a packet-to-channel scheduling policy. Under the saturated traffic condition (*i.e.*, packets are always supplied at the transmitter), delay of a packet is measured by the duration between the instant at which the packet is transmitted for the first time and the time it departs from the resequencing queue at the receiver. Using simulations, we investigate the performance of the average packet delay for SABP and the impact of different channel scheduling policies on the average packet delay performance.

The main contributions of this paper are introduction of a MIMO system model and a multichannel radio link control protocol, and the performance evaluation of the multichannel radio link control protocol under static and dynamic channel scheduling policies. Simulation results show that the dynamic scheduling always outperforms the static scheduling. With the dynamic scheduling policy, the average packet delay increases with the average of error rates of the parallel channels, but decreases with the variance in the error rates; with the static scheduling policy, the average packet delay increases with either the average error rate or the variance in the error rates. In addition, if the average error rate among parallel channels remains fixed, the number of parallel channels has an insignificant impact on the average packet delay when the dynamic scheduling policy is applied. However, the average packet delay is severely affected by the number of parallel channels when the static scheduling policy is used.

The rest of this paper is organized as follows. Section 2 describes a MIMO system model. A multichannel radio link control protocol and two channel scheduling policies are introduced in Section 3. Simulation results for the average packet delay are presented and discussed in Section 4, followed by the final section concluding this study.

2   MIMO System Model

In this section, we describe a MIMO system model, where a multichannel radio link control protocol (to be elaborated in Section 3) operates.

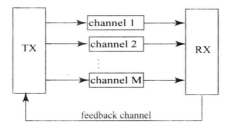

TX and RX denote transmitter and receiver, respectively.

Fig. 1. MIMO System Model

A MIMO system consists a transmitter and a receiver. The transmitter-receiver pair communicates data packets for one communication session (*e.g.*, a video file transfer). As illustrated in Fig. 1, the forward link from the transmitter to the receiver consists of M ($M \geq 2$) channels that transmit data packets simultaneously with the multiple antennas equipped in the transmitter and the receiver. Each of the channels is identified with channel i for $i = 1, 2, \cdots, M$, and each channel i is characterized by a data transmission rate and a packet error rate p_i. (The transmission rate of a channel is measured by the maximum number of bytes of data that can be transmitted over that channel during a specified time period; the packet error rate of a channel characterizes the packet loss property of the channel when transmitting packets.) We assume that the packet loss property of a channel is time-invariant, which means that the error rate p_i for channel i is a real number in $(0, 1)$ representing the probability that a packet transmitted over the channel is erroneously received or simply lost. Packet errors that occur in different channels are assumed to be independent. In addition, a high-rate cyclic redundancy check (CRC) error-detection code and a feedback channel are provided in the system. We assume that an erroneous packet can always be detected and that the feedback channel is error-free for transmitting acknowledgement frames.

Each packet to be transmitted is identified by a unique integer number, referred to as the sequence number. We assume that the transmitter has a buffer, referred to as the transmission queue, where there are always packets waiting for transmission. That is, an infinite number of packets are waiting in the transmission queue for first-in-first-out transmission and retransmission with respect to their sequence numbers. Another buffer, referred to as the resequencing queue, is provided at the receiver to temporarily store unqualified packets. An unqualified packet is referred to as a correctly received packet with the property that at least one packet with a smaller sequence number has not been correctly received. All channels have the same transmission rate, and the M channels are time-slotted with one unit (or slot) equal to the transmission time of a packet over a channel. Therefore, the transmission rate of each channel is one packet per slot. All packets, when transmitted from the transmitter to the receiver, have a fixed round trip time (RTT) equal to $(\tau - 1)$ slots, which is assumed to be an even number of slots. A packet experiences the same propagation delay in forward and feedback channels, which is $(\tau - 1)/2$ slots. The transmitter sends multiple packets at a time, one per channel. All channels share the same set of sequence numbers of the packets in packet-to-channel scheduling (to be discussed in Section 3.2). The M channels have possibly different error rates. That is, the packet error rate p_i of channel i, for $i = 1, \cdots, M$, might be different from the packet error rate p_j of channel j when $i \neq j$. By assuming that a perfect channel estimation is accomplished, the transmitter has knowledge about the condition (e.g., the error rate) of each channel, according to which a dynamic scheduling (to be discussed in Section 3.2) can be implemented at the transmitter. A multichannel radio link control protocol (MRLC), which will be detailed in the next section, is used for traffic flow and packet error control.

3   Multichannel Radio Link Control (MRLC)

In this section, we elaborate a SR-ARQ based radio link control protocol and two different channel scheduling policies for traffic flow and error control in the MIMO system described in Section 2.

3.1   SABP: A SR-ARQ Based Link Control Protocol for MIMO

At the beginning of each slot, the transmitter starts transmitting a block of M packets to the receiver and completes transmission at the end of the slot. The receiver receives the block of M packets, which were transmitted in slot t for $t = 0, 1, \cdots$, at the end of slot $t + (\tau - 1)/2$ (see Fig. 2). The packet transmitted over channel i is received erroneously or simply lost with probability p_i. At the receiver, an erroneously received or lost packet corresponds to a negative acknowledgement (NACK), while a correctly received packet corresponds to a positive acknowledgement (ACK). Then the receiver sends an acknowledgement frame containing exactly M acknowledgements (ACKs/NACKs) corresponding to the most recently received block of M packets, to the transmitter. We assume that transmission of the acknowledgement frame takes no time at the receiver and is completed at the end of slot $t + (\tau - 1)/2$.

After sending the acknowledgement frame, the receiver discards erroneously received packets, delivers the qualified packets, and stores the unqualified packets in the resequencing buffer. A qualified packet is a correctly received packet with a sequence number such that all packets with a smaller sequence number have been correctly received. The transmitter receives the acknowledgement frame, which is associated with the block of M packets transmitted at slot t, at the end of slot $t + \tau - 1$. It checks each acknowledgement in the acknowledgement frame, and prepares the next block of M packets to transmit at slot $t + \tau$ according to the following rule: If there is no NACK in the acknowledgement frame, the next block to transmit is composed of M new packets; if the acknowledgement frame contains one or more, for example k, NACKs, the next block of M packets consist of those k old packets, which are negatively acknowledged by the receiver, and $M - k$ new packets (see Fig. 2). Meanwhile, the transmitter removes these positively acknowledged packets from the transmission queue. These selected M packets are to be transmitted in slot $t + \tau$ according to one of the following packet-to-channel scheduling policies.

3.2   Packet-To-Channel Scheduling

To simultaneously transmit a block of M packets over the M channels in a slot, either one of the following two packet-to-channel scheduling policies: dynamic scheduling and static scheduling, can be applied. The dynamic scheduling is illustrated in Fig. 2, where $p_1 \leq p_2 \leq p_3$ is assumed, and works as follows. The best channel (*i.e.*, a channel with the smallest error rate) is assigned to the packet associated with the smallest sequence number in the block; the second best channel is assigned to the packet associated with the second smallest sequence number; and so forth.

The counterpart of the dynamic scheduling is the static scheduling, which is illustrated in Fig. 3 with $p_1 \leq p_2 \leq p_3$. With the static scheduling policy, an old packet (*i.e.*, a packet to be retransmitted) is always assigned to the same channel for retransmission as the originally assigned one, while a new packet (*i.e.*, a packet to be transmitted for the first time) is assigned to a uniformly chosen channel among those available for transmitting new packets. As will be shown from simulation results presented in the next section, the dynamic scheduling achieves a better protocol performance than the static scheduling.

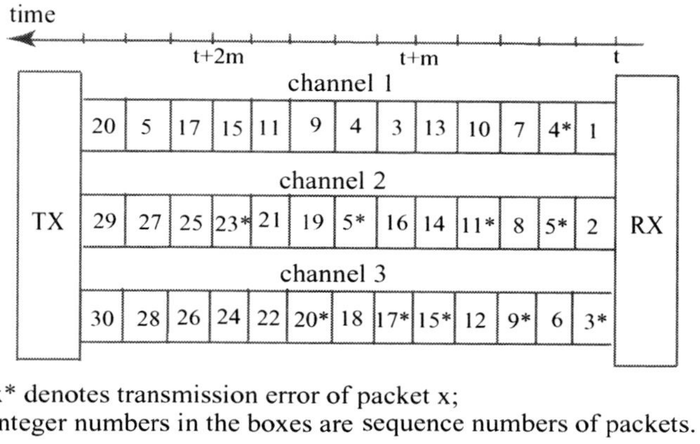

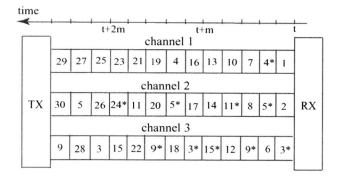

x* denotes transmission error of packet x;
integer numbers in the boxes are sequence numbers of packets.

Fig. 2. Dynamic Channel Scheduling ($M = 3; \tau = 5$)

Fig. 3. Static Channel Scheduling ($M = 3; \tau = 5$)

4 Performance Evaluation of MRLC

In this section, we conduct a simulation study to evaluate the performance of the multichannel radio link control protocol with either dynamic or static channel scheduling. The performance metric that we consider is the average packet delay. The delay of a packet is defined as the amount of time (*i.e.*, the number of slots) between the instant at which the packet is transmitted for the first time and the instant at which it departs from the resequencing queue in the receiver. We investigate the impact of the channel scheduling policies and the protocol parameters on the average packet delay performance through simulations.

4.1 Simulation Environment

We use the SimPy simulator [16], which is an object-oriented, process-based discrete-event simulation platform based on the standard programming language

Python. SABP is at first implemented with SimPy. Then two individual processes, one considered as the transmitter and the other as the receiver, form
an M-channel MIMO system. Each process independently operates an object of
SABP. The transmitter continuously sends data packets and receives acknowledgement frames, and the receiver receives data packets and sends out acknowledgement frames. Data packets are transmitted over M parallel channels, while
acknowledgement frames are transmitted via a separate feedback channel with
no errors.

In the following simulation analysis, the round trip time of a packet is 4 slots,
or $\tau = 5$. We use Δ_i to represent the ratio of p_{i+1} to p_i for $i = 1, \cdots, M - 1$,
i.e.,

$$\Delta_i = \frac{p_{i+1}}{p_i}, \quad i = 1, \cdots, M - 1. \tag{1}$$

It is clear that, the larger the value of Δ_i, the greater the difference between
the error rates of channels i and $i + 1$. In addition, we let $\Delta = \Delta_1 = \cdots =
\Delta_{M-1}$. Then, the triad (M, Δ, p) will uniquely determine the error rate sequence
$(p_1, p_2, \cdots, p_M)$.

4.2   Simulation Results

We plot the simulation results of the average packet delay for SABP with the
dynamic and static scheduling in Fig. 4, Fig. 5 and Fig. 6. An important observation in these plots is that, compared with the static scheduling, the dynamic
scheduling improves the packet delay performance in the MIMO system. For
instance, for $M = 16$, the average packet delay performance can be improved as
much as up to 70% when the packet scheduling policy changes from the static
scheduling to the dynamic scheduling. When $\Delta = 1.5$, the average packet delay with the dynamic scheduling can be only one third of that with the static
scheduling.

The average packet delay is plotted in Fig. 4 for $\Delta = 1.2$, $p = 0.25$, and M
varying from 2 to 16. As we expect, the difference of the average delay between
the two scheduling policies becomes larger with the increase of M. Meanwhile,
as M increases, the average packet delay with the dynamic scheduling slightly
increases at first and then slightly decreases. This shows that, under the saturated traffic condition, the overall impact of the number of parallel channels
on the packet delay performance is insignificant when the dynamic scheduling
is applied. Since the average packet delay approaches a constant limit as the
number of channels increases, the use of parallel channels will be a favorable
option for high-data-rate MIMO system with SABP for error control. It is noted
that, for the multichannel protocol under non-saturated traffic conditions, packet
end-to-end delay includes another delay component, the packet waiting time at
the transmitter, in addition to the packet delay defined in this study. Under a

non-saturated traffic condition, it is clear that the increase of the transmission rate mainly results in the reduction of the packet waiting time at the transmitter, and hence the packet end-to-end delay. So the above observation corroborates the fact that the increase of the number of parallel channels leads to the increase of the transmission rate but the decrease of the overall packet delay for MIMO systems with non-saturated traffic.

In Fig. 5, we plot the average packet delay when $M = 8$, $\Delta = 1.2$, and p varying from 0.05 to 0.45. The average packet delay increases as p does, while the increasing rate with the dynamic scheduling is smaller than that with the static scheduling. The average packet delay is shown in Fig. 6 when $M = 8$, $p = 0.25$, and Δ varying from 1.1 to 1.7. As Δ increases, the average packet delay decreases when the dynamic scheduling is applied, but it increases when the static scheduling is used. For example, when Δ increases from 1.1 to 1.5, the average packet delay with the dynamic scheduling decreases almost 50%, but the average packet delay with the static scheduling increases 100%. This is because the greater the variance in the error rates, the smaller the error rates of the first few channels. (For instance, in Fig. 6, the error rates of channels 1 to 4 when $\Delta = 1.2$ are smaller than the corresponding ones when $\Delta = 1.1$.) Intuitively, the packets transmitted over the first few channels have a larger probability of being correctly received (and delivered to the upper layer). This results in a smaller possibility for the other packets to be queued in the resequencing buffer. Therefore, the average waiting time of a packet queued in the resequencing queue is reduced, and so is the total average packet delay.

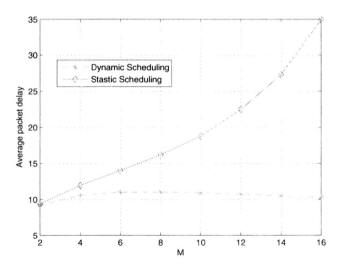

Fig. 4. Average Packet Delay vs. M ($\Delta = 1.2$, $p = 0.25$)

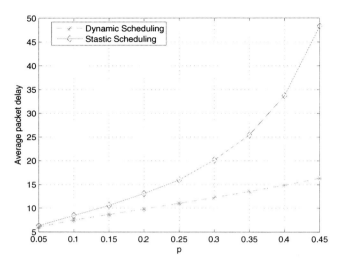

Fig. 5. Average Packet Delay vs. p ($\Delta = 1.2, M = 8$)

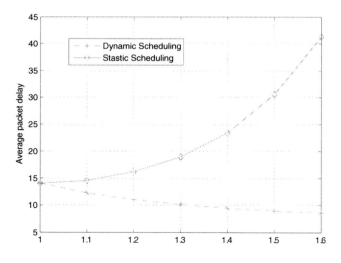

Fig. 6. Average Packet Delay vs. Δ ($M = 8, p = 0.25$)

5   Conclusion

In this paper, we introduced a MIMO system model, where our proposed multichannel radio link control protocol and a channel scheduling policy operate. We performed a simulation analysis of the average packet delay for the multichannel link control protocol with two different channel scheduling policies: dynamic and static scheduling. From simulation results, we concluded that the dynamic scheduling always achieves a better packet delay performance than the static scheduling. The average packet delay with the dynamic scheduling increases with the average error rate of all channels, but decreases with the variance in the error rates of the parallel channels. More interestingly, we observed that the number of parallel channels has only an insignificant impact on the average packet delay, when the dynamic scheduling is applied in the MIMO system, and hence the use of parallel channels is a favorable option for multichannel packet data networking.

Acknowledgement. This work was supported by Defence Research and Development Canada (DRDC) (under the project entitled "Self-Healing Networked Control Systems For Enhanced Reliability And Safety Of Multivehicle Missions").

References

1. Part 16: Air Interface for Fixed Broadband Wireless Access Systems, IEEE Standard for Local and Metropolitan Area Networks, 802.16 (2004)
2. 3GPP TS 25.321 V7.6.0, Medium Access Control (MAC) Protocol Specification (Release 7), 3GPP Technical Specification Group Radio Access Network (2007)
3. 3GPP TS 36.201, Evolved Universal Terrestrial Radio Access (E-UTRA): Long Term Evolution (LTE) Physical Layer, 3GPP Technical Specification Group Radio Access Network, source (2008),
   http://www.3gpp.org/ftp/Specs/html-info/36-series.htm
4. 3GPP TS 25.322 V5.3.0, Radio link control (RLC) protocol specification (release 5). 3GPP Technical Specification, source (2002), http://www.3gpp.org
5. Chang, J.-F., Yang, T.-H.: Multichannel ARQ Protocols. IEEE Transactions on Communications 41(4), 592–598 (1993)
6. Ding, Z.: ARQ Techniques for MIMO Communication Systems. Ph.D. thesis, Department of Electrical and Computer Engineering, Brigham Yong University Provo (2006)
7. Ding, Z., Rice, M.: ARQ Error Control for Parallel Multichannel Communications. IEEE Transactions on Wireless Communications 5(11), 3039–3044 (2006)
8. Forkel, I., Klenner, H., Kemper, A.: High Speed Downlink Packet Access (HSDPA) – Enhanced Data Rates for UMTS Evolution. Computer Networks: The International Journal of Computer and Telecommunications Networking 49(3), 325–340 (2005)
9. Fujii, S., Hayashida, Y., Komatu, M.: Exact Analysis of Delay Performance of Go-Back-N ARQ Scheme over Multiple Parallel Channels. Electronics and Communications in Japan, Part 1 84(9), 27–41 (2001)

10. Ghosh, A., Classon, B., Cudak, M., Jalloul, L.A.: Multi channel stop and wait ARQ communication method and apparatus. United States Patent No. 7,065,068, http://www.patentstorm.us/patents/7065068.html

11. Ghosh, A., Wolter, D.R., Andrews, J.G., Chen, R.: Broadband Wireless Access with WiMax/8O2.16: Current Performance Benchmarks and Future Potential. IEEE Communication Magazine 43(2), 129–136 (2005)

12. Hu, T., Afshartous, D., Young, G.: Parallel Stop and Wait ARQ in UMTS - Peformance and Modeling. In: Proceedings of the 2004 World Wireless Congress, San Francisco, CA (2004)

13. Jacobus, J.C.: Multi-channel automatic retransmission query (ARQ) method. United States Patent No. 6,021,124, http://www.patentstorm.us/patents/6021124.html

14. Li, J., Zhao, Y.Q.: Resequencing Analysis of Stop-and-Wait ARQ for Parallel Multichannel Communications. IEEE/ACM Transactions on Networking 17(3), 817–830 (2009)

15. Li, J., Zhao, Y.Q.: Packet Delay Analysis for Multichannel Communication Systems with MSW-ARQ. Performance Evaluation 66(7), 380–394 (2009)

16. Matloff, N.: Introduction to Discrete-Event Simulation and the SimPy Language, http://heather.cs.ucdavis.edu/~matloff/156/PLN/DESimIntro.pdf

17. Redi, J., Watson, B., Ramanathan, R., Basu, P., Tchakountio, F., Girone, M., Steenstrup, M.: Design and Implementation of a MIMO MAC protocol for ad hoc Networking. In: Proceedings of SPIE 2006, Orlando, FL., vol. 6248, 624802.1–624802.12, Florida, USA (2006)

18. Shacham, N., Shin, B.C.: A Selective-Repeat-ARQ Protocol for Parallel Channels and Its Resequencing Analysis. IEEE Transactions on Communications 40(4), 773–782 (1992)

19. Winters, J.H.: On the Capacity of Radio Communication Systems with Diversity in a Rayleigh Fading Environment. IEEE Journal on Selected Areas in Communications SAC-5(5), 871–878 (1987)

20. Wu, W.-C., Vassiliadis, S., Chung, T.-Y.: Performance Analysis of Multi-Channel ARQ Protocols. In: Proceedings of the 36th Midwest Symposium on Circuits and Systems, vol. 2, pp. 1328–1331 (1993)

21. Zheng, H., Lozano, A., Haleem, M.: Multiple ARQ Processes for MIMO Systems. EURASIP Journal on Applied Signal Processing 5, 772–782 (2004)

Improving Data Dissemination in Multi-hop Cognitive Radio Ad-Hoc Networks

Mubashir Husain Rehmani[1], Aline Carneiro Viana[2],
Hicham Khalife[3], and Serge Fdida[1]

[1] LIP6/UPMC Sorbonne Universités, France
{mubashir.rehmani,serge.fdida}@lip6.fr
http://www.lip6.fr/
[2] INRIA, France
aline.viana@inria.fr
http://www.inria.fr/
[3] LaBRI/ENSEIRB, Université de Bordeaux, France
hicham.khalife@labri.fr
http://www.labri.fr/

Abstract. In this paper, we present SURF, a distributed channel selection strategy for efficient data dissemination in multi-hop cognitive radio ad-hoc networks (CRNs). SURF classifies the available channels on the basis of primary radio unoccupancy and the number of cognitive radio neighbors using the channels. Through extensive NS-2 simulations, we compare the performance of SURF with three related approaches. Simulation results confirm that SURF is effective in selecting the best channels for efficient communication and for highest dissemination reachability in multi-hop CRNs.

Keywords: multi-hop cognitive radio networks, channel selection, data dissemination.

1 Introduction

Data dissemination is commonly defined as the spreading of information to multiple destinations through broadcasting. The main objective is to reach the maximum number of neighbors with every sent packet. In this communication scheme, no routing is required, thus neither routing tables nor end-to-end paths are maintained. Among different applications where data dissemination can be useful, we focus in this work on networking scenarios where providers disseminate non-urgent messages with limited cost and complexity through the network, such as: services, updates (e.g., new code to re-task a provided service), or any kind of publicity message. However, guaranteeing reliability of data dissemination in wireless networks is a challenging task. Indeed, the characteristics and problems intrinsic to the wireless links add several issues in the shape of message losses, collisions, and broadcast storm problem, just to name a few. Particularly in the context of Cognitive Radio Ad-Hoc Wireless Networks (CRN) [1], where

D. Simplot-Ryl et al. (Eds.): ADHOCNETS 2011, LNICST 89, pp. 117–130, 2012.

channels for transmission are opportunistically selected, reliability is difficult to achieve. This is due to the inherent features of such networks. First, in addition to the already known issues of wireless environments, the diversity in the number of channels that each cognitive node can use adds another challenge by limiting node's accessibility to its neighbors. Second, Cognitive Radio (CR) nodes have to compete for the residual resources left by the Primary Radio (PR) nodes on many channels and use them opportunistically. Besides, CR nodes should communicate in a way that do not disturb the reception quality of PR nodes by limiting CR-to-PR interference.

Due to lack of centralized entity and the difficult coordination between CR nodes, the selection of a common channel by CR transmitters and receivers is a challenging task in multi-hop CRNs. In this context, we argue that the data dissemination reachability in such networks can be improved if (1) the chances for both transmitter and receivers, selecting the same channel for operating is increased and (2) the use of the best channel in terms of communication opportunities is prioritized. A lot of works have been carried out for dynamic channel management in CRNs. These approaches focus on single-hop CRNs [2,3,4,5], the presence of central entity, or the coordination with PR nodes in their channel selection decision. A proposal/solution related to our approach is Selective Broadcasting (SB) [6], however, SB requires more than one transceiver, resulting in bigger and more complex devices, as for military applications [7]. Besides, transmissions over a set of channels without considering the PR activity may increase the probability of interference with PR nodes.

In this paper, we propose SURF, a distributed and intelligent channel selection strategy for multi-hop CRNs. SURF classifies the available channels and uses them efficiently to create a multi-hop CRN, connected with high probability. The classification is done on the basis of PR unoccupancy and the number of CR neighbors using the channels. The objective of every CR node is to select the best channel ensuring a maximum connectivity and consequently, allowing the largest data dissemination reachability in the network. Hence, solutions should on the one hand select channels having low primary radio nodes (PRs) activities and achieve reliability by selecting spectrum bands that have high number of CR neighbors on the other hand. Moreover, SURF keeps track of previous wrong channel state estimation and accordingly adapts future channel selection decision. Usually channel selection strategies provide a way for nodes to select channels for transmission. SURF however, endues CR nodes to select best channels not only for transmission but also for overhearing. As a result, both sender and receiver tune with high probability to the same channel for effective and reliable data dissemination.

Through extensive NS-2 simulations, we show that SURF is effective in selecting the best channels for efficient communication. SURF offers the highest dissemination reachability in multi-hop CRN when compared with three other approaches i.e., Random, Highest Degree, and Selective Broadcasting [6]. Additionally, thanks to SURF, the amount of collision with the PR nodes is considerably reduced. In fact, SURF protects the PR nodes during channel selection decision. The simplicity and decentralized nature of SURF makes it usable in ad-hoc CRNs deployed to convey services, updates, or any kind of publicity messages.

The remainder of this paper is organized as follows: we discuss system model and assumptions in Section 2. We then give a general overview of SURF in Section 3. Section 4 and 5 deal with the description of SURF. Performance analysis is done in section 6, section 7 discuss related work, and finally, section 8 concludes the paper.

2   System Model and Assumptions

We consider a Cognitive Radio Ad-Hoc Network, which is composed of a set of PR nodes and a set of CR nodes [8]. In this type of network setting, we assume that no centralized network entity is available. Such entity could facilitate CR nodes in different network operations like spectrum sensing, channel selection decision etc. Instead, we consider these previous tasks are performed by the CR nodes themselves. We assume that CR nodes are equipped with a single transceiver, where a single channel can be selected at a time and used exclusively for transmission or overhearing. Such operating mode reduces the operational cost of the CR device [9] and avoids potential interference between co-located transceivers due to their close proximity [10]. We consider the set of C total frequency channels. CR nodes can communicate using licensed or unlicensed bands, whichever bands are available. The use of licensed bands by cognitive radio nodes is however, only possible when the bands are *idle*, i.e. unoccupied by the PR nodes. We denote by idle the temporal availability of a channel. In some cases, it can happen that a CR node starts a transmission in the same time when PR becomes active. Since, we consider here CR transmissions should not generate harmful interference at PR receivers [11], CRs shall interrupt their transmissions.

We assume that spectrum sensing and the detection of the PR signal are not performed by SURF. These tasks are responsibility of the spectrum sensing block [12], which in turn provides PR spectrum unoccupancy information. In this case, SURF will work on the list of available channels resulted from the spectrum sensing. We further assume that SURF requires the information about CR neighbors and this neighbor discovery is not the part of SURF. CR neighbors can be discovered by using a Common Control Channel (CCC) [13] or with any other neighbor discovery mechanism, such as [14].

3   Channel Selection Strategy SURF

3.1   Rationale

SURF is a packet-based channel selection scheme for data dissemination and not a routing algorithm. SURF classifies available channels on the basis of primary radio unoccupancy and the number of CR neighbors using the channels. More precisely with SURF, every CR node autonomously classifies available channels based on the observed PR-unoccupancy over these channels. This classification is then refined by identifying the number of CRs over each channel. The best channel for transmission is the channel that has the lowest PR activity and a highest number of CR neighbors. Indeed, choosing a channel with few CRs increases the probability of having a disconnected network. Practically, every CR after classifying available channels, switches dynamically to the best one and broadcasts the stored message. Moreover, SURF tries to learn with previous wrong channel state estimation. This learning process allows better tuning the future estimations and helps CR nodes to recover from their bad channel selection decisions.

Additionally, CRs with no messages to transmit implement the SURF strategy in order to tune to the *best* channel for data reception. Clearly, using the same strategy implemented by the sender increases the chance that receivers in close geographic areas select the same used-to-send channel for overhearing. This is also due to the fact that, intuitively, it is likely that CRs in the sender's vicinity have the same PR unoccupancy. Hence, channels available to a CR sender are also available, with high probability, to its neighbors [15]. In this way, SURF increases the probability of creating a connected topology. Once a packet is received, every CR receiver undergoes again the same procedure to choose the appropriate channel for conveying the message to its neighbors.

3.2   Channel's Weight Calculation Formula

SURF strategy classifies channels by assigning a weight $P_w^{(i)}$ to each observed channel i in the channel set C. Thus, every cognitive radio running SURF, locally computes the $P_w^{(i)}$ using the following equation:

$$\forall i \in C : P_w^{(i)} = PR_u^{(i)} \times CR_o^{(i)} \tag{1}$$

$P_w^{(i)}$ describes the weight of a channel i and is calculated based on the unoccupancy of PR (i.e. $PR_u^{(i)}$) and CR occupancy (i.e. $CR_o^{(i)}$) over channel i (c.f. section 4 and section 5). Then, the channels are ranked according to their weights and the best channel (i.e., the one providing highest $P_w^{(i)}$) is selected.

Practically, the computed weight in Eq. (1) increases with the PR unoccupancy and the CR occupancy. These two behaviors are directly related to the two objectives the SURF strategy needs to satisfy. The major objective of protecting the ongoing PR activity is mapped as a function of PR unoccupancy. The higher the probability of channel being in OFF state, i.e. $PR_u^{(i)}$, the higher the weight will be. The second objective of increasing connectivity is implemented in the second term of Eq.(1). More precisely, the weight increases with the number of CR neighbors i.e. $CR_o^{(i)}$. We now discuss each objective in detail.

4   Primary Radio Unoccupancy

The primary radio activity, i.e. presence or absence of the PR signal, can be modeled as continuous-time, alternating ON/OFF Markov Renewal Process (MRP) [16], [17]. The authors in [18] validate this model for the presence of the PR signal. Fig. 1 illustrates the wireless channel model. The ON state, i.e. busy state, indicates that the channel is currently occupied by the PR node, while the OFF state, i.e. idle state, indicates that the channel is currently unoccupied by PRs.

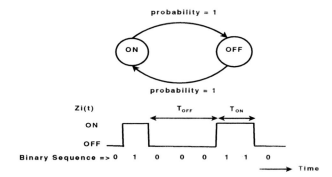

Fig. 1. Wireless channel model: Alternating Markov Renewal Process for PR activity

As in [16], [19], we consider the channels ON and OFF periods are both exponentially distributed with p.d.f. $f_X(t) = \lambda_X \times e^{-\lambda_X t}$ and $f_Y(t) = \lambda_Y \times e^{-\lambda_Y t}$ respectively. Since our goal is to select the channel that will be unoccupied at time t, we only consider $P_{OFF}(t)$, the probability that the channel i will be in OFF state at time t. Therefore $P_{OFF}(t)$, is calculated as:

$$P_{OFF}(t) = \frac{\lambda_X}{\lambda_X + \lambda_Y} + \frac{\lambda_Y}{\lambda_X + \lambda_Y} e^{-(\lambda_X + \lambda_Y)t} \qquad (2)$$

The best channel at time t is the one that has very high probability of being in OFF state. It may be possible that the next estimated channel state mis-matches with the real state of the channel. This leads to bad channel selection decision and causes harmful interference to PR nodes. Next, we detail how the learning of previous wrong estimations are used to tune future estimations.

4.1   Recovery from Bad Channel Selection Decisions

The main challenges we deal with in this paper reside in making efficient and reliable channel selection decisions on-the-fly and in recovering from bad channel selection decisions. Clearly, keeping track of wrong channel state estimations can help CR nodes to recover from their bad channel selection decisions, which ultimately enhance the reliability and the performance. To achieve this goal, nodes maintain the history of their wrong channel state estimations and the observed

Table 1. Estimated and Current States of the Channel

Event	Estimated State	Current State	Probability
P_{UM}	OFF	ON	P_{MD}
	ON	OFF	P_{FA}

current state of the channels. CR nodes then use this history to calculate the probability of unsuccessfully matched state P_{UM}. P_{UM} is defined as the probability that the estimated channel state mis-matches with the actual channel state or simply how often the channel states estimation become erroneous. CR nodes then give the feedback of P_{UM}, while calculating the next channel state (cf. Fig. 2). More specifically, the accuracy of the SURF state estimation of channels depends upon the estimated state and the measured current state of the channel. Table. 1 provides the possible combinations between these two values.

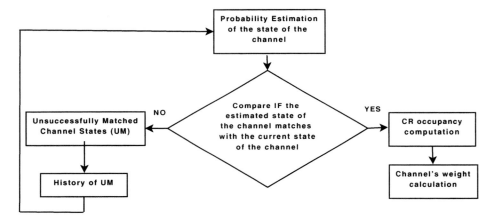

Fig. 2. Flow chart showing the corrective measure taken by CR nodes in the case of detection of unsuccessfully matched channel states i.e. P_{UM}

The probability P_{UM} is expressed as: $P_{UM}^{(i)} = \frac{x_{nt}}{N}$, where x_{nt} is the number of times the estimated channel state does not match with the actual channel state i.e. how often the channel states estimation was erroneous, and N is the number of coin flips. We further decompose $P_{UM}^{(i)}$ into $P_{MD}^{(i)}$ and $P_{FA}^{(i)}$ as: $P_{UM}^{(i)} = \frac{x_{nt}}{N} = P_{MD}^{(i)} + P_{FA}^{(i)}$, where P_{MD} refers to the *Probability of Miss-Detection* and occurs when P_{OFF} estimation is OFF and the observed current channel state is ON. In P_{MD}, CR node declares the busy channel as unoccupied. This will lead to harmful interference with PR nodes. Whereas, P_{FA} is the *Probability of False-Alarm* and occurs when P_{OFF} estimation is ON and the observed current channel state is OFF. In P_{FA}, CR node declares that the unoccupied channel is busy. This will lead to refraining CR nodes from transmitting and thus, wasting precious spectrum opportunity.

Table 2. Wireless channel parameters used in the simulations

	Ch 1	Ch 2	Ch 3	Ch 4	Ch 5	Ch 6	Ch 7	Ch 8	Ch 9	Ch 10
λ_X	1.25	0.4	1	0.4	0.5	2	1	0.18	0.5	0.67
λ_Y	0.67	2	1	0.33	1	0.29	0.25	2	1.33	0.5

Consequently, the lower the $P_{UM}(t)$, the more accurate will be the channel state estimation. Putting things together, we estimate the primary radio un-occupancy $P^*_{OFF}(t)$, which considers the probability of unsuccessfully matched state during the channel state estimation, as follows:

$$PR_u^{(i)} = P^*_{OFF}(t)^{(i)} = P^{(i)}_{OFF}(1 - P^{(i)}_{FA}) + P^{(i)}_{MD}(1 - P^{(i)}_{OFF}) \qquad (3)$$

In the case of a perfect channel estimation (i.e., $P_{FA} = 0$ and $P_{MD} = 0$), $P^*_{OFF}(t)=P_{OFF}(t)$. In the presence of channel estimation errors, the probability of channel (i) being in OFF state is given by Eq. (3). Note that when the channel has high weight but at time t is occupied, SURF reacts (i) by not transmitting the packet on the best weighted channel, (ii) by selecting the next best weighted channel for packet transmission/overhearing, and (iii) by recomputing P_{FA} and P_{MD}. Also note that when all the channels are occupied, no message is sent.

5   Cognitive Radio Occupancy

CR occupancy reflects the number of CR neighbors, which means the number of CR nodes using the channel i at time t. In SURF, special consideration is given to selecting those channels that have higher number of CR neighbors. Higher number of CR neighbors provides good level of network connectivity and consequently increases the transmission coverage of CR nodes. The CR occupancy $CR_o^{(i)}$ of channel i is estimated as: $CR_o^{(i)} = CR_n^{(i)}$, where, $CR_n^{(i)}$ is the number of CR neighbors using the channel i. As mentioned earlier, SURF requires information about CR neighbors, which can be discovered by using a Common Control Channel (CCC) [13] or with any other neighbor discovery mechanism, such as [14].

6   Performance Analysis

We analyze the performance of SURF through extensive simulations. We show here some results and we ask readers to refer to [21] for more detailed analysis. We enhanced the Cognitive Radio Cognitive Network (CRCN) patch [22] of NS-2 to include the PR activity model. Practically, each channel alternates between ON and OFF states with rate parameters λ_X and λ_Y respectively (cf. Table 2).

We compare SURF with random strategy (RD), highest degree strategy (HD) and selective broadcasting, proposed in [6] with multiple transmissions (SB). In RD, channels are randomly selected to be used by CR nodes for transmission and/or overhearing, without any consideration to the ongoing PR and CR activity over these channels. HD approach only considers CR activities and is

inspired by SB approach. In HD, CR nodes select the highest CR degree channel for transmission and overhearing, without any consideration of PR activity.
The highest degree channel covers, consequently, the highest number of neighbors in the available list of channels. In SB, each CR node calculates a minimum
set of channels, Essential Channel Set (ECS), for transmission that covers all
its geographic neighbors, without considering the PR unoccupancy. In SB, a CR
node transmits on multiple channels in round-robin fashion present in the ECS
list, until all neighbors are covered. Note that in [6] nothing is mentioned about
how nodes overhear over the channels. Therefore, we consider nodes select for
overhearing the highest degree channel from their ECS list only. If more than one
option is available, a random choice for transmission/overhearing is performed
among those channels with the same degree.

Since, our goal is to efficiently disseminate the data and to protect the PR
nodes from harmful interference, we define three performance metrics:

1. *Harmful Interference Ratio (HIR)*: This metric is defined in order to capture
   the notion of collision with PR nodes. HIR is defined as the ratio of the total
   number of times the channel is found to be occupied by PRs after the channel
   selection decision over total number of times the channel selection occurs.
2. *Average Delivery Ratio*: This metric measures the data dissemination process. It represents the ratio of packets received by a particular CR node over
   total packets sent in the network.
3. *Ratio of Accumulative CR Receivers*: This metric also evaluates the data
   dissemination process. It is defined as the average ratio of accumulative
   CR receivers per hop over the accumulative effective neighbors per hop.
   Accumulative CR receivers per hop are the number of CR receivers per hop
   that successfully received the message, while accumulative effective neighbors
   per hop are the CR neighbors that selects the same channel for overhearing
   as the sender node used for transmission. By accumulative ratio we mean:
   at each new hop n, the receivers and effective neighbors of all previous hops
   $l < n$ are summed up to the ones at hop n.

The transmission range of CR nodes is set to $R = 250m$. The number of CR
nodes is fixed to N=100 and CRs are randomly deployed within a square area
of $a^2 = 700\text{x}700m^2$. Simulations run for 1000 seconds. Total 1000 packets are
sent, where each packet is sent by a randomly selected source node after every
1 second. All results are obtained with a confidence interval of 95%.

We consider 5 (Ch=5) and 10 (Ch=10) total number of channels, that allow varying the neighborhood density d_{avg} between 11.3 (when Ch=5) and 20.1
(when Ch=10). Note that this density is computed *after* the spectrum sensing
provides the list of available channels and *before* the CRs select the channel to
transmit/overhear. In this case, it is worth mentioning that, at the following simulation studies, the neighborhood density varies in function of the CRs' channel
selection and is lower than the above ones. *TTL* is introduced to disseminate
the message in the whole network. It is the maximum number of hops required
for a packet to traverse the whole network, i.e., $\lceil \frac{2a}{R} \rceil$, and is set to $TTL = 6$ in

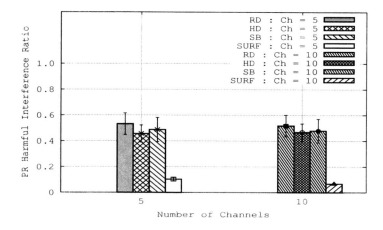

Fig. 3. PR harmful interference ratio for RD, HD, SB and SURF

our simulation scenario. Details on the used wireless channel parameters can be found in Table. 2, which were measured by authors in [19].

In summary, at each packet transmission event, the PR unoccupancy per channel i, $(PR_u^{(i)})$, is calculated by each CR node. Then, each CR node locally computes the CR occupancy $(CR_o^{(i)})$ and the weight $(P_w^{(i)})$ of each channel i. The channel with the highest weight is then selected for transmission and/or over-hearing. The message dissemination phase then starts, during which a randomly selected CR node disseminates the message on the selected channel by setting a *TTL* at the message. CR neighbor nodes that are on the same channel will overhear the message, decrease the *TTL*, redo the spectrum sensing, select the best available channel, and disseminate the message to the next-hop neighbors until *TTL=0*.

Harmful Interference Ratio. Fig. 3 compares the harmful interference ratio for the four strategies i.e. RD, HD, SB and SURF, for Ch=5 and Ch=10. It can be clearly seen in the figure that SURF, as expected, causes less harmful interference to PR nodes, compared to RD, HD, and SB. This is primarily because, when using SURF, CR nodes select those channels that have very high probability of being in OFF state, reducing thus PR interference. Note that in SURF, if all channels are occupied, the CR transmission will not take place. Thus, the lower HIR value for SURF in Fig. 3 is shown only to represent the cases where all channels were occupied by PRs and a probable interference is to be caused if a transmission takes place. In addition, when the number of channels is low, i.e. Ch=5, the value of HIR is higher than Ch=10. This is due to the fact that a lower number of channels also reduces the chances for CR nodes finding PR-unoccupied channels for their transmission. As a result, SURF protects PR nodes, by reducing the amount of collisions with primary radios.

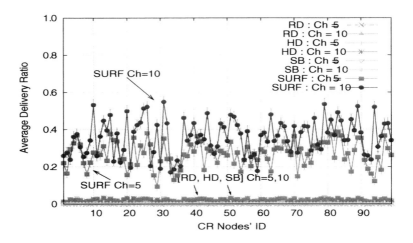

Fig. 4. CR Nodes' ID and average delivery ratio

Average Delivery Ratio. Fig. 4 compares the average delivery ratio of RD, HD, SB and SURF, for Ch=5 and Ch=10. SURF increases considerably the delivery ratio compared to the other solutions. In particular, for Ch=5, SURF guarantees a maximum delivery ratio of approximately 40% compared to almost 0% in the case of RD, HD, and SB. And when Ch=10, SURF allows some nodes to reach a maximum delivery ratio of 50%, while in RD, it is almost 0% and 2% in HD and SB. In fact, RD, HD, and SB, do not guarantee that the selected channel is unoccupied for transmission thus causing a severe decrease in the delivery ratio. While in SURF, the average delivery ratio is higher because CR nodes selects the channel that has higher $P_{OFF}^*(t)$ and higher CR neighbors. It is worth mentioning that the diversity in terms of available channels and PR activities, and the consequent lower neighborhood density after CRs local channel selection result in the creation of different topologies (i.e., dynamic neighborhood) at each transmission/overhearing of CR nodes. These issues make hard the achievement of a higher delivery ratio than SURF.

In order to better observe the impact on delivery ratio of such dynamic neighborhood, Fig. 5 shows the average delivery ratio per node ID for Ch=5 and Ch=10 when PR activity equals to 0. Similarly, Table 6 summarizes the overall average delivery ratio of Fig 4 and Fig. 5. The results attest the obtained low delivery ratios are mainly due to the creation of different topologies resulted from the multi-channel availability and distributed channel selection by CRs. More specifically, even when no PR competition exists, the maximum average delivery ratio is lower than 35%. Nevertheless, it is worth to note that SURF is the approach less impacted by the PR activities: By intelligently taking profit of channels availabilities, SURF is able to ensure a stable delivery ratio even when CRs transmission is competing with the PR ones.

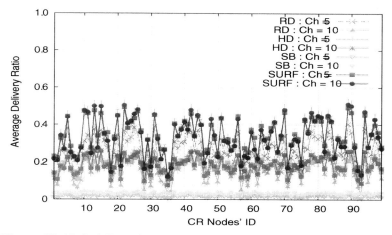

Fig. 5. CR Nodes' ID and average delivery ratio, when PR activity is zero

Table 3. Overall average delivery ratio (in %)

Strategy Name	PR=0		PR ≠ 0 (cf. Table 2)	
	Ch=5	Ch=10	Ch=5	Ch=10
RD	0.25	0.16	0	0
HD	0.18	0.18	0.02	0.02
SB	0.02	0.03	0	0
SURF	0.34	0.33	0.27	0.36

Most importantly, it is worth noting that with the increase of the number of channels, SURF performance is also enhanced. This result is counterintuitive since adding more channels makes the synchronization between the sender and the receiver (i.e selecting the same channel) harder to achieve. However, by using the appropriate metric and mainly employing the same strategy at the sender and the receiver, SURF achieves better results when more channels are available.

Ratio of Accumulative Receivers. Fig. 6 compares the ratio of accumulative receivers at each hop of communication (i.e until $TTL = 0$) for RD, HD, SB, and SURF. SURF outperforms the 3 other techniques in all hops. At the 1st-Hop, due to the first transmission of the message, no collision is present. In this case, SURF provides a ratio of 95% receivers for Ch=10 (80% for Ch=5), against 5% for RD, 12% for HD, and 2% for SB. With the message propagation and its natural replication in the network, the probability of collisions increases and consequently, the receivers ratio at each new hop decreases, for all the strategies. Still, SURF provides a better dissemination ratio than other strategies. This is obtained thanks to the SURF channel selection, which selects channels providing high probability for good delivery as well as for good reception.

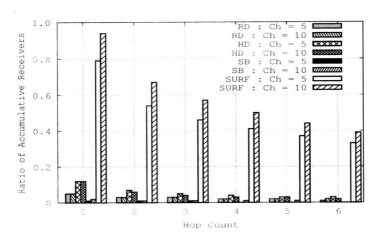

Fig. 6. Hop count and Ratio of accumulative receivers

In summary, results in Fig. 4 and Fig. 6 confirm that SURF can provide higher network reachability, suitable for increasing dissemination reliability in multi-hop cognitive radio networks.

7   Related Work

Recently, a lot of work has been carried out for dynamic channel management in cognitive radio networks [3,4,5,15,20,25,26]. However, all these approaches focuses on single-hop cognitive radio networks and either requires the presence of any central entity or coordination with primary radio nodes in their channel selection decision. For instance, [3] proposed an efficient spectrum allocation architecture that adapts to dynamic traffic demands but they considered a single-hop scenario of Access Points (APs) in Wi-Fi networks. An approach that use non-continuous unoccupied band to create a high throughput link is discussed in [4]. In [5], authors proposed a proactive channel selection strategy for TV-broadcast networks, which is single-hop and requires strong co-ordination with TV receivers in their channel selection decision.

A very few works has been done for channel selection in the context of multi-hop cognitive radio ad hoc networks so far [6,23,24]. We compared SURF with Selective Broadcasting [6], in which each CR node calculates a minimum set of channels i.e. Essential Channel Set (ECS) for transmission that covers all its geographic neighbors, without considering the PR unoccupancy. In [23,24], the authors proposed a dynamic resource management scheme for multi-hop cognitive radio networks. In fact, their approach is a route/channel selection for delay sensitive applications such a multimedia streaming, while SURF is a channel selection scheme for data dissemination and not for routing.

8   Conclusion and Future Work

We have introduced SURF, a channel selection strategy for reliable data dissemination in multi-hop CRNs. Simulation results in NS-2 confirmed that SURF, when compared to random-based, highest degree and selective broadcasting strategies, is effective in selecting the best channels. Furthermore, we show that unlike other solutions, SURF performance is enhanced with the increase of the number of existing channels. This is due to its intelligent selection mechanism. We intend in future to consider the traffic and data rates of CR nodes in the channel's weight calculation formula, as well as time needed to disseminate messages in the network.

References

1. Akyildiz, I.F., Lee, W.-Y., Vuran, M.C., Mohanty, S.: Next generation/dynamic spectrum access/cognitive radio wireless networks: a survey. Computer Networks: The International Journal of Computer and Telecommunications Networking 50(13), 2127–2159 (2006)
2. Nguyen, G.D., Kompella, S., Wieselthier, J.E., Ephremides, A.: Channel sharing in cognitive radio networks. In: MILCOM (2010)
3. Yang, L., Cao, L., Zheng, H., Belding, E.: Traffic-aware dynamic spectrum access. In: Proceedings of The Fourth International Wireless Internet Conference (WICON 2008), Hawaii, USA, November 17-19 (2008)
4. Rahul, H., Kushman, N., Katabi, D., Sodini, C., Edalat, F.: Learning to share: Narrowband-friendly wideband wireless networks. In: ACM SIGCOMM, vol. 38(4), pp. 147–158 (2008)
5. Acharya, P.A.K., Singh, S., Zheng, H.: Reliable open spectrum communications through proactive spectrum access. In: TAPAS (2006)
6. Kondareddy, Y.R., Agrawal, P.: Selective Broadcasting in Multi-Hop Cognitive Radio Networks. In: IEEE Sarnoff Symposium (April 2008)
7. Younis, O., Kant, L., Chang, K., Young, K.: Cognitive manet design for mission-critical networks. IEEE Communications Magazine, 64–71 (2009)
8. Akyildiz, I.F., Lee, W.-Y., Chowdhury, K.R.: Crahns: Cognitive radio ad hoc networks. Ad Hoc Networks 5 (July 2009)
9. Harada, H.: A small-size software defined cognitive radio prototype. In: Proceedings of the IEEE International Symposium on Personal, Indoor and Mobile Radio Communications (PIMRC), Cannes, France, September 15-18, pp. 1–5 (2008)
10. Shin, K.G., Kim, H., Cordeiro, C., Challapali, K.: An experimental approach to spectrum sensing in cognitive radio networks with off-the-shelf ieee 802.11 devices. In: 4th IEEE Consumer Communications and Networking Conference, CCNC 2007, January 11-13, pp. 1154–1158 (2007)
11. Khalife, H., Malouch, N., Fdida, S.: Multihop cognitive radio networks: to route or not to route. IEEE Networks, 20–25 (August 2009)
12. Yucek, T., Arslan, H.: A survey of spectrum sensing algorithms for cognitive radio applications. IEEE Com. Surv. and Tutorials 11(1), 116–130 (2009)
13. Loukas Lazos, S.L., Krunz, M.: Spectrum opportunity-based control channel assignment in cognitive radio networks. In: 6th IEEE SECON, Rome, Italy, June 22-26 (2009)

14. Arachchige, C., Venkatesan, S., Mittal, N.: An asynchronous neighbor discovery algorithm for cognitive radio networks. In: 3rd IEEE Symposium on New Frontiers in Dynamic Spectrum Access Networks, DySPAN 2008, pp. 1–5 (2008), doi:10.1109/DYSPAN.2008.78

15. Zhao, Q., Tong, L., Swami, A., Chen, Y.: Decentralized cognitive mac for opportunistic spectrum access in ad hoc networks: A POMDP framewrok. IEEE JSAC 25(3), 589–600 (2007)

16. Min, A.W., Shin, K.G.: Exploiting multi-channel diversity in spectrum-agile networks. In: IEEE INFOCOM (April 2008)

17. Lee, W.-Y., Akyildiz, I.: Optimal spectrum sensing framework for cognitive radio networks. IEEE Trans. on Wir. Commun. 7(10), 3845–3857 (2008)

18. Geirhofer, S., Tong, L., Sadler, B.M.: Dynamic spectrum access in wlan channels: Emperical model and its stochastic analysis. In: ACM TAPAS (August 2006)

19. Kim, H., Shin, K.: Efficient discovery of spectrum opportunities with mac-layer sensing in cognitive radio networks. IEEE Trans. on Mobile Comp. 7(5), 533–545 (2008)

20. Niyato, D., Hossain, E.: Competitive spectrum sharing in cognitive radio networks: A dynamic game approach. IEEE Transactions on Wireless Communications 7(7), 2651–2660 (2008)

21. Rehmani, M.H., Viana, A.C., Khalife, H., Fdida, S.: SURF: A distributed channel selection strategy for data dissemination in multi-hop cognitive radio networks. INRIA, Technical Report (2011), http://hal.inria.fr/inria-00596224/en/

22. http://stuweb.ee.mtu.edu/~ljialian/

23. Zhao, J., Zheng, H., Yang, G.H.: Distributed coordination in dynamic spectrum allocation networks. IEEE Trans. Veh. Tech. 58(2), 941–953 (2009)

24. Shiang, H.P., Schaar, M.V.D.: Delay-sensitive resource management in multi-hop cognitive radio networks. IEEE DySpan (2008)

25. Cordeiro, C., Challapali, K., Birru, D., Shanka, S.N.: IEEE 802.22: An introduction to the first wireless standard based on cognitive radios. Journal of Communications 1(1), 38–47 (2006)

26. Hoyhtya, M., Pollin, S., Mammela, A.: Classificaiton-based predictive channel selection for cognitive radios. In: IEEE ICC (May 2010)

Cooperative MAC Scheduling
in CDMA-MANETs with Multiuser Detection⋆

Jun Li, Yifeng Zhou, Mathieu Déziel, and Louise Lamont

Communications Research Centre Canada
3701 Carling Ave. Ottawa, ON. K2H 8S2 Canada
{jun.li,yifeng.zhou,mathieu.deziel,louise.lamont}@crc.gc.ca

Abstract. Code division multiple access mobile *ad hoc* networks (CDMA-MANETs) will be a next-generation wireless networking architecture to connect various military platforms. The classic contention-based MAC protocols are inappropriate for tactical *ad hoc* networks, where more rigid requirements for the quality of service (QoS) (*e.g.*, guaranteed packet delivery) have to be satisfied. In this paper, we propose a contention-free medium access control (MAC) scheduling framework for CDMA-MANETs where each mobile unit is capable of multiuser detection (MUD) as well. In this MAC scheduling scheme, how and when a pending data packet is going to be transmitted are cooperatively determined by the respective transmitter-receiver pair. Furthermore, to fully utilize the functionality provided by multiuser detection, our proposed cooperative MAC scheduling scheme is able to schedule multiple transmitters to simultaneously transmit packets to a same receiver. Computer simulations are carried out to demonstrate the performance of the proposed cooperative MAC scheduling framework. It is confirmed from simulation results that the packet average delay increases with either the packet generation rate or the network size. More importantly, the proposed cooperative MAC scheduling framework is more suitable for MUD-enabled CDMA-MANETs with heavier network traffic and possibly a larger number of network nodes.

Keywords: Code division multiple access (CDMA), mobile *ad hoc* networks (MANETs), multiuser detection (MUD), medium access control (MAC), packet scheduling, cooperative communications.

1 Introduction

Multiuser detection (MUD) techniques can significantly improve the performance and capacity of code division multiple access (CDMA) networks, which have long been used in both the military and the civilian domain for one-hop communications [7]. Recently multi-hop mobile *ad hoc* networks (MANETs) are receiving increasing research attention due to their ubiquitous applications to military and civilian networks [15]. It is envisioned that multi-hop code division

---

⋆ This work was supported by Defence Research and Development Canada (DRDC).

D. Simplot-Ryl et al. (Eds.): ADHOCNETS 2011, LNICST 89, pp. 131–146, 2012.

multiple access mobile *ad hoc* networks (CDMA-MANETs) will serve as a next-generation networking architecture used to network various military platforms, such as manned/unmanned aerial vehicles, manned/unmanned ground vehicles, and soldiers, and thus some more recent research has focused on this specific type of *ad hoc* network. (See, *e.g.*, [3,5,6,8,9,11,13,17,18] for studies on the data link layer and [4,10,12,14] for studies on the network layer.)

It is noted that a majority of studies [3,6,8,9,11,13,17,18] on the medium access control (MAC) layer have been based on the RTS/CTS handshaking mechanism, as used in the IEEE 802.11 standard [2], to scheduling transmission of packets, and are contention-based scheduling in nature. Some drawbacks of contention-based MAC schemes include that they experience a high packet collision probability under heavier network traffic and the quality of service (QoS) cannot be guaranteed in general. In a military CDMA-MANET, However, it is often explicitly specified that one or more rigid QoS requirements (*e.g.*, guaranteed delivery of command and control data with a delay limit) have to be satisfied, and thus it is impractical to use a contention-based MAC scheduling protocol in such a network. Recently, some non-contention based MAC designs have been reported in the literature. Among them is a hybrid token CDMA MAC protocol based on token-passing schemes [5]. By circulating the token around the network in a pre-defined order, a node with packets to transmit obtains a CDMA code dynamically and is ensured to transmit without contending to access channels. The multiuser detection techniques were not considered in [5].

In this paper, we propose a cooperative MAC scheduling framework in the context of military CDMA-MANET where each mobile unit is capable of multiuser detection. In the network, a unique control message, referred to the token frame, circulates continuously around the network in a non-predetermined order. Through circulating the token frame, each node obtains the information required for the MUD functionality, and based on the traffic information of the neighborhood, a potential transmitter-receiver pair cooperatively determines how and when a pending packet is going to be transmitted. To fully utilize the functionality provided by multiuser detection, our proposed cooperative MAC scheduling scheme schedules multiple transmitters to simultaneously transmit packets to a same receiver. Computer simulations are carried out to demonstrate the performance of the proposed cooperative MAC scheduling framework. It is confirmed from simulation results that the packet average delay increases with either the packet generation rate or the network size. More importantly, the proposed cooperative MAC scheduling framework is more suitable for MUD-enabled CDMA-MANETs with heavier network traffic and possibly a larger number of network nodes.

The rest of the paper is organized as follows: In Section 2, we describe a CDMA *ad hoc* network model and the problem to be solved in this study. A cooperative MAC scheduling framework is proposed in Section 3. Performance evaluation of the proposed cooperative MAC scheduling scheme is carried out in Section 4 using simulations. Finally, concluding remarks are given in Section 5.

2   Network Model and Problem Statement

In this section, we describe a CDMA-MANET model followed by a statement of the problem to be studied in this paper.

2.1   Network Setup and Assumptions

As shown in Fig. 1, a number N of nodes, which can be aircraft, or ground vehicles, or soldiers, are deployed in the battlefield and form a military mobile *ad hoc* network. All nodes are synchronized at packet level. The synchronization can be achieved by tracing a common timing source such as the global positioning system (GPS). The distribution of codes is shown in Fig. 2. A total of $M + 1$ CDMA codes are allocated for message transmissions, among which M codes (code 1 to M in Fig. 2) are assigned for data packets and one code, referred to as the Common Control Channel (CCC) in Fig. 2, is for disseminating control packets. Each node is equipped with two half-duplex transceivers of a same transmission range. One transceiver operates on code 1 to M and is capable of CDMA multiuser detection; the other is a simplified system that operates on CCC, and is not required to have the multiuser detection capability. All wireless links are assumed to be error-free so that only the node mobility can cause the link breakage, *e.g.*, two nodes are out of the transmission range of each other.

The network is assumed to be (fully or partially) connected although the network topology changes over time due to the mobility of the nodes in the network. It is also assumed that one of the mobile nodes is selected as the backbone node (BN), as shown in Fig. 1. BN typically has long-lasting power and serves as a gateway to another network, such as the secured Internet. We assume that BN is alive all the time. In the proposed MAC, the backbone node also plays the role of the token lead who initiates the token. In addition, the MUD capacity of a node is assumed to be greater than the maximum number of neighboring nodes of the node. The MUD capability of a node refers to the maximum number of transmission sources that the node can jointly detect. The assumption of greater MUD capability allows simultaneous transmissions of all neighbors of a node. When a node has data packets to transmit, it needs a CDMA code to be assigned by a code assignment mechanism. Because of the limited size of CDMA code set, reuse of a code is desired and necessary in CDMA *ad hoc* networks. To avoid collisions between two simultaneous transmissions, a code assignment mechanism has to guarantee that any two nodes that are either one- or two-hop away from each other are not assigned to a same code. In this paper, we assume that the code assignment mechanism (CAM) in [16] is implemented in each node through broadcasting control messages (*i.e.*, the token frame detailed in Section3.1).

2.2   Problem Statement

In CDMA-MANETs, the implementation of multiuser detection at the MAC layer has the following two requirements.

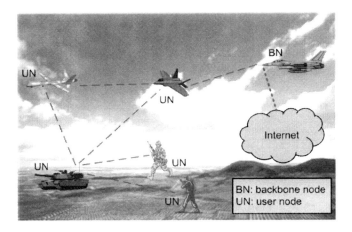

Fig. 1. Military CDMA Mobile Ad Hoc Network

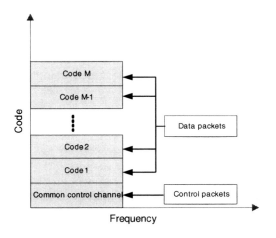

Fig. 2. Channel Structure

1. **Knowledge of code at the receiving side:** For a data transmission process to be conducted for a transmitter-receiver pair, the receiver has to know the corresponding code assigned to the transmitter for the transmission. Due to the dynamic feature of code assignment in CDMA-MANETs, the receiver does not have knowledge of code until the transmitter has been explicitly assigned one. Therefore, after assignment of code at the transmitter, a MAC scheduling mechanism is required to inform the receiver of the code that this transmission uses.

2. **Starting time of an expected communication:** Due to a limited capacity of multiuser detection (*i.e.*, the number of packets that the receiver can simultaneously receive is limited), the receiver needs to decide when a

data transmission process can start and inform the transmitter the starting time of the expected communication. This is done by a MAC scheduling mechanism as well.

In this paper we propose a MAC scheduling scheme, which explicitly considers the above requirements, for CDMA-MANETs with multiuser detection. By fast circulating the token frame, a type of scheme control message, the proposed scheduling scheme belongs to the group of contention-free scheduling mechanisms and enables cooperative scheduling of multiple transmissions destined to a same receiver which is enabled for multiuser detection.

3   Cooperative MAC Scheduling

In this section, we first define control messages, scheme buffers and scheme timers that are needed by our MAC scheduling scheme. We then elaborate the cooperative MAC scheduling scheme that fully utilizes the MUD capability in CDMA-MANETs.

3.1   Scheme Control Messages

Below we introduce two types of control messages, token frame and HELLO message, to be used in the proposed cooperative MAC scheduling scheme. Due to the use of a dedicated transceiver operating on CCC, there are no collisions between data and control packets, and parallel processing of data and control packets is allowed. The parallel processing of data and control packets is expected to improve the scheme performance such as a decreased packet delay and an increased system throughput. The token frame is created by BN at the beginning of the network operation. The token continuously circulates around the network. HELLO messages are transmitted in one hop, *i.e.*, between neighboring nodes.

Token Frame. As shown in Fig. 3, the token frame contains in total seven fields that start with the *preamble* field used for piloting/synchronization and end up with the *end_of_token* field indicating the end of the token. The *source* field is the address of the node that forwards the token, while the *destination* field contains the address of the node to which the token is forwarded. The *RTR* (ready to receive) field is used to indicate whether the *source* node is ready to receive data packets. The *NOC* (number of codes) field is an integer number representing the number of code indices listed in the *code_list* field. The *assigned_code* field contains the index of the code assigned to the *source* node, or a number, referred to as *NaC* (not a code), if no code is assigned to the *source* node. The *code_list* field lists all indices of the codes currently available for assignment.

We shall note that, among these fields in the token frame, *NOC* and *code_list* fields are exclusively used by the code assignment mechanism in [16], which is assumed in this study. As will be seen in Section 3.4, all other fields in the token frame will be used in our proposed cooperative MAC scheduling scheme to schedule transmission of data packets.

preamble	source	destination	RTR	NOC	assigned_code	code_list	end_of_token

Fig. 3. Token Frame

HELLO Message As shown in Fig. 4, a HELLO message contains three fields starting with *preamble* and ending up with *end_of_message*. The *source* field is the address of the node that broadcasts the HELLO message. The size of a HELLO message is very small. In addition, a node broadcasts a HELLO message only when it loses connection to the network (see Section 3.6). Hence, the chance that the token frame collides with a HELLO message is very small. In this paper, we assume that the token frame and HELLO messages are never colliding with each other.

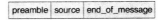

preamble	source	end_of_message

Fig. 4. HELLO Message

3.2   Scheme Buffers

Two buffers, successor list (SL) and transmitter list (TL), are created in a node to facilitate operation of our proposed MAC scheduling scheme in the node.

Successor List (SL). SL in a node contains all neighbors of the node and provides information about the destination to which the node forwards the token. As will be seen from the scheme, the neighbor on the top of SL will always be chosen as the *destination* of the token. Under the assumption that the network is always connected, SL is never empty. In addition, when a node overhears the token circulating among the network, SL in the node is updated accordingly.

Transmitter List (TL). TL in a node maintains the information about the nodes that have data to transmit to the node as well as the codes to be used by these transmitters. In other words, each item in TL, containing the address of a node and a code index, corresponds to a transmission to be started.

3.3   Scheme Timers

As a result of node movements, a link between two nodes can be up and down. In addition, a node could enter an area where all its neighbors are new. To deal with these two possible changes in the network topology, we set the following two timers in our proposed MAC scheduling scheme

Timer for Link Breakage (*TimerOne*). For each time a node forwards the token to its successor, the node activates *TimerOne* and sets the value to 3τ, where τ represents the one-way transmission and processing time of the token from the source to its successor. The value of τ can be obtained from the last round of the token circulation. *TimerOne* is deactivated when the node overhears transmission of the token by its successor. If the timer is active and expires, the node assumes that the recent token forwarding has failed due to link breakage, in which case the node will retransmit the token to a next successor.

Timer for Entering the Network (*TimerTwo*). For each time a node forwards the token to its successor, the node sets the value of *TimerTwo* to $3N\tau$. When *TimerTwo* expires, the node assumes that it has lost connection to the network. That is, the links previously connecting the node to its neighboring nodes are down and all current neighbors of this node are new. In this case, the node initiates the *entering* procedure to rejoin the network, which is detailed at the end of Section 3.4.

3.4   MAC Scheduling Scheme

In this section a cooperative MAC scheduling scheme is proposed for CDMA-MANETs with the capability of multiuser detection.

The key idea in our proposed cooperative MAC scheduling scheme is the "receive-forward" module. This is a major difference between our proposed MAC scheduling scheme and a classical token ring MAC protocol (*e.g.*, IEEE 802.5 [1]) that is based on the "receive-hold-forward" module. In the "receive-hold-forward" module, only a node capturing the token can transmit data, and the node, after capturing the token, holds the token until the transmission process is terminated. In comparison, with the "receive-forward" module, a node, when receiving the token, will not hold the token during a data transmission process, but simply forward the token to a successor (*i.e.*, *destination* of the node), disregarding the status of the node (*i.e.*, transmitting, receiving or idle state). The token successor corresponds to the address at the top of SL in the node. Due to dynamic updates of the successor list, the token circulates in a non-predetermined order. The core part of the cooperative MAC scheduling scheme is described as follows.

If the current node A destined by the token is idle and has data packets to transmit to a node C, which is one neighbor of A, A obtains a code via CAM and moves C to the top of A's successor list. If A is transmitting, it removes the top node from SL to the *destination* field of the token and sets the RTR field to 0 (meaning not ready for data reception). Otherwise (i.e., A is either receiving data packets or idle), it removes the top node from SL to the *destination* field of the token frame and sets the RTR field to 1 (meaning ready for data reception). After the modification of the token frame, A sets itself as *source* of the token frame and forwards the token to its successor. After receiving the token, the successor repeats modification of the token frame according to the above description and forwards it to a next successor. While transmitting the token, all neighboring nodes of source node A will overhear the token, from which whether data transmission to A can be conducted will be determined from the RTR field of the token. If a neighboring node finds that the RTR field is one, and if it has data packets to transmit to A, is currently idle, and has been assigned to a code for this data transmission, it starts to transmit data packets to A immediately. Otherwise, the overheard token frame is ignored. We assume that this "receive-forward" module is processed almost instantaneously in each node such that a source node can always overhear the token transmitted by its successor.

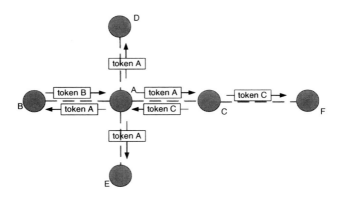

Fig. 5. A Network with Cooperative MAC Scheduling

Fig. 5 illustrates the MAC scheduling scheme described above. We assume that, when receiving the token from B (token B in Fig. 5), A is idle and has data packets to transmit to C. The nodes in A's SL is (B, D, C, E) with B on the top of buffer and E in the bottom. TL in A is empty. Then, A moves B to the bottom of SL so that the list becomes (D, C, E, B). Moreover, since A has data packets for C, C is moved to the top of SL in A, which results in (C, D, E, B) in A's SL. A then acquires a code via CAM and assigns its corresponding code index x to $assigned\_code$ of the token. Since A is not transmitting at the moment, RTR of the token is set to 1. The the resulting token to be sent by A (token A in Fig. 5) is shown in Fig. 6, where the NOC and $code\_list$ fields are addressed in CAM. Node A also moves C to the bottom of its SL after the token is sent out. Each of the neighbors of A (B, C, D, E in Fig. 5) overhears the token and moves node A to the bottom of the SL in the node. Moreover, when receiving the token sent by A, C updates its TL by running the TL_update procedure in Algorithm 2, after which an item $(A; x)$ is added in C's TL. Given that node C is not transmitting at the moment, C signals its neighbors that it is ready for receiving data packets by setting RTR to 1. (If C is transmitting, RTR is set to zero.) The contents of the token sent out by C (token_C in Fig. 5) is shown in Fig. 7. When A overhears the token sent by C, A will start to transmit data packets to C using the channel code of index x.

Using an algorithmic format the cooperative MAC scheduling scheme is summarized in Algorithm 1. We assume that the algorithm is run by some node A, which can be either the BN or a UN. Besides the core part described above, the scheme also includes the following procedures.

Algorithm 1. Cooperative MAC Scheduling Scheme

---

while *(algorithm running in A)* **do**

  if *(TimerOne is active and expires)* **then**

    remove the node, referred to as X, in the bottom of A's SL from the list;

    if *(A's TL has an item containing X)* **then** remove the item from the list;

    set the node on the top of A's SL as *destination* of the token and move that node to the bottom of the list;

    send the token to A's successor;

    reset the value of *TimerOne* to 3τ;

  end

  if *(A is a UN and its TimerTwo expires)* **then**

    empty SL and TL in A;

    call *entering* procedure in Section 3.6;

  end

  if *(A overhears token sent by B)* **then**

    if *(TimerOne in A is active)* **then** deactivate *TimerOne*;

    if *(B is in A's SL)* **then**

      move B to the bottom of A's SL;

    else

      add B to A's SL in the bottom of the list;

    end

    if *(RTR of the token is 1 and A is idle and A has data waiting for transmission to B and A has been assigned to a code)* **then** A starts data transmission to B;

    if *(A is the destination of the token)* **then**

      if *(A is a UN)* **then** deactivate *TimerTwo*;

      if *(assigned_code is not NaC)* **then** perform *TL_update* procedure (Algorithm 2);

      if *(A is idle and A has data to transmit to C)* **then**

        move C to the top of A's SL;

        obtain a code via CAM and set the code index to *assigned_code* of the token;

      else

        set *assigned_code* to NaC;

      end

      if *(A is transmitting)* **then**

        set the RTR field of the token to 0;

      else

        set the RTR field of the token to 1;

      end

      assign A as *source* of the token;

      set the node at the top of SL as *destination* and move that node to the bottom of A's SL;

      send the token to its successor;

      activate *TimerOne* and set the value to 3τ;

      if *(A is a UN)* **then** set *TimerTwo* to $3N\tau$;

    end

  end

end

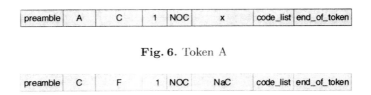

| preamble | A | C | 1 | NOC | x | code_list | end_of_token |

Fig. 6. Token A

| preamble | C | F | 1 | NOC | NaC | code_list | end_of_token |

Fig. 7. Token C

3.5   Update of Scheme Buffers

The scheme buffers need to be updated accordingly in the MAC scheduling scheme. First of all, both SL and TL in a node are updated if either $TimerOne$ or $TimerTwo$ of the node expires. For instance, when $TimerTwo$ of node A expires, A's SL and TL will be emptied. Because SL in node A is a priority list of A's neighbors, A will update its SL each time the token frame sent by a node, denoted by B, is overheard. That is, B will be put into the bottom position of A's SL. In addition, the node associated with the *destination* field of the token sent by A has to be moved to the bottom of A's SL. When A is the destination of the token sent node B, A's TL is updated according to Algorithm 2. That is, if the *assigned_code* field in the token contains a valid code index, A looks up its TL. If TL does not contain an item corresponding to node B, a new item containing B and code index equal to *assigned_code* is created and added to A's TL. If TL contains an item corresponding to node B, then B's code index in that item is reassigned to *assigned_code*.

Algorithm 2. *TL_update* Procedure

---

begin
    if *(A's TL has an item containing B)* **then**
        | replace B's code index with *assigned_code* of the token;
    else
        create a new item containing B and *assigned_code*;
        add the item to A's TL;
    end
end

3.6   Management of Node Mobility:

Some node X that wants to enter the network has to initiate the *entering* procedure. In the procedure, node X starts to periodically broadcast a *HELLO* message, which contains the address of node X, over the common control channel. If a neighboring node Y that is already in the network receives the *HELLO* message, node Y updates the successor list by simply adding X to the top of Y's SL. In the next time node Y receives the token, node X will be Y's successor who receives the token. By this way, node X joins the network.

4   Performance Evaluation

In this section, we describe a performance study on the proposed cooperative MAC scheduling scheme using simulations implemented in MATLAB.

4.1   Simulation Setup

In simulations the network size N varies between 4 and 24 nodes. The wireless channel connecting a pair of nodes is assumed to be bidirectional and has a constant data rate 1 $Mbps$. Due to the mobility of the network nodes, the wireless channel between the pair of nodes is up and down over time. The period of channel status changes is set to 40 milliseconds, which equals the duration of one slot. We assume that the network topology changes over time according to a Markov model. That is, the channel status process $\{X_{ij}(t) : t = 1, 2, \cdots\}$ for a pair of nodes i and j is a two-state (*i.e.*, up and down) Markov chain with the transition probability matrix $\mathbf{P} = \begin{bmatrix} 0.8 & 0.2 \\ 0.1 & 0.9 \end{bmatrix}$. The parameter t in the process denotes the slot numbers in discrete time. In addition, two channel status processes for two different pairs are assumed to be independent of each other. All data packets are assumed to have the same size of 2500 bytes, which corresponds to a transmission delay of 20 ms for each data packet. The size of a control packet is 62.5 bytes, which corresponds to a transmission delay of 0.5 ms for each control packet. During a simulation run each node generates data packets with the number of data packets generated per second being a binomial random variable with parameters $(10, p)$. The arrival probability p varies between 0.1 and 1 in simulations. This implies that the packet arrival rate in each node is between 1 and 10 packets per second. Each simulation runs 300 seconds, and we consider the following two performance metrics.

1. **Packet Average Delay:** The packet average delay is the average duration between the time a data packet is generated and the time of reception by its destination. The packet delay of a data packet is the sum of waiting time of the packet in its source node and the transmission time, which is assumed to be a constant of 20 ms in this study.
2. **Packet Delivery Ratio:** The packet delivery ratio is defined as the ratio of the total number of packets received by all network nodes to the total number of packets generated by them.

4.2   Simulation Results

In Fig. 8 we plot the packet average delay results when packet arrival rate varies from 1 to 10 and the network size N is fixed as 16. The solid line segments correspond to the simulation results of our proposed cooperative MAC scheduling scheme when multiuser detection is enabled in network nodes, while the dashed line segments correspond to the results when network nodes are not capable of multiuser detection. As we expect, the packet average delay increases with the packet arrival rate. This is because, on average, a data packet will wait longer for service in its source node for a larger packet arrival rate. Meanwhile, it is observed from Fig. 8 that the packet average delay results for MUD enabled networks are always smaller than these for networks without MUD capability. This is because multiple transmitters can simultaneously transmit packets to a same receiver in a MUD enabled network, which in turn results in a reduced packet waiting time in the source node. Furthermore, the larger the value of the packet arrival rate, the larger the gap between the MUD enabled packet delay results and the delay results without MUD capability. When the packet arrival rate becomes larger, there are more chances that more than one node have data packets destined to a same receiver at the same time, and thus the MUD capability can be more frequently utilized in the network. This shows that our proposed cooperative MAC scheduling can be more beneficial for MUD CDMA-MANETs with heavier traffic.

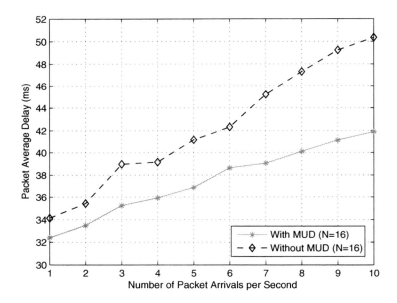

Fig. 8. Packet Average Delay versus Arrival Probability p

Fig. 9 plots the packet average delay results for the network size varying from 4 to 24 and p set to 0.4. The bottom curve in the figure corresponds to the network with MUD while the top curve corresponds to the network without MUD. It is observed that the packet average delay increases with the network size. For a network with a fixed size N, the packet average delay with MUD is smaller than that without MUD. The gap between these two results is more or less the same for different network sizes. This shows that our proposed cooperative MAC scheduling is suitable for MUD CDMA-MANETs of a large network size.

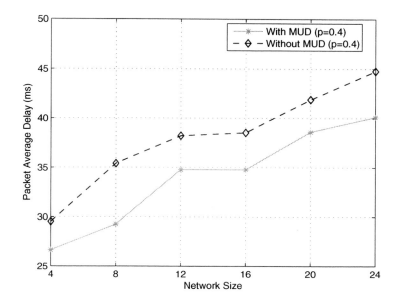

Fig. 9. Packet Average Delay versus Network Size

We plot the simulation results of the packet delivery ratio in Fig. 10 for the packet arrival rate varying from 1 to 10 and N equal to 16. There are two reasons which cause a data packet to not be received by its destination. One reason is due to changes in the network topology. If the channel between a packet's source node and its destination is down when the packet is to be transmitted by the source node, the packet will not be received by the destination node. The other reason is due to longer waiting times of packets in their source nodes. At the end of a simulation run, if a data packet, which has been generated before that time, has not been transmitted due to too many packets waiting for transmission, the packet will not be counted in the total number of received packets. In this simulation work, the ratio of the undelivered packets caused by the first reason is the same for both MUD-enabled and -disabled networks. Then a major difference of the packet delivery ratio between MUD-enabled and -disabled networks results from the second cause. It is observed from Fig. 10 that the packet delivery ratio in a network with MUD is always larger than that in a network without MUD as a consequence of a smaller packet average delay in the MUD enabled network. The simulation results of the packet delivery ratio are plotted in Fig. 11 when the network size varies from 4 to 24 and p is set to 0.4. We observe that the packet delivery ratio with MUD is never larger than that without MUD for each network size value.

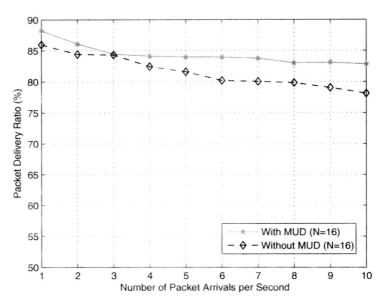

Fig. 10. Packet Delivery Ratio versus Arrival Probability p

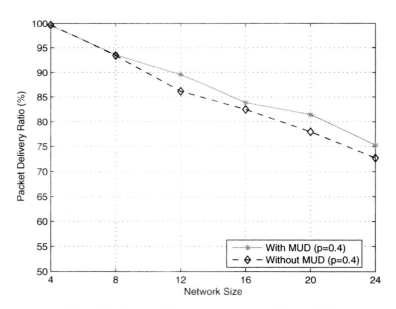

Fig. 11. Packet Delivery Ratio versus Network Size

5   Conclusion

In this paper, we proposed a MAC scheduling scheme that cooperatively schedules transmission of data packets in CDMA-MANETs with multiuser detection. Different from commonly used MAC schemes in wireless networks, the proposed cooperative MAC scheduling belongs to the group of non-contention based ones. By continuously circulating the token around the network, multiuser detection capability of the network can be fully utilized by each network node, for which multiple transmitters are allowed to transmit data to a same receiver at the same time. Simulation results are presented to demonstrate the performance of our proposed cooperative MAC scheduling scheme. It is observed from simulation results that the packet average delay increases with either network size or the intensity of network traffic. More importantly, it is shown that our proposed cooperative MAC scheduling is appropriate for MUD CDMA-MANETs with intense network traffic and possibly a large network size.

References

1. IEEE Standards Board. IEEE 802.5 - Token ring access method and physical layer specifications (March 1985)
2. IEEE Standards Board. IEEE 802.11: Wireless LAN medium access control (MAC) and physical layer (PHY) specifications (August 1999)
3. Al-Meshhadany, T., Ajib, W.: New CDMA-based MAC protocol for ad hoc networks. In: Proc. of the IEEE 66th Vehicular Technology Conference (VTC 2007-Fall), pp. 91–95 (September 2007)
4. Comaniciu, C., Poor, H.V.: On the capacity of mobile ad hoc networks with delay constraints. IEEE Transactions on Wireless Communications 5(8) (August 2006)
5. Liu, I.S., Takawira, F., Xu, H.J.: A hybrid token-CDMA MAC protocol for wireless ad hoc networks. IEEE Transactions on Mobile Computing 7(5), 557–569 (2008)
6. Moon, Y., Syrotiuk, V.R.: A cooperative CDMA-based multi-channel MAC protocol for mobile ad hoc networks. Computer Communications 32(17), 1810–1819 (2009)
7. Moshavi, S.: Multi-user detection for DS-CDMA communications. IEEE Communications Magazine 34(10), 124–136 (1996)
8. Muqattash, A., Krunz, M.: CDMA-based MAC protocol for wireless ad hoc networks. In: Proc. of the 4th ACM International Symposium on Mobile Ad Hoc Networking & Computing (MobiHoc 2003), pp. 153–164 (June 2003)
9. Naqvi, S.H., Patnaik, L.M.: A medium access protocol exploiting multiuser-detection in CDMA ad-hoc networks. Wireless Networks 16(6), 1723–1737 (2010)
10. Nie, N., Comaniciu, C.: Energy efficient AODV routing in CDMA ad hoc networks using beamforming. In: Proc. of the IEEE 61th Vehicular Technology Conference (VTC 2005-Spring), vol. 4, pp. 2449–2453 (May 2005)
11. Qian, X.C., Zheng, B.Y., Yan, Z.Y., Yu, G.J.: Algorithm and application of multiuser detection for CDMA-based MANET. Journal of Shanghai University (English Edition) 11(2), 148–152 (2007)
12. Sankaran, C., Ephremides, A.: The use of multiuser detectors for multicasting in wireless ad hoc CDMA networks. IEEE Transactions on Information Theory 48(11), 2873–2887 (2002)

13. Su, Y.S., Su, S.L., Li, J.S.: Receiver-initiated multiple access protocols for spread spectrum mobile ad hoc networks. Computer Communications 28(10), 1251–1265 (2005)
14. Xiao, L.: CDMA bus lane: A cross-layer protocol for QoS routing in CDMA based mobile ad hoc networks. Ph.D. thesis, Department of Electronic Engineering, Queen Mary, University of London (September 2007)
15. Yi, J.: A survey on the applications of MANET. Technical report,
    http://www.jiaziyi.com/documents/20080229_
    A_Survey_on_the_Applications_of_MANET.pdf
16. Zhang, J., Dziong, Z., Kadoch, M., Gagnon, F.: Enhanced broadcasting and code assignment in multihop mobile ad hoc networks. In: Proc. of the 11th World Multi-Conference on Systemics, Sybernetics and Informatics (WMSCI 2007) (July 2007)
17. Zhang, J., Dziong, Z., Gagnon, F., Kadoch, M.: Receiver initiated MAC design for ad hoc networks based on multiuser detection. In: Proc. of the 5th International ICST Conference on Heterogeneous Networking for Quality, Reliability, Security and Robustness (QShine 2008) (July 2008)
18. Zhang, J., Dziong, Z., Gagnon, F., Kadoch, M.: Multiuser detection based MAC design for ad hoc networks. IEEE Transactions on Wireless Communications 8(4), 1836–1846 (2009)

MobileR: Multi-hop Energy Efficient Localised Mobile Georouting in Wireless Sensor and Actuator Networks

Nicolas Gouvy[1] and Nathalie Mitton[2]

[1] Univ Lille Nord de France, USTL, CNRS UMR 8022, LIFL, INRIA, France
nicolas.gouvy@lifl.fr
[2] INRIA Lille-Nord Europe, Univ Lille Nord de France, USTL,
CNRS UMR 8022, LIFL, France
nathalie.mitton@inria.fr

Abstract. This paper addresses the usage of actuators (sensors with controlled mobility) for routing in wireless sensor and actuator networks. Different routing protocols have been proposed to improve routing in terms of energy efficiency through the use of controlled mobility enabled sensors . We introduce MobileR. Unlike literature proposals also using actuators, MobileR considers the cost of a full path toward one of its neighbours instead of the cost of the direct edge toward it. To do so, MobileR computes in advance the possible routing paths over the next hops relying on the one-hop neighbours and their possible relocations. Moreover MobileR is fully localised and stateless. We evaluate our solution in terms of cumulative energy consumption with regard to network density. Experiments show that, with sufficient node degree, energy used for routing is significantly reduced and so network lifetime is extended.

Keywords: mobile sensor network, localised algorithm, controlled mobility routing, energy efficiency, connectivity preservation, multi-hop path computation.

1 Introduction

Wireless sensor networks (WSN) are characterised with the use of constrained devices powered by batteries and with low computational power and very little memory. As a consequence it is essential to propose routing algorithms which take into account those limitations in order to improve network lifetime. Considering that radio transmission is the most energy consuming factor in WSN, a common solution is to increase sensor density in order to decrease communication range. A more recent approach is to introduce mobile sensors, since it has been proven [3] to be as efficient as the density increasing. However, only a handful of routing protocols ([8,5]) relies on the usage of mobile sensors in order to extend the global network life. Those protocols are geographical routing protocols with cost-over-progress (COP) [12] heuristics. They are position-based, and compute possible relocations of each node on the routing path.

D. Simplot-Ryl et al. (Eds.): ADHOCNETS 2011, LNICST 89, pp. 147–161, 2012.
© Institute for Computer Sciences, Social Informatics and Telecommunications Engineering 2012

In this paper we propose MobileR routing protocol. MobileR is also a position based COP geographic routing protocol. However, unlike previous solutions, MobileR does not select the best node to forward a packet in the same way. As in [10], our solution evaluates at each step of the routing all possible multi-hop paths over its neighbourhood toward the destination. Moreover MobileR takes into account mobility deeper than any other routing protocol. It computes all associated relocations on each multi-hop path and their consequences in term of energy. MobileR comes in two variants, $MultipleORouting$ and $MultipleMove_R$, similarly to [8]. These variants differ in the relocation pattern they use, in order to permit further energy savings. Each variant fits better some energy models. Both variants respect the following properties:

- Localised: routing decision is taken only based on neighbour and destination location
- Scalable: routing process is stateless which allows it to be transposable to large networks as no information is stored neither in the message nor in the network nodes.
- Loop free: routing loops are avoided in order to protect network lifetime
- Energy efficient: MobileR takes into account all the costs associated with the routing process, transmission and moving costs. Transmission cost *and* displacement cost are evaluated with regard to the geographic progress.

The paper is organized as follows. Section 2 presents the related works. Simulation models are detailed in Section 3. We present the principle of MobileR in details in Section 4. Section 5 exposes two different heuristics and their uses in MobileR. Performance evaluation results are presented in Section 6. Finally, we conclude our work in Section 7.

2   Related Work

Position Based Routing. Those routing algorithms rely on the assumption that every node is aware of its own location, the location of its one-hop neighbours, and the location of the destination of the message. This made possible greedy routing [1] in which the message to route is forwarded to its neighbour which is the closest to the destination. It has been further optimized with COP [12] routing. It ensures that the ratio of energy used for sending a message to a node to the measured reduction in distance to the destination is minimized.

Other routing algorithms were proposed which ensure the packet delivery, like GFG [4], LOAFR [9] or ETE [10]. LOAFR chooses the first node being closer to the destination than the current one, this node is a relay node. Then LOAFR computes an energy shortest path (using Dijkstra) between the current node and the relay. Message is accordingly modified to include the computed path, and forwarded along that path until it reaches relay node. And so on. Recovery is done through Face-Routing. ETE is a routing algorithm which computes the energy weighted shortest path (SP) over the one-hop neighbourhood in the forward direction. In ETE computed path is not forwarded. Loops are avoided by considering in the path computing only nodes in the forwarding direction of the destination. ETE makes each node on the routing path compute its own SP according to its neighbourhood knowledge, as it allows further optimization on each step. So only the data is forwarded to the first node on the SP.

Routing in Mobile Sensor Networks. The topic of mobility is a main concern in ad hoc and wireless sensor networks since the beginning of this research topic. But most part of the extensive investigation on this topic focused on adapting to *consequences* of mobility. The first attempt of routing with the use of *controlled* mobility is the introduction of a mobile sink which gathers data from the sensors by one-hop radio communication [13]. The mobile sink then carries the data to a fixed base station. This approach requires the nodes to buffer their data between each visit of the sink. Same authors also propose a multi-sink scenario in which each sink moves randomly and collects data from sensors in its range.

A handful of more recent approaches considers the cases in which all sensors are mobile sensors (robots or actuators) or at least a significant part. Most of them [5,6] use an existing protocol to find an initial path, and then move each node on this path to the midpoint of its predecessor and successor on the routing path. MobileCOP [5] relies on three step. *1)* It builds a path from the source to the destination, electing at each node the next hop on the route in a COP fashion. *2)* Once the destination has been reached, a route confirmation packet is sent from the destination to the source, relocating nodes on the path at this moment by placing them on the line from source to destination and equidistantly placed. *3)* Finally, the data is sent along the pre-defined path. A major drawback of this approach is that the path has to be memorised to allow further relocation of nodes. And it may cause node's memory overhead. Moreover this routing algorithm does never take into account neither the moving cost nor the network connectivity, and so can disconnect the network. However, relocation pattern in [6] may cause useless zig-zag movements.

The CoMNet [8] routing algorithm is localised and stateless. It is COP fashioned, with both sending cost and relocation cost included. CoMNet comes with three relocation patterns: *1)* CoMNet *ORouting On the Move* which aims to align nodes on the routing path on a virtual line between source and destination, *2)* CoMNet $Move_{(r)}$ which equally spaces nodes on the routing path with the optimal radio range *3)* CoMNet $Move_{DSR}$ which aligns nodes and spaces them according to the optimal number of hops of the path at once. CoMNet relies on the use of a Connected Dominated Set (CDS) to guarantee network connectivity.

Connectivity Preservation. Mobility is a double-edged sword. If it can be used to improve routing, mobility must be used with caution since it may provoke network disconnection through the relocation of one single node. In CoMNet [8] - and MobileR- connectivity of the network is guaranteed through the computation of a Connected Dominated Set (CDS). If a node determines that it belongs to the CDS, it will never move. Those nodes, called dominant, are used to define a "skeleton". The other nodes, called dominated, are free to move while they remain in transmission range of at least dominant. In other words, mobility is only allowed for dominated nodes and under a one hop radio range of the skeleton. This mechanism ensures that there is always a path from one node to another in the network whatever the movements of the nodes.

3   Models

System Model

The system is composed of a set of wireless sensor nodes. Each of them can be either a static sensor or an actuator. In our context, we call a static sensor a sensor which can not move by itself but can communicate through a radio device. An actuator is a wireless sensor node which can communicate through radio and moreover can move in response to the reception of a displacement order in a controlled way. Furthermore, each node of the network, either static sensor or actuator, is capable to adjust its transmission range between 0 and R to save energy. All nodes are aware of their location through an hardware device such as GPS or any other location mean.

Notation

Let $N(u)$ be the neighbourhood of node u: the physical set of nodes which are in the transmission range of node u. We also define as $N_d(u)$ the subset of $N(u)$ in which each node is closer to node d than u itself, *i.e.* such that:

$$N_d(u) = \{v \in N(u) \text{ such as } dist(v, d) \leq dist(u, d)\} \tag{1}$$

Node's X relocation is noted as X'.
We define here a set of functions used in the following:

location(): returns the location where a node should move, based on MobileR variant,
dist(): gives the Euclidean distance between two nodes location.
isCoveredByDominant(): returns TRUE if a location is in the radio range of a dominant node, FALSE otherwise.

Energy Costs

It is worth noting that MobileR is energy model independent. Nevertheless, in order to measure MobileR performance, we use the most common energy model to compute the cost of the radio transmission of a packet, such as defined in [2]:

$$cost_s(r) = c + r^\alpha \tag{2}$$

where r to the Euclidean distance the signal has to cover, c corresponds to the activation cost of the radio device, and where α is a real constant ($1 < \alpha < 8$) which represents the signal attenuation.

The moving cost model we employ is the one used in previous similar works [5]:

$$cost_m(r) = a \times r \tag{3}$$

in which r is the Euclidean distance between the actual actuator location and the location the actuator is ordered to reach (*i.e.* the distance $dist(A, A')$ the actuator has to travel). a is a numerical constant determined by the engine used.

4   MobileR General Idea

Unlike previous solutions such as [5] and [8], MobileR does not simply compute the best node toward the destination and relocate it before routing. On the contrary, MobileR computes recursively all possible paths through relocations over the one hop neighbours in forward direction. Those computations aim to anticipate all possible routing paths over next hops toward destination. In Figure 1 node S computes the shortest path toward each of its neighbour, taking into consideration only nodes A,C and B which are towards D, in order to avoid routing loops. Transmission and relocation costs relative to each path are considered with regard to the total progress in a COP-fashion. Relocation of a node is done accordingly to a relocation pattern, and only if possible. MobileR can use any relocation pattern, but does always use the same over a network. MobileR selects the best path (BP) computed : the path which minimizes the COP.

Assuming that $x_0x_1...x_ix_{i+1}..x_n$ is the node sequence on the computed path from $a = x_0$ to $b = x_n$, its cost can be defined as follows:

$$cost(a, b) = \sum_{i=0}^{n} (cost_s(x_i, x'_{i+1}) + cost_m(x_{i+1}, x'_{i+1})) \tag{4}$$

where x'_i or x'_{i+1} are the new positions of respectively node x_i and node x_{i+1}, while the progress of this path is defined as:

$$progress = dist(a, D) - dist(x_n, D) \tag{5}$$

However MobileR does not communicate the BP from one node on the to another. It forwards the message to route to the first node on the path without any computed information about BP. It allows each node on the routing path to compute its BP toward the destination according to its neighbourhood knowledge. So, only one node may move at each set of the routing process, even if computed BP includes multiple nodes relocation.

We first describe the MobileR routing algorithm and then illustrate it through an example. MobileR makes a node x_s which has a message to route consider its neighbours in the forward direction. In first step, starting from current node position $location(x_s)$, it tries to virtually relocate one of its neighbour x_a. The relocation of x_a is in x'_a according to the relocation pattern used. And so MobileR has virtually built a path $x_sx'_a$ and can compute its associated cost-over-progress. Recursively, MobileR tries to extend the path $x_0x'_a$, starting from its end, the

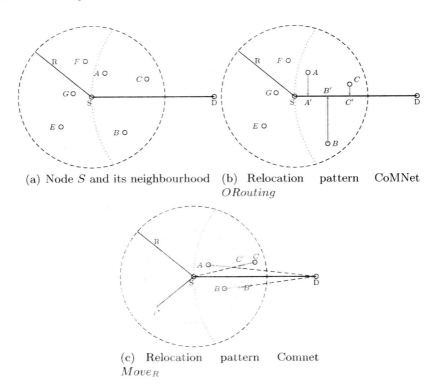

(a) Node S and its neighbourhood   (b) Relocation   pattern   CoMNet
$ORouting$

(c) Relocation   pattern   Comnet
$Move_R$

Fig. 1. Illustration of relocation patterns for a routing from S to D

x'_a location. As before, MobileR chooses a common neighbour of x'_a and x_s in forward direction, for example x_b and relocate it in x'_b. It makes possible the COP evaluation of path $x_s x'_a x'_b$. And so on, with each possible neighbour at each step, computing all possible paths starting from x_s. It is important to notice that x_s -which runs MobileR - does never know the real x'_a neighbourhood. It only knows a subset of them: the subset of its (*i.e* node x_s) neighbours which are closer to the routing destination than x'_a. With destination D it can be noted as:

$$N_D(x'_a) = N_D(x_s) \cap \{v \in N(x'_a) \text{ such as } dist(x'_a, D) \leq dist(x_s, D)\}$$

This enables possible energy saving by anticipating the routing over possible few hops only with the one hop knowledge.

Let's illustrate MobileR with an example, linked to Algorithm 1. Considering Figure 1, MobileR will act as follows. In this particular case source node S has to send a data packet to destination node D. The first step of MobileR is to make S compute the subset of nodes of its neighbourhood closer to the destination D than itself: $N_D(S)$ (Alg. 6, Line 16), *i.e.* in our example $N_D(S) = \{A, B, C\}$. If this set is empty, the greedy routing fails (Alg. 1 Line 14). Following a relocation pattern (*MultipleORouting* or *MultipleMove_R*), S then computes the relocation of each node belonging to $N_D(S)$ (Alg. 1 Line 17 / Alg. 2).

Algorithm 1. $Compute(s, d)$

1: $x \leftarrow s, min \leftarrow \infty$
2: **while** $x \neq d$ and $ok = 1$ **do**
3:     **if** $N_d(u) \neq \emptyset$ **then**
4:         Routing error
5:     **else**
6:         **for all** $v \in N_d(u)$ **do**
7:             $C \leftarrow rCompute(location(s), 0, v, s, d)$
8:             **if** $C < min$ **then**
9:                 $min \leftarrow C, x \leftarrow$ first node on $BP(x, v)$
10:            **end if**
11:        **end for**
12:    **end if**
13: **end while**
14: **return** x

A will be virtually relocated in A', B in B' and C in C' with radio and displacement costs computed (Alg. 2, l1-2). S then computes the COP of this $S \leftarrow A'$ path. Then, using A' new location, MobileR makes S do a recursive path computation: A' is the new start of the path. $N_D(A')$ is computed, but according to the neighbourhood knowledge of S (Alg. 2 line l6).

$$N_D(A') = N_D(S) \cap \{v \in N(A') \text{ such as } dist(A', D) \leq dist(S, D)\}$$

MobileR so makes S compute relocation of nodes in this set (Alg. 2 l7) in a recursive way in order to extend the $S- > A'$ path if possible. And so on. In Figure 1(c) the path $S- > A'- > C'$ can be built.

However, if for any reason (node is dominant, node is not a mobile sensor, relocation of a node is not covered by a dominant) a node x_i can't be moved, $x'_i = x_i$ as shown in Algorithm 3.

S finally selects the path which minimizes the COP (Alg. 2, l8-9 / Alg. 1, l8-9). This BP is the best possible path in terms of COP, based on S knowledge. S then forwards the packet to the first node on the BP, like in [10]. None other information previously computed (Alg. 1-l14) is sent to the next hop. It makes each node routing the message to compute its own BP based on its neighbourhood knowledge.

MobileR so computes a multi-hop path over it's one neighbourhood toward the destination of routing. It attempts to optimize routing by trying to figure out what would be the routing path over the next hops.

In order to improve energy efficiency in the routing process, two different relocation patterns have been considered (Figure 1). Each variant has its own advantages according to the energy consumption model and/or the application. On the one hand MobileR-$MultipleORouting$ relocates the first node on BP (with a beacon) before forwarding the message. This mechanism is used in order to reduce

Algorithm 2. $rCompute(prevNodeReloc, prevCost, nodeToConsider, origin, dest)$

1: $sCost \leftarrow cost_s(dist(prevNodeReloc, location(nodeToConsider)))$
2: $mCost \leftarrow cost_m(dist(location(nodeToConsider), relocation(nodeToConsider)))$
3: $cost \leftarrow sCost + mCost + prevCost$
4: $progress \leftarrow dist(origin, d) - dist(relocation(nodeToConsider), d)$
5: $min \leftarrow \frac{cost}{progress}$
6: **for all** $z \in (N_d(relocation(nodeToConsider)) \cap N_d(origin))$ **do**
7:     $C \leftarrow rCompute(relocation(nodeToConsider), cost, z, d)$
8:     **if** $C < min$ **then**
9:         $min \leftarrow C$
10:    **end if**
11: **end for**
12: **return** min

Algorithm 3. $relocation(nodeToConsider)$

1: $x \leftarrow location(nodeToConsider)$
2: $x' \leftarrow$ *new position according to relocation pattern*
3: **if** $(isCoveredByDominant(x')$ **AND** $(!isDominant(nodeToConsider))$ **then**
4:     **return** x'
5: **else**
6:     **return** x
7: **end if**

transmission costs by reducing radio range before sending message. On the other hand, MobileR-*MultipleMoveR* sends the relocation order with the message. It aims to reduce moving distance costs while optimizing the sending cost.

5   MobileR Variants

5.1   MobileR-*MultipleORouting*

Illustrated in Figure 2, this heuristic aims to align all nodes on the path from the source to the destination as it provides the best energy saving ([8],[5]) for sending. The relocation principle here consists in relocating a node to its orthogonal projection on the source-destination virtual line since the orthogonal projection is the shortest distance to travel.

The relocation order is sent first through a beacon. And then, when relocation of the neighbour is done, the message is sent. We consider that a message is significantly bigger than a beacon. With a negligible beacon cost -compared to the message-, the transmission costs are reduced since the relocated node is closer than before. The cost of each path is composed by the relocation cost of each node on the path (from X to X') and the transmission cost between each node on the path (from X' to Y' for instance). Figure 2 illustrates all the possible logical paths. The path from S to D by A' is direct $S \rightarrow A'$ since there is no possibility to have any energy shorter path. There are only two possibilities to use B: $S \rightarrow B'$,

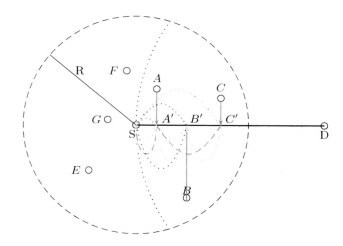

Fig. 2. Illustration of relocations in MobileR-*MultipleORouting* (red arrows). Some of the possible paths considered between S and the relocations of its neighbours are also depicted.

or $S \rightarrow A' \rightarrow B'$ since A is closer to S than B. All possible paths from S to C' are the following ones: $S \rightarrow C', S \rightarrow A' \rightarrow C', S \rightarrow B' \rightarrow C', S \rightarrow A' \rightarrow B' \rightarrow C'$. At each step of path computations, only nodes which are closer to the destination than the last one on the current computed path are considered to avoid routing loops.

5.2   MobileR-*MultipleMove_R*

An illustration can be found in Figure 3. This relocation pattern relies on the idea to equally space each node on the path. Moreover, nodes' relocation is such that the distance between two nodes on the path is equal to the optimal radio range of their transmission device [8]. This range is extracted from the common energy model for radio transmission $cost(r) = r^\alpha + c$ and is equal to $r^* = \sqrt[\alpha]{\frac{c}{\alpha-1}}$ [11]. In this variant, relocation order is added to the message. As a consequence, relocation is done after message reception.

The relocation of a node X is on the intersection point of the X-destination virtual line and the circle $C(S)_{r^*}$ of radius r^* centred in S if $|SX| \leq r^*$. Otherwise, relocation is on the intersect between $C(S)_{r^*}$ and SX.

Figure 3 illustrates a step in the path computations, and demonstrates the possible relocations of a node engendered by the relocation of another. Furthermore, the higher the $\frac{r^*}{maximal\ range}$ ratio is, the further the path computation is. And so a node can predict more accurately the optimal path toward the destination on multiple hops. In this heuristic, the message is sent *with* the relocation order in it.

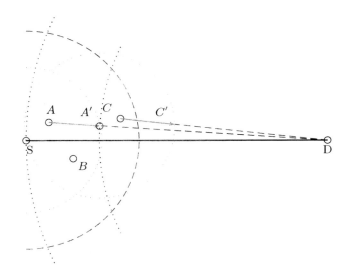

Fig. 3. Relocation principle MobileR-$MultipleMove_R$ (red arrows). The relocation of A in A' makes possible the relocation of C in C' and as a consequence the evaluation of the path $S \rightarrow A' \rightarrow C'$.

6   Performance Evaluation

Simulations are performed using WSNet network simulator[1]. Since we focus on the network layer, simulations are conducted with no interferences and/or collisions. On the network point of view, nodes are deployed uniformly on a 1000×1000 square topology. Each of the node is able to tune its transmission range R between 0 and 250 and can obtain their location precisely on the simulation map. We use the algorithm found in [7] for CDS computation. This algorithm is fully local and only requires knowledge of one hop neighbourhood. Nevertheless any CDS computation algorithm is possible.

6.1   Routing Success Rate

Figure 4 represents the percentage of success routing with respect to network node density. Results show that MobileCOP is outperformed by every solution in low densities. MobileR-$MultipleMoveR$ and MobileR-$MultipleORouting$ and their one-hop variant (respectively CoMNet *Mover* and CoMNet *ORouting On the Move*) are equivalent with a slight improvement for MobileR. It suggests that the path anticipation in MobileR might decrease coverage hole.

---

[1] http://wsnet.gforge.inria.fr/

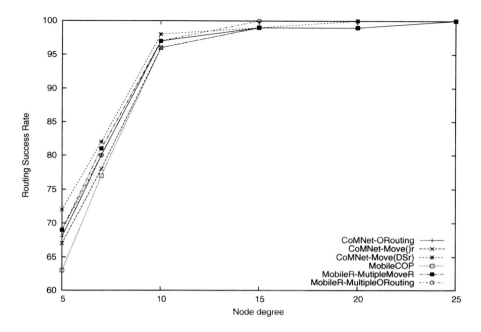

Fig. 4. Routing success rates of different routing algorithms

6.2   Energy Consumption

We set the simulation parameters to the common values used in literature. On the one hand we used the values in $c = 3^8$ and $\alpha = 4$ in the energy model (Eq. 2). On the other hand, we use the same approach as the one developed in [8] regarding the moving cost model (Eq. 3). With E_T the radio transmission cost and E_D the displacement cost, three different cases can be envisaged:

- $E_T << E_D$: case in which the displacement cost over a distance d equals the transmission cost over the same distance. In that case we set the a parameters in (Eq. 2) such as $100 \times cost_s(d) = cost_m(d)$
- $E_T == E_D$: where $cost_s(d) = cost_m(d)$,
- $E_T >> E_D$: in which the radio transmission cost is much energy-hungry than the relocation cost over a same distance. a is here set such as $cost_s(d) = 100 \times cost_m(d)$

The simulator runs the different routing algorithms with the same source-destination couple for 10 consecutive times over 1000 maps.

With Respect to the Number of Routings
Figure 5 displays the energy consumption as a function of the number of successive routings. Each mobility model is presented. Density is set to $\delta = 25$. As nodes may move on second or more iteration of routing with some of the algorithms, we decide to integrate both transmission and displacement costs in order to make possible true comparisons.

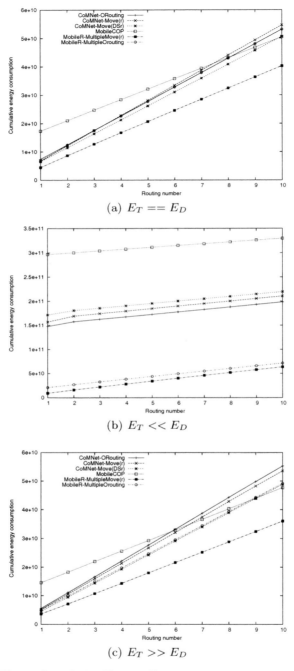

(a) $E_T == E_D$

(b) $E_T << E_D$

(c) $E_T >> E_D$

Fig. 5. Cumulative Energy Consumption over 10 routes

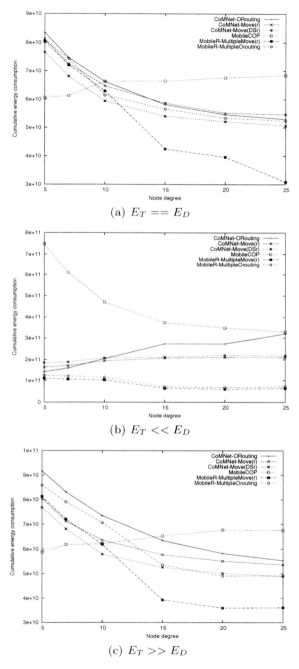

(a) $E_T == E_D$

(b) $E_T << E_D$

(c) $E_T >> E_D$

Fig. 6. Energy consumption used for routing with regard to node degree

As expected, for all models, in any case, MobileR *MultipleMoveR* and MobileR *Multiple ORouting* outperform their CoMNet variant. This is due to their recursive computation of paths over their one hop neighbourhood. It permits MobileR variants to anticipate routing over few hops in best cases. And so they are able to perform better choices than the previously existing algorithms in most cases. Moreover, MobileR *MultipleMoveR* appears to perform the best in most cases, as it aims to minimize both transmission and relocation costs.

Compared to MobileCOP, our approach is significantly better in terms of energy saving. This is due to the fact that MobileCOP does not take into account the cost of mobility. This is particularly obvious when displacement costs are expensive, see Figure 5(b). Moreover, as MobileCOP relies on a route request and then a route confirmation with relocation before message sending, its initial cost is higher than any other. On the one hand, route request and confirmation are the reason of the initial cost when transmission cost are the most expensive (Figure 5(c)). But on the other hand, the nodes relocation during route confirmation explain the initial cost when displacement cost are a lot more expensive than transmission ones(Figure 5(b)). MobileCOP and CoMNet heuristics tend to converge over the successive routing.

With Respect to Network Density
Figure 6 displays the cumulative energy for ten consecutive routings along the same path by each algorithm as a function to network density. The presence of the CDS explains that MobileCOP outperforms our approach for low densities networks ($\delta \leq 10$) and when transmission costs are less or as costly than displacement costs. This is because most of the nodes are member of the CDS and thus can not move. With the increase of node density, more and more nodes are free to move, and thus they perform similarly to MobileCOP. Anyway, MobileCOP is outperformed when the moving costs are significantly higher: it does not take into account the cost of mobility.

Results show that MobileR *MultipleMoveR* and MobileR *MultipleOrouting* consume the same ($\delta < 10$) or less ($\delta > 10$) energy than their one hop CoMNet variant, respectively CoMNet $Move_r$ and CoMNet $ORouting$. In fact, the higher the density is, the lower the energy consumed for routing is. Once a minimum density is reached ($\delta \equiv 10$), the required nodes for the CDS are selected, and so there are more nodes available for routing and Best Path computation.

7   Conclusion

MobileR routing protocol promises to lower the energy consumption of the routing process in wireless sensor and actuator networks by taking advantage of node mobility. Furthermore, MobileR is fully localised, scalable, energy efficient and guarantee network connectivity. It comes with two different relocation principles adapted to different traffic schemes. The performance of the these heuristics has been analysed based upon the results of exhaustive simulations. Future works include the consideration of multiple and concurrent simultaneous routing from different sources, and the guarantee of delivery. Future experiments will be conduced using realistic parameters before experimenting on the very large scale open wireless sensor network plateform Senslab.

Acknowledgements. This research is supported by a grant from CPER Nord-Pas-de-Calais/FEDER Campus Intelligence Ambiante.

References

1. Fin, G.G.: Routing and addressing problems in large metropolitan internetworks (1987)
2. Rodoplu, V., Meng, T.: Minimizing energy mobile wireless networks. IEEE JSAC 17(8), 1333–1347 (1999)
3. Wang, W., Srinivasan, V., Chua, K.C.: Extending the lifetime of wireless sensor networks through mobile relays. IEEE/ACM Trans. Netw. 16(5), 1108–1120 (2008)
4. Bose, P., Morin, P., Stojmenovi, I., Urrutia, J.: Routing with Guaranteed Delivery in ad hoc Wireless Networks. Wireless Networks (2001)
5. Liu, H., Nayak, A., Stojmenović, I.: Localized Mobility Control Routing in Robotic Sensor Wireless Networks. In: Zhang, H., Olariu, S., Cao, J., Johnson, D.B. (eds.) MSN 2007. LNCS, vol. 4864, pp. 19–31. Springer, Heidelberg (2007)
6. Goldenberg, D.K., Lin, J., Morse, A.S.: Towards mobility as a routing primitive. In: Mobihoc, pp. 163-174 (2004)
7. Carle, J., Simplot-Ryl, D.: Energy efficient area monitoring by sensor networks. IEEE Computer Magazine 37, 40–46 (2004)
8. Hamouda, E., Mitton, N., Simplot-Ryl, D.: Ensuring Connectivity for Energy Efficient Mobile Routing in Actuator and Sensor Networks. In: 10th International Conference on Ad Hoc Networks and Wireless. AdHocNow (2011)
9. Sanchez, J.A., Ruiz, P.M.: Exploiting Local Knowledge to Enhance Energy-Efficient Geographic Routing. In: Cao, J., Stojmenovic, I., Jia, X., Das, S.K. (eds.) MSN 2006. LNCS, vol. 4325, pp. 567–578. Springer, Heidelberg (2006)
10. Elhafsi, E.H., Mitton, N., Simplot-Ryl, D.: End-to-End energy efficient geographic path discovery with guaranteed delivery in ad hoc and sensor networks. In: Personal, Indoor and Mobile Radio Communications (2008)
11. Stojmenovic, I., Lin, X.: Power-aware localized routing in wireless networks. IEEE TPDS 12(11), 1122–1133 (2001)
12. Kuruvila, J., Nayak, A., Stojmenovic, I.: Progress and location based localized power aware routing for ad hoc sensor wireless networks. IJDSN 2, 147–159 (2006)
13. Shah, R.C., Roy, S., Jain, S., Brunette, W.: Data MULEs: Modeling and Analysis of a Three-tier Architecture for Sparse Sensor Networks. Ad Hoc Networks 1(2-3), 215–233 (2003)
14. http://www.senslab.info

Neighbour Selection and Sensor Knowledge: Proactive Approach for the Frugal Feeding Problem in Wireless Sensor Networks

Elio Velazquez and Nicola Santoro

School of Computer Science, Carleton University, Canada
{elio_velazquez,santoro}@scs.carleton.ca

Abstract. This paper examines new proactive solutions to the Frugal Feeding Problem (FFP) in Wireless Sensor Networks. The FFP attempts to find energy-efficient routes for a mobile service entity to rendezvous with each member of a team of mobile robots. Although the complexity of the FFP is similar to the Traveling Salesman Problem (TSP), we propose an efficient solution, completely distributed and localized for the case of a fixed rendezvous location (i.e., service facility with limited number of docking ports) and mobile capable sensors. Our proactive solution reduces the FFP to finding energy-efficient routes in a dynamic Compass Directed Gabriel Graph (CDGG) or Compass Directed Relative Neighbour Graph (CDRNG). The proposed graphs incorporate ideas from forward progress routing and the directionality of compass routing in an energy-aware graph. Navigating the CDGG or CDRNG guarantees that each sensor will reach the rendezvous location in a finite number of steps. The ultimate goal of our solution is to achieve energy equilibrium (i.e., no further sensor losses due to energy starvation) by optimizing the use of a shared recharge station. We also examine the impact of critical parameters such as transmission range, number of recharge ports and sensor knowledge for the two proposed graphs.

1   Introduction

The problem of achieving continuous operation in a robotic environment by refueling or recharging mobile robots has been the focus of attention in recent research papers. In particular, [8,9] presents this problem as the Frugal Feeding Problem (FFP), for its analogy with occurrences in the animal kingdom. The FFP attempts to find energy-efficient routes for a mobile service entity, also called "tanker", to rendezvous with every member of a team of mobile robots. The FFP has several variants depending on where the "feeding" or refueling of the robots takes place: at each robot's location, at a predefined location (e.g., at the tanker's location) or anywhere. Regardless of which variant is chosen, the problem is how to ensure that the robots reach the rendezvous location without "dying" of energy starvation during the process.

D. Simplot-Ryl et al. (Eds.): ADHOCNETS 2011, LNICST 89, pp. 162–176, 2012.
© Institute for Computer Sciences, Social Informatics and Telecommunications Engineering 2012

In this paper we study the FFP in a wireless sensor network scenario where mobility capabilities are added to the sensors and static recharge facilities are deployed throughout the sensing area. In this variant of the FFP, the sensors are responsible for maintaining the overall health of the network and the service facilities play a passive role. The rendezvous between sensors and facilities should take place at the closest facility's original position (i.e., static location). The maximum number of sensors that can rendezvous with a facility at any given time is determined by the number of docking ports or recharge sockets available at the facility. Our problem can be seen as the "tanker absorbed" version of the FFP. A similar problem is addressed in [14].

1.1   Related Work

In the FFP, as introduced in [8], specialized robots, also called tankers, have to rendezvous with a team of mobile robots for refueling purposes. The main goal is to minimize the amount of fuel (i.e., energy) required to move the robots and tankers to the rendezvous locations. The problem can have several variants: 1) robot-absorbed case. The rendezvous takes place at the robot's location. The robots in need of energy do not move but instead wait for the refueling tanker to come to their rescue. 2) tanker-absorbed case. The rendezvous takes place at the tanker's location and the robots should move to the tanker's original location. 3) General case. The rendezvous takes place at locations that do not coincide with the initial robot or tanker locations. The FFP also has a combinatorial component pertaining to the order in which the robots should be recharged. Finding a solution to the FFP that guarantee that no robots die of energy starvation is an NP-Hard problem (as shown in [8]).

Examples of the robot-absorbed FFP can be found in [1,2,10]. In all cases, a charger robot is responsible for delivering energy to a swarm of robots. The recharging strategy is completely reactive (i.e., robots are only recharged when they become out of service and cannot move). The simulations results presented in [2] showed that in a network with 64 robots and one charger station with only one docking port; there will be a large number of robots either abandoned or dead due to battery depletion. However, increasing the number of docking ports to 2, affects the performance dramatically by decreasing the number of robot deaths and improving the exploring/dead time ratios. The solution presented in [10] creates clusters based on the number of available chargers. The experimental results with this approach show that a network with 76 sensors deployed in an area of $1000x1000m^2$ requires at least 3 chargers to keep the network alive. The network is considered dead when more that 50% of the sensors die due to battery depletion.

Reactive vs. proactive strategies for energy restoration in WSN are discussed in [13,14]. In particular, examples of proactive strategies for the tanker-absorbed FFP can be found in [14] along with the impact of several network parameters such as transmission range, locomotion costs and recharge station role.

1.2   Contributions

This paper emphasizes the use of a proactive approach to solve the Frugal Feeding Problem (FFP) in WSN. We propose an efficient solution, completely distributed and localized for the case of a fixed rendezvous location (i.e., service facility with limited number of docking ports) and mobile sensors. In particular, we propose to reduce the tanker-absorbed FFP with a fixed rendezvous location in a sensor network of arbitrary topology to finding energy-efficient routes in a dynamic Compass Directed Gabriel Graph (CDGG) or Compass Directed Relative Neighbour Graph (CDRNG). We prove that energy-aware mobility strategies built on the CDGG and CDRNG are loop-free, guaranteeing that the sensors will reach the recharge station within a finite number of moves. The experimental analysis of our solution confirms that energy equilibrium (i.e., no further losses due to energy starvation) can be achieved in a network of 100:1 sensor/station ratio with one station containing two docking ports. Our experiments also examine the impact of critical parameters such as topology, transmission range, number of docking ports and sensor knowledge. This paper also starts a discussion on proactive solutions to the FFP in the presence of obstacles.

The main differences between our proposed solution to the FFP and the existing literature in the area of autonomous robot recharging are: 1) Our solution is completed distributed and localized; there is no need for an entity with global knowledge. Sensors are only aware of their immediate neighbors and the location of the closest facility. 2) Our approach is completely proactive. The sensors act before their batteries reach a critical level to minimize coverage holes by making the shortest possible trip to the recharge station. 3) The algorithms for route selection and logical topologies used are dynamic and adaptive. 4) Our analysis considers the impact of critical network parameters such as neighbour information, transmission range and number of recharge ports.

2   Proactive Alternatives to the Facility-Absorbed FFP

This paper extends some results previously presented in [14]. The general requirement for our theoretical model is to maximize the network operating life by the autonomous recharging of low energy sensors. However, the ultimate goal is to achieve a state of energy equilibrium where no further losses are reported. In general, the model includes the following key components: 1) A set of N sensors, $S = \{s_1, ..., s_N\}$ randomly distributed in an area of unspecified shape. 2) A randomly located static recharge facility F (i.e., rendezvous location). The facility is equipped with a fixed number of recharging ports or sockets. This represents the maximum number of simultaneous sensors at the rendezvous location.

It is assumed that sensors can determine their own positions by using GPS or other localization methods. Sensors can communicate with other sensors within their transmission range R and they all move at the same speed. The distance to the closest facility should be within the sensors' mobility range to guarantee a successful round-trip to the station with one battery charge. All communications are asynchronous; there is no global clock or centralized entity to coordinate communications or actions. The communication environment is contention and error free (i.e., no need to retransmit data) and there is no interference produced by receiving simultaneous radio transmissions (i.e., ideal MAC layer).

We consider the sensors to be static in terms of their sensing requirements.In other words, from the point of view of the application (i.e., functional requirements), the sensors are static and placed at a specific set of coordinates. However, they all have the capability of moving if they decide to go to the service station to recharge their batteries. Consequently, a pro-active behaviour implies that the sensors decide to act before their batteries reach a critical level. The general idea is that sensors will try to get closer to the rendezvous location by swapping positions with higher energy sensors that are closer to the station and eventually making the shortest possible trip when their batteries reach a critical level. Every time a sensor visits the recharge station, a coverage hole is created. The duration of the hole depends on the recharging time plus the length of the round-trip. In order to minimize coverage holes sensors will attempt a gradual approach towards the rendezvous location by swapping positions with higher energy sensors. The operating life of a sensor is divided in three stages depending on its battery status: 1) a BATTERY_OK or normal operation, 2) BATTERY_LOW or energy-aware operation and 3) BATTERY_CRITICAL or recharge-required operation. A sensor in a BATTERY_OK state will perform its regular sensing functions as well as accept any swapping proposal from other sensors with less energy. When the battery level falls below a fixed threshold, the sensor switches to the BATTERY_LOW state. In this state, the sensor will start its migration towards the service station, proposing swapping operations to sensors with higher energy levels. Finally, a sensor in the BATTERY_CRITICAL state will contact the service station and wait until a socket or docking port has been secured, then it will travel to the station and recharge.

The objective of the sensor during migration is to reach the recharge facility in an effective timely manner, while relying solely on local information. This can be done by allowing the sensor to explore energy-aware routes leading to the recharge facility. The chosen routes are based on a logical Compass Directed Gabriel Graph (CDGG) or a Compass Directed Relative Neighbour Graph (CDRNG).

Definition 1. *Let $G = (V, E)$ be a Unit Disk Graph with vertices V and a set of edges E. A graph $G = (V' \cup F, E)$ with $V' \subseteq V$ and $E' \subseteq E$ is called Compass Directed Gabriel Graph (CDGG) if $\forall$ pair of sensors $s_i, s_j \in V'$ and recharge facility F, the edge $s_i \rightarrow s_j \in E'$ iff the following conditions are satisfied:*

1. *Unit graph criterion: $d(s_i, s_j) \leq R$ where d denotes the Euclidean distance and R is the transmission range.*
2. *Proximity criterion: $d(s_j, F) < d(s_i, F)$ and $d(s_i, S_j) < d(s_i, F)$*
3. *Directionality criterion: $\exists s_{jp}$ such that $\overrightarrow{s_j s_{jp}} \cdot \overrightarrow{s_i F} = 0$ and $d(s_i, s_{jp}) + d(s_{jp}F) = d(s_i, F)$*
4. *Gabriel neighbour criterion: $\nexists s_k \in V'$ such that $d(s_k, \frac{s_i + s_j}{2}) < d(s_i, \frac{s_i + s_j}{2})$*

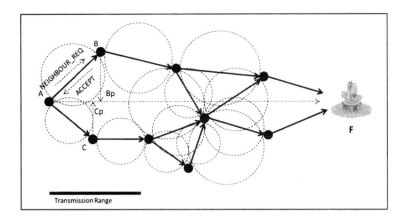

Fig. 1. Compass Directed Gabriel Graph

Definition 2. *Let $G = (V, E)$ be a Unit Disk Graph with vertices V and a set of edges E. A graph $G = (V' \cup F, E)$ with $V' \subseteq V$ and $E' \subseteq E$ is called Compass Directed Relative Neighbour Graph (CDRNG) if $\forall$ pair of sensors $s_i, s_j \in V'$ and recharge facility F, the edge $s_i \to s_j \in E'$ iff the following conditions are satisfied:*

1. *Unit graph criterion: $d(s_i, s_j) \leq R$ where d denotes the Euclidean distance and R is the transmission range.*
2. *Proximity criterion: $d(s_j, F) < d(s_i, F)$ and $d(s_i, s_j) < d(s_i, F)$*
3. *Directionality criterion: $\exists s_{jp}$ such that $\vec{s_j s_{jp}} \cdot \vec{s_i F} = 0$ and $d(s_i, s_{jp}) + d(s_{jp} F) = d(s_i, F)$*
4. *Relative neighbour criterion: $\not\exists s_k \in V'$ such that $d(s_i, s_k) < d(s_i, s_j)$ and $d(s_k, s_j) < d(s_i, s_j)$*

Routing algorithms use the hop count as the metric to measure effectiveness. In this case, the hop count would be equivalent to the number of swapping operations between sensors in our CDGG or CDRNG. Our solution to the FFP can be divided into two main stages: 1) the construction of the CDGG/CDRNG and 2) the incremental swapping approach (i.e., migration) towards the rendezvous location.

2.1   Creating the CDGG and CDRNG

Figure 1 shows an example of the proposed CDGG for three sensors A,B,C and a facility F. In the first stage of the algorithm, it is assumed that all sensors have the required levels of energy to construct the CDGG. The process can be summarized by the following actions:

1. Sensors position themselves at some initial fixed location that depends on the task at hand.

2. Sensor A sends a NEIGHBOUR_REQUEST broadcast message inviting other sensors to participate.
3. Upon receiving a NEIGHBOUR_REQUEST message from sensor A, immediate neighbours verify the neighbouring criteria according to the following rules:
   a) Proximity: $d(A,F) > d(B,F)$ and $d(A,B) < d(A,F)$.
   b) Directionality: For example, B and C are neighbours of A if the corresponding projections B_p and C_p on line $\overline{AF}$ intersect the line segment $\overline{AF}$.
4. If the conditions a) and b) are met, then sensors B and C send a NEIGHBOUR_ACCEPT message. Otherwise they send a NEIGHBOUR_DENY message.

Up to this point, the process is the same as the creation of the CDG introduced in [13,14]. However, to guarantee that only the Gabriel neighbours are selected as graph neighbours, the sensor should implement the following actions:

1. Upon receiving a NEIGHBOUR_ACCEPT message from a potential Gabriel neighbour S', the receiving sensor S verifies if there is already a graph neighbour in the disc with center $(\frac{S_x+S'_x}{2}, \frac{S_y+S'_y}{2})$ and radius $\frac{d(S,S')}{2}$. If such a neighbour exists, then sensor S sends a NEIGHBOUR_DENY message to S'.
2. If no existing graph neighbour is found in the previous step, this means that sensor S' is in fact a Gabriel neighbour. However, some of the existing graph neighbours could be affected by this newly accepted sensor and they are no longer Gabriel neighbours. If the newly accepted sensor S' falls in the diametric disc between sensor S and one of the existing graph neighbours S_i, the neighbour in question should be excluded by sending it a NEIGHBOUR_DENY message.

The creation of the CDRNG follows the same pattern with only one minor change to verify the relative neighbouring criterion:

1. Upon receiving a NEIGHBOUR_ACCEPT message from a potential relative neighbour S', the receiving sensor S verifies if there is already a graph neighbour in the Lune created by intercepting the discs with centers in S and S' and radius $d(S,S')$. If such a neighbour exists, then sensor S sends a NEIGHBOUR_DENY message to S'.
2. If no existing graph neighbour is found in the previous step, this means that sensor S' is in fact a relative neighbour. However, some of the existing graph neighbours could be affected by this newly accepted sensor and they are no longer relative neighbours. If the newly accepted sensor S' falls in the Lune between sensor S and one of the existing graph neighbours S_i, the neighbour in question should be excluded by sending it a NEIGHBOUR_DENY message.

Algorithm 1. GDGG Construction: sensor S and facility F

(* In State $INIT$: *)
send $NEIGHBOUR\_REQUEST$ broadcast message
become $BATTERY\_OK$
(* In State $BATTERY\_OK$: *)
if receiving $NEIGHBOUR\_REQUEST$ from S' **then**
    if $distance(S, F) < distance(S', F)$ and $distance(S, S') < distance(S', F)$ and
$DistancePointToLineIn(S, S', F, distanceToLine)$ **then**
        $parentList.Add(S')$
        send $NEIGHBOUR\_ACCEPT$ to S'
    end if
end if
if receiving $NEIGHBOUR\_ACCEPT$ from S' **then**
    $midPoint.X = (S.CoordX + S'.CoordX)/2$
    $midPoint.Y = (S.CoordY + S'.CoordY)/2$
    while $i \leq numNeighbours$ **do**
        if $S.distance(midPoint) \geq neighbourPositions[i].distance(midPoint)$ **then**
            send $NEIGHBOUR\_DENY$ to S'
            become $BATTERY\_OK$
        end if
    end while
    while $i \leq numNeighbours$ **do**
        $midPoint.x = (S.CoordX + neighbourPositions[i].CoordX)/2$
        $midPoint.y = (S.CoordY + neighbourPositions[i].CoordY)/2$
        if $S.distance(midPoint) \geq S'.distance(midPoint)$ **then**
            send $NEIGHBOUR\_DENY$ to $neighbour[i]$
            $neighbourList.Remove(i)$
        end if
    end while
    $rankingPar = d(S, S')$
    $neighbourList.Add(S', rankingPar)$
    $neighbourList.rank()$
end if

The main interactions required for the construction of the CDGG are summarized by Algorithm 1. A detailed description of the CDRNG construction is omitted for space limitations but it follows the same idea with only minor modifications.

At the end of this phase each sensor will have two routing tables: one containing its children (i.e., sensors from which NEIGHBOUR_ACCEPT messages were received) with their corresponding ranking and a second table containing its parents (i.e., sensors to which NEIGHBOUR_ACCEPT messages were sent). The routing tables are just partial maps of the network indicating the position of their children and parents. The identity of the sensors in the routing tables is dynamic and will be updated every time a swapping operation occurs. This property, along with a neighboring criteria that incorporates ideas from forward progress and compass routing [11,7,6] in an energy-aware unit graph, ensure the following lemma:

Lemma 1. *The proactive solution to the FFP using a CDGG or CDRNG guarantees that all sensors reach the rendezvous location within a finite number of swapping operations.*

Proof. Let $G = (V, E)$ be a CDGG or CDRNG with a set of vertices $V = \{S_1, ..., S_N, F\}$ where S_i, $1 \leq i \leq N$ represent sensors and F denotes the rendezvous location. Let E be a set of edges of the form $S_i \rightarrow S_j$ where S_j is neighbor of S_i. By definition, G satisfies the conditions of proximity (2) and directionality (3).

Without loss of generality, we can assume that for any path $P_i = < S_i, ..., S_K, F >$ leading to the recharge station F, with $1 \leq i < K \leq N$, the sub-path containing the sensors $< S_i, ..., S_K >$ does not contain any cycles. This claim can be proved by contradiction.

Let us assume that the rendezvous location cannot be reached. This means that at some point during the execution of the algorithm a given sensor finds itself in a loop (i.e., a cycle C of arbitrary length L is found). Let $C = \{S_i, S_{(i+1)} ..., S_{(L-1)}\} \bigcup \{S_L, S_i\}$ with $1 \leq i < L \leq N$. If such a cycle C exists, sensor S_i must be neighbor of sensor S_L which means that $d(S_i, T) < d(S_L, T)$. This contradicts the proximity criterion (2)(triangular inequality). Hence, the Lemma holds. □

3 Increasing Sensor Knowledge

Another possible enhancement to improve the overall performance of the proactive strategy and help low energy sensors reach the recharge station faster is to add additional information about the energy levels of the 2-hop graph neighbours. Regardless of the topology chosen (i.e., CDG, CDGG, or CDRNG), having the 2-hop neighbouring information combined with the 1-hop greedy strategy should lead to a more energy efficient path selection. To implement this new approach, a series of changes to the existing algorithms is necessary. For example, the neighbouring information stored by each sensor s needs to change to include the tuple $(s_i, E_{S_i}, E_{S_{i_{2hop}}})$ where s_i is the i-th 1-hop neighbour of s. E_{S_i} represents the energy level and $E_{S_{i_{2hop}}}$ represents the average energy levels of the 1-hop graph neighbours of s_i.

The information about existing 1-hop graph neighbours will be appended to the NEIGHBOUR_ACCEPT messages sent during the graph creation phase. When a sensor sends a NEIGHBOUR_ACCEPT message to its parent, the message will now include the average energy level of its existing 1-hop neighbours. This new piece of information will have to be updated once the migration or swapping phase is initiated. Consequently, two swapping sensors will exchange this new piece of information as part of the swapping process. Furthermore, sensors reacting to a SWAP_COMPLETE message will generate a new message NEIGHBOUR_2HOP_UPDATE to inform their parents about the changes of their 2-hop graph neighbours.

Let us examine the example shown in Figure 2 to illustrate the new interactions required during a swapping operation. In this example, sensors

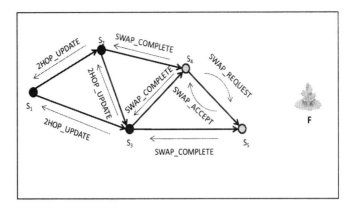

Fig. 2. Sensor swapping with 2-hop neighbours updates

S_4 and S_5 have agreed to swap positions after the corresponding exchange of SWAP_REQUEST and SWAP_ACCEPT messages. Once the sensors arrive at the location occupied by their swapping partners, both sensors (i.e., S_4 and S_5) will send SWAP_COMPLETE messages to their parents S_2 and S_3. The SWAP_COMPLETE message received by sensor S_2 contains the tuple $(S_4, E_{S_4}, E_{S_{4_{2hop}}})$. After updating its neighbouring information with the newly received information, S_2 computes the combined energy level of its 1-hop graph neighbours: $E_{S_{2_{2hop}}} = \frac{E_{S_3} + E_{S_4}}{2}$ and sends a new NEIGH-BOUR_2HOP_UPDATE $(S_2, E_{S_4}, E_{S_{2_{2hop}}})$ message to its parent S_1.

It is clear from the previous example that for each successful swapping operation there will be an overhead produced by the new NEIGH-BOUR_2HOP_UPDATE messages. The density of the graph, determined by the neighbour selection criteria and the sensor transmission ranges, will have a great impact on how many of these new notification messages are generated. The next section examines the impact of this added knowledge, its relationship with the underlying topology chosen, its potential benefits and possible drawbacks.

4   Simulation Results

Previous work on energy consumption of wireless sensor networks and protocols such as 802.11, have found that the energy required to initiate communication is not negligible. In particular, loss of energy due to retransmissions, collisions and acknowledgments is significant [4,5]. Protocols that rely on periodic probe messages and acknowledgments are considered high cost. It is also noted in the literature that sensors' energy consumption in an idle state can be as large as the energy used when receiving data [5]. On the other hand, the energy used in transmitting data could be between 30-50% more than the energy needed to receive a packet.

A common consideration for any solution involving mobile entities is how to accurately represent the energy spent when moving from one location to another. Locomotion cost depends on many factors such as the weight of the electronic components, irregularities in the terrain, obstacles, etc. For simplicity, in [8,14], the weighted Euclidean distance between origin and destination is used as the cost of relocating a robot. In particular, in [14] is observed that the energy required to move their robotic sensors was 54x the energy required to send a packet over the same distance and the energy spent in communications (i.e., send/receive) was 25% more than the battery drain in the idle state.

The simulation scenarios are implemented in Omnet++ [12] along with the mobility framework extension [3]. For all experiments, the sensors and charging facilities were randomly placed in an area of $1000 \times 1000m^2$. The analysis of our simulated results centers on two important aspects of the solutions: 1) Whether or not a state of equilibrium is achieved and the number of sensor losses until such condition is met and 2) Impact of several variables such as: underlying topology, transmission range, number of recharge sockets/ports and sensor knowledge.

In an ideal system, all sensors will reach the BATTERY_CRITICAL state when they are exactly at one-hop distance from the rendezvous location. When the trip to the recharge station is made from a one-hop position (i.e., there are no graph neighbors), it is called a "one-hop run" or "optimal run". Contrarily, if the final trip is made from any other location, it is called a "panic run" [13]. In all the simulated scenarios, the quality of the strategy is measured in terms of optimal runs vs. panic runs. Constant cost values are assigned to each basic operation (i.e., send, receive, idle and move). Initial values for these operations are based on some of the observations found in [14,4,5].

4.1   Topology Comparison

This test was designed to determine whether our proactive solution to FFP reaches a state of equilibrium when the new proposed CDGG and CDRNG are used as the underlying topologies for the mobility strategies. The experiment measured the cumulative number of sensor losses until energy equilibrium is reached. Figure 3(a) shows the result of a simulation involving 100 sensors and one service facility. The facility is equipped with two sockets, which allow only two sensors to be recharged at the same time. The sensor transmission range is now fixed at 100m and the energy ratio for sending/receiving a packet is set to a constant $(E : E/2)$. Locomotion costs were based on the weighted Euclidean distance with a weight factor of $\frac{1}{5}E$ per meter traveled. For all the tests performed on the three different topologies, the mobility strategy selected was the greedy closest-first swapping where a low energy sensor chooses its closest graph neighbour as a swapping partner during its migration towards the recharge station.

As expected, the closest-first swapping strategy on the three topologies chosen (i.e., CDG, CDGG and CDRNG) reached the state of equilibrium. The CDGG and CDRNG are sub-graphs of the CDG and according to the experimental results presented in [14], even the single path (i.e., single neighbour) approach

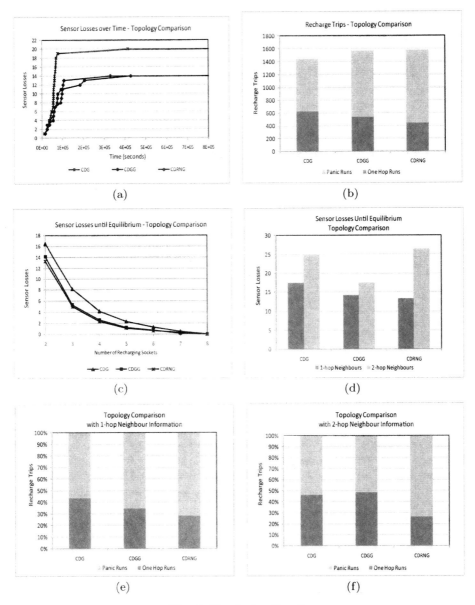

Fig. 3. Simulation Results

reached the state of equilibrium. However, the interesting finding is that although the three topologies reached the state of equilibrium at the same time approximately, the CDGG and CDRNG reported fewer sensor losses due to battery depletion. This is an important observation that implies that fewer but better selected graph neighbours will yield better results if the main goal is to minimize the number of permanent failures due to battery depletion.

Unfortunately, the CDGG and CDRNG did not report any improvements in terms of optimal trips to the recharge station. Figure 3(b) shows the number of recharge trips and breakdown between optimal and panic runs for the three topologies in question. For the CDGG and CDRNG there was a small increase in the number of recharge visits compared to the CDG and a small decrease in the number of optimal runs. This decrease is somehow expected since the number of neighbours for both topologies (i.e., CDGG and CDRNG) is more restrictive than the CDG. Once more, choosing different topologies for the migration strategy exposed a trade-off between permanent coverage holes due to battery depletion and more short-lived temporary holes due to more frequent visits to the facility.

The next part of this test was designed to measure the impact of the recharge sockets on the cumulative number of losses until equilibrium and verify whether the perfect equilibrium can be reached by increasing the number of sockets or docking ports in the recharge station. Figure 3(c) shows the result for this test where the closest-first swapping strategy on the three topologies showed the same progression towards perfect equilibrium. The total number of recharge sockets needed for the perfect equilibrium is the same for the three topologies but the CDGG and CDRNG showed an improvement on the number of sensor losses over the CDG as the number of recharge sockets increased.

4.2   Sensor Knowledge

The goal of this set of tests is to verify the impact of added sensor knowledge, as introduced in 3, and compare it with the 1-hop information greedy strategies on the three topologies (i.e., the CDG proposed in [14] and the CDGG and CDRNG). The network parameters are the same as in the previous tests, with fixed transmission range at 100m. The closest-first swapping strategy is applied on the three topologies (i.e., CDG, CDGG and CDRNG) with information about the energy levels of 1-hop graph neighbours only and 2-hop graph neighbours respectively.

Figure 3(d) shows the number of sensor losses until equilibrium for the three topologies tested with 1-hop neighbour information vs. 2-hop neighbour information. In each case, there was an increase in the number of sensor losses when the migration strategy included the 1-hop neighbour information. When 2-hop information is used, the best performer was the CDGG with losses similar to the 1-hop CDG. This is a rather surprising result, which seems to imply that "knowing more individually" about the network is less useful for the collective effort than "knowing less". Knowing more in this case has a direct impact on the number of control messages required to maintain the underlying topology in a consistent state. This phenomenon will be more evident as the graph degree increases. The graph maintenance overhead related to keeping 2-hop neighbour information proved to be crucial to the point that counteracts any possible improvement when compared to keeping 1-hop information only.

The idea of adding extra knowledge to the sensors aimed to improve the path selection strategy and increase the number of optimal runs or 1-hop trips to the recharge station. The simulation results shown in 3(f) confirmed our expectations. Added knowledge had, in fact, a positive impact on the selection of a better energy-efficient migration strategy towards the recharge station. There was some marginal improvement on the number of optimal runs for the CDG and CDRNG with a real improvement for the CDGG. The CDGG proved again to be the best performing topology in terms of cumulative sensor losses until equilibrium and breakdown between panic and optimal runs when using 2-hop neighbour information.

The last test involving the added-knowledge scenario examined the impact of the sensors transmission range on the overall performance. For this test, the closest-first swapping strategy on the CDG with 2-hop neighbour information was implemented on the network of 100:1 sensor/facility ratio with various transmission ranges (e.g., 50m, 100, 200m, 300m).

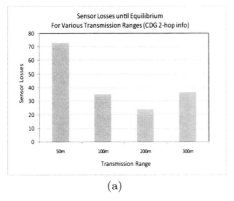 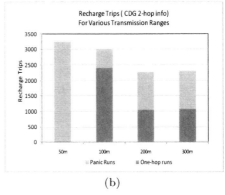

(a)   (b)

Fig. 4. Simulation Results - Variable Range

Figure 4(a) shows the cumulative number of sensor losses until equilibrium for each range value. The behaviour is very similar to the results for the 1-hop neighbour information scenario presented in [14]. The transmission range of 50m was too restrictive, which means that most of the sensors were isolated and the number of 1-hop and 2-hop neighbours in the CDG was too small to guarantee a gradual approach towards the recharge station. By increasing the transmission range, the number of losses decreased dramatically. However, for the 300m range there was a decline on the overall performance, which is consistent with the 1-hop information scenario.

The number of recharge trips and breakdown between panic and optimal runs is shown in Figure 4(b). Following the same behaviour as in the 1-hop information scenario, for a transmission range of 50m, most of the trips could be considered panic runs since there is almost no migration due to the lack of 1-hop neighbours. The best breakdown between one-hop and panic runs occurs with the 100m range. However, there are more visits to the recharge location, when compared to the 200m and 300m cases, which reported more balanced results in terms of the number and type of visits to the facility.

5   Conclusions and Future Work

In this work we have enhanced existing proactive strategies to solve the facility-absorbed Frugal Feeding Problem (FFP). Our novel approach proposed the introduction of new underlying topologies with different neighbour selection processes (e.g., Compass Directed Gabriel Graph and Compass Directed Relative Neighbor Graph). The proposed graphs guarantee that sensors will reach the rendezvous location within a finite number of swapping operations with a loop-free migration trajectory. We have also proposed to enhance sensor capabilities and decision making by adding information about energy levels of the 2-hop graph neighbours. All decisions made by the sensors regarding the next swapping operation are based on local knowledge.However, a new look-ahead parameter that includes the combined energy levels of the 2-hop neighbours is taken into account in the selection of the swapping partner.

The simulation results of the modified proactive solution to the FFP show that:

1. For networks of 100:1 sensor/facility ratio, the network survivability rate can be improved by using a CDGG or CDRNG as an underlying topology for the migration strategy.
2. Adding the energy levels of the 2-hop graph neighbours improves a sensor's individual migration strategy towards the facility. There is an increase in the number of optimal trips. However, the number of losses until equilibrium also increases, which results in lower network survivability.
3. If 2-hop neighbour information is available, the proposed CDGG outperforms the other proposed topologies in terms of network survivability at the point of equilibrium and distance traveled to the facility.
4. The transmission range has a positive impact on the network survivability at the point of equilibrium and the number of optimal trips to the facility. However, for higher transmission ranges that result in higher degree graphs, there is a clear negative impact on the key quality indicators (i.e., sensor losses, optimal trips, total number of recharge trips).
5. In general, the simulations exposed several trade-offs between the key variables (i.e., topology, transmission range, locomotion cost, sensor knowledge and station role)

Future enhancements to this work may explore in more detail the proposed proactive strategies in the presence of obstacles and the cost of applying obstacle avoidance strategies. Another possibility may also include the study of other instances of the Frugal Feeding Problem based on the mobility capabilities of sensors and recharge stations under more realistic MAC layers such as 802.11 CSMA/CA.

References

1. Arwin, F., Samsudin, K., Ramli, A.R.: Swarm robots long term autonomy using moveable charger. In: Proceedings of the 2009 International Conference on Future Computer and Communication, pp. 127–130 (2009)
2. Drenner, A., Papanikolopoulos, N.: Docking station relocation for maximizing longevity of distributed robotic teams. In: Proceedings of the 2006 IEEE International Conference on Robotics and Automation, pp. 2436–2441 (2006)
3. Drytkiewicz, W., Sroka, S., Handziski, V.: A mobility framework for omnet++. In: Proceesings of the 3rd International OMNeT++ Workshop (2003)
4. Feeney, L.: An energy consumption model for performance analysis of routing protocols for mobile ad hoc networks. Mobile Network Applications 6, 239–249 (2001)
5. Feeney, L., Nilsson, M.: Investigating the energy consumption of a wireless network interface in an ad hoc networking environment. In: Proceedings of the 20th Annual Joint Conference of the IEEE Computer and Communications Societies (IEEE Infocom 2001), vol. 3, pp. 1548–1557 (2001)
6. Frey, H., Ruhrup, S., Stojmenovic, I.: Routing in wireless sensor networks. In: Guide to Wireless Sensor Networks, ch. 4, pp. 81–111 (2009)
7. Kranakis, E., Singh, H., Urrutia, J.: Compass routing on geometric networks. In: Proceedings of the 11th Canadian Conference on Computational Geometry, pp. 51–54 (1999)
8. Litus, Y., Vaughan, R., Zebrowski, P.: The frugal feeding problem: energy-efficient, multi-robot, multi-place rendezvous. In: Proceedings of the 2007 IEEE International Conference on Robotics and Automation, pp. 27–32 (2007)
9. Litus, Y., Zebrowski, P., Vaughan, R.T.: A distributed heuristic for energy-efficient multirobot multiplace rendezvous. IEEE Transactions on Robotics 25, 130–135 (2009)
10. Sharifi, M., Sedighian, S., Kamali, M.: Recharging sensor nodes using implicit actor coordination in wireless sensor actor networks. Wireless Sensor Network 2, 123–128 (2010)
11. Stojmenovic, I., Lin, X.: Power-aware localized routing in wireless networks. IEEE Transactions on Parallel and Distributed Systems 12, 1122–1133 (2001)
12. Vargas, A.: The omnet++ discrete event simulation system. In: Proceedings of the European Simulation Multi-conference (ESM 2001), pp. 319–324 (2001)
13. Velazquez, E., Santoro, N.: Mobility-based strategies for energy restoration in wireless sensor networks. In: Proceedings of the 6th International Conference on Mobile Ah-hoc and Sensor Networks (MSN 2010), pp. 161–168 (2010)
14. Velazquez, E., Santoro, N., Lanthier, M.: Pro-active Strategies for the Frugal Feeding Problem in Wireless Sensor Networks. In: Par, G., Morrow, P. (eds.) S-CUBE 2010. LNICST, vol. 57, pp. 189–204. Springer, Heidelberg (2011)

Connectivity of Vehicular Ad Hoc Networks in Downtown Scenarios

Shigeo Shioda

Graduate School of Engineering, Chiba University,
1-33 Yayoi, Image, Chiba, 263-8522 Japan
shioda@faculty.chiba-u.jp
http://www.qos.tu.chiba-u.jp

Abstract. We study the connectivity in vehicular ad-hoc networks in a downtown scenario, where the mobility of vehicles is constrained on a lattice-shaped road network. We theoretically investigate the connectivity under the Poisson-positioning assumption, where vehicles are positioned according to a Poisson process on each road at any arbitrary instants. We find that the Poisson-positioning assumption allows the existence of the finite critical-vehicle density; that is, if (and only if) the density of vehicles is greater than the finite critical density, then there exists a large (theoretically infinite) cluster of vehicles and an arbitrary pair of vehicles in the cluster is connected in single or multiple hops. Under the Poisson-positioning assumption, we derive two approximation formulas for the critical density, which are given as a function of the transmission range of each vehicle and the distance between intersections. We also consider the connectivity under more realistic movement patterns of vehicles where the Poisson-positioning assumption does not hold. We numerically find that, even in non-Poisson-positioning cases, there exists the critical vehicle density, which is larger than the one under the Poisson-positioning assumption. The effectiveness of deploying roadside-relay stations to provide better connectivity between vehicles is also investigated.

Keywords: connectivity, VANET, critical density, bond percolation, Poisson, NETSIM.

1 Introduction

Vehicular ad hoc networks (VANETs) have recently received considerable attention for their potential of improving the safety and the comfort of drivers through infrastructure-less communications among vehicles. Since VANETs allow vehicles to propagate information about their speed and movement direction to vehicles in their vicinity, drivers can quickly detect potentially dangerous events such as lane changes or sudden slow-down [1,16,14]. VANETs also allow vehicles to inform approaching vehicles about situations of traffic congestion, drivers can take alternative routes to reach their destination when original routes are heavily congested.

The connectivity is a fundamental performance measure of ad-hoc networks or sensor networks. For VANETs, the connectivity is very important as a measure to see

D. Simplot-Ryl et al. (Eds.): ADHOCNETS 2011, LNICST 89, pp. 177–192, 2012.

the reliability of information propagation from vehicles to vehicles. Most of previous works on the connectivity of sensor or ad-hoc networks [3,6,11,5] were conducted based on the assumption that the nodes are randomly deployed according to a Poisson process on free two-dimensional space. This assumption does not hold in VANETs in two following senses; first, in VANETs, the mobility of vehicles is constrained along roads. Second, vehicles would not be randomly positioned according to a Poisson process because of the nature of vehicle's mobility; for example, a cluster of vehicles emerges around an intersection when the signal is on red. These properties (constraint along roads and non-randomness) of vehicle positions in VANETs might yield conclusions different with previous works obtained on the connectivity of sensor or ad-hoc networks.

The aim of this work is to study the fundamental characteristics of the connectivity in VANETs. In particular, we investigate what influence is made on the connectivity by the constraint along road or non-randomness of vehicle positions. First, we theoretically investigate the connectivity under the assumption that vehicles are positioned on roads according to a Poisson process at any arbitrary instants, which we call the *Poisson positioning assumption* in this paper. We find that, under the Poisson-positioning assumption, there exists the finite critical-vehicle density; that is, if (and only if) the density of vehicles is greater than the critical density, then a large set (theoretically a set of infinite size) of vehicles would emerge almost surely and an arbitrary pair of vehicles in the set is connected in single or multiple hops. We derive two approximation formulas for the critical density, which are expressed by the transmission range of each vehicle and the distance between intersections.

Next, we consider the connectivity when vehicles move according to the NETSIM model, under which the Poisson-positioning assumption does not hold anymore. We numerically find that, even in non-Poisson-positioning cases, there still exists the critical vehicle density. The critical density in the NETSIM model is, however, larger than the one obtained under the Poisson-positioning assumption. We also investigate the efficiency of deploying roadside relay stations to provide better connectivity between vehicles.

Note that several studies have been made on the connectivity of VANETs [17,4,13] in highway scenarios, where vehicles are positioned along the one-dimensional space (line). Most of these studies attempt to provide better connectivity by deploying stationary or mobile gateways to the Internet, and their focuses are different with our study. We also note that finite critical density does not exist in one-dimensional case. This paper is the extended version of our previous work [15]; an approximation formula (4) for the critical density is newly derived through the notion of weakly open edge in the current manuscript and related numerical results are presented. The proofs of lemmas, used to derive main results, are also presented in the current manuscript.

This paper is organized as follows; in Section 2, we explain the model of road maps, mobility model, and channel model. In Section 3, we investigate the connectivity of VANETs under the Poisson-positioning assumption. In particular, we prove the existence of the critical density and derive two approximation formulas for the critical density; one gives the strict upper bound of the critical density and the other gives estimates lower than the first one. In Section 4, we numerically investigate the connectivity of VANETs when vehicles move according to the NETSIM model by simulation. In

Section 5, we study how the deployment of the roadside relay stations would improve the connectivity. Finally, we conclude this article in Section 6.

2   Network and Channel Model

2.1   Road Network Model

In this paper, we assume a downtown scenario where roads cross each other in a lattice shape. In the following, we refer a section of road between neighboring intersections to as *edge*. Each edge is assigned an index, and let d_i denote the length of edge i. The lengths of edges are not necessarily the same but its maximum is bounded from above; that is $d_{sup} \overset{def}{=} \sup\{d_i,\ i = 1, 2, \ldots\} < \infty$. We also assign an index to each road.

The mobility of vehicles is constrained along roads. We neglect the width of roads, but we assume that two vehicles facing in the opposite direction on a road can move without crash. In this paper we consider the single-lane case, but the extension to multiple-lane cases is possible.

2.2   Channel Model

In this paper, we use the following simplified channel model; when a vehicle transmits a message, all nodes within distance r from the sender correctly receives the message with positive probability, while any nodes out of distance r from the sender cannot receive the message at all. Although the above channel model may look too simple, it would capture the most relevant feature of wireless transmission. This channel model is often called "Boolean Model" [12,3].

We refer the circular region of radius r centered at a vehicle to as the *transmission area* and refer the circular region of radius $r/2$ centered at a vehicle to as the *communication area* (Fig. 1). If the communication areas of two vehicles have an intersection, then two vehicles are directly reachable from each other. We refer a connected region which is made of communication areas to as *cluster* (Fig. 2). Vehicles contained in a common cluster are mutually reachable by single or multiple hops at the physical (MAC) layer.

3   Connectivity under Poisson Positioning Assumption

3.1   Connectivity

In this work, we use the term "connectivity" in the sense of reachability at the physical (MAC) layer. Thus, as explained in Section 2.2, two vehicles are "connected", if and only if they are contained in the common cluster. The connectivity at the physical layer is a necessary condition for the connectivity at the network (and higher) layer. We are interested in the fundamental characteristics of physical-layer connectivity, such as how it depends on the density of vehicles or the structure of the underlying road networks, and we do not consider the influence of routing protocols or transport protocols on the connectivity. The overheads caused by routing protocols are also neglected.

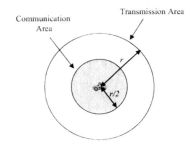

Fig. 1. Transmission area and communication area

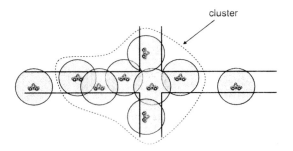

Fig. 2. Cluster

3.2   Poisson-Positioning Assumption

In this section, we investigate the connectivity under the following *Poisson-positioning assumption*:

(1) Vehicles are positioned according to a Poisson process on a road at any arbitrary instants.
(2) The density of vehicles on each road is constant.
(3) The minimum density of vehicles among roads is positive; that is

$$\lambda \stackrel{\text{def}}{=} \inf\{\lambda_s, \ s = 1, \ldots\} > 0,$$

where λ_s is the vehicle density on road s.

3.3   Critical Density

The connectivity is closely related to how large clusters are composed in the network. It follows from the percolation theory of Boolean models that, if vehicles are freely positioned according to a Poisson process in a two-dimensional infinite area, then there exists the finite critical density of vehicles, above which the unique infinite-size cluster emerges almost surely [12]. This fact has been used for analyzing the coverage property

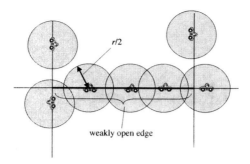

Fig. 3. Weakly open edge

of sensor networks or the connectivity of ad-hoc networks where mobile nodes are randomly positioned in the network [3,6,11]. The existence of the finite critical density was also proved for ad-hoc networks with more complicated channel models [5].

The aim of this section is to prove the existence of the finite critical density under the road topology-limited positions of vehicles. We also attempt to obtain some analytical formulas giving an estimate of the critical density. Note that few results have been obtained concerning analytical formula of the critical density in general Boolean percolation models.

3.4 Existence of the Critical Density for VANETs

We first consider a simple road network, where all edges have the same length d and the densities of vehicles on roads are all equal to λ. We call this road network model the *basic model*. Meanwhile, road network models, which are not the basic model but satisfy the conditions mentioned in Sec. 3.2, are called *general models*.

Definition 1. An edge is called *weakly open* if and only if it is completely covered by a cluster of communication areas (Fig. 3). An edge is called *strongly closed* if and only if it is not weakly open.

Definition 2. An edge is called *strongly open* if and only if it is completely covered by a cluster of communication areas, each of which is produced by a vehicle positioned on the edge itself (Fig. 4). An edge is called *weakly closed* if and only if it is not strongly open.

An edge is weakly open if it is strongly open; the converse is false. Figure 3 shows an example of the edge, which is weakly open but is not strongly open. Note that each edge is strongly open or not, independently of all other edges. An edge being weakly open or not is however associated (positively correlated) with the statuses (weakly open or not) of neighbor edges.

Let p_w (p_s) denote the probability that an edge is weakly (strongly) open. The theory of coverage process [8] on a one-dimensional space leads to the following lemma.

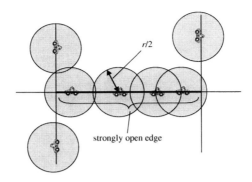

Fig. 4. Strongly open edge

Lemma 1.

$$p_w \geq p_1(\lambda; d, r) \overset{\text{def}}{=} 1 + \sum_{j=1}^{\lfloor (d/r)+1 \rfloor} \frac{(-1)^j}{j!} \{\lambda(d - (j-1)r)\}^{j-1}$$
$$\times \ e^{-jr\lambda} \{\lambda(d - (j-1)r) + j\}, \tag{1}$$

where $\lfloor x \rfloor$ denotes the largest integer not greater than x.

Proof. See Appendix.

Lemma 2.

$$p_s \geq p_2(\lambda; d, r)$$
$$\overset{\text{def}}{=} \begin{cases} (1 - e^{-\lambda r/2})^2 p_1(\lambda; d - r, r) & \text{for } d > r, \\ 1 - e^{-(r-d)\lambda} + e^{-(r-d)\lambda}(1 - e^{-(d-\frac{r}{2})\lambda})^2 & \text{for } r \geq d > r/2, \\ 1 - e^{-d\lambda} & \text{for } r/2 \geq d. \end{cases}$$
$$\tag{2}$$

Proof. See Appendix.

The well known result of the homogeneous and independent bond percolation on a square lattice (Fig. 5) gives a simple proof of the existence of the finite critical density. In a homogeneous and independent bond percolation model, each edge is open with probability p and closed otherwise, independently of all other edges. A finite or infinite connected sequence of edges is referred to as *path*. It is known that if $p > 0.5$, then there exists the unique infinite-length path using open edges only almost surely [10,7].

The basic model can be considered as a homogeneous and independent percolation model on the square lattice. Note that the Poisson positioning assumption is very essential because, only under this assumption, each edge is strongly open or not, independently of all other edges.

Lemma 3. If $p_2(\lambda; d, r) > 0.5$ in the basic model, then the unbounded cluster emerges almost surely.

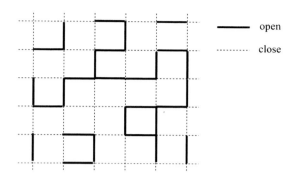

Fig. 5. Bond percolation on a square lattice

Proof. According to the theory of the bond percolation on the square lattice, if $p_s \geq p_2(\lambda; d, r) > 0.5$, then there exists the unique infinite-length path using strongly open edges only almost surely. This infinite-length (strongly) open path is completely covered by the unbounded cluster, which completes the proof.

Lemma 2 reveals that, if $p_2(\lambda; d, r) > 0.5$, then there exists the set of infinite number of vehicles, mutually connected at physical layer, almost surely. Since $p_2(\lambda; d, r)$ is a strictly increasing function of λ, we can define

$$p_2^{-1}(0.5; d, r) \stackrel{\text{def}}{=} \inf \{\lambda; p_2(\lambda; d, r) \geq 0.5\} < \infty.$$

The above discussion shows that, if the density of vehicles is larger than $p_2^{-1}(0.5; d, r)$, then the set of infinite number of vehicles, mutually connected at physical layer, emerges almost surely. This fact proves the existence of the finite critical density in the basic model.

The existence of the finite critical density in the basic model readily proves the existence of the finite critical density in general models.

Lemma 4. If $\lambda_{inf} > p_2^{-1}(0.5; d_{sup}, r)$, then the set of a large (theoretically infinite) number of vehicles, which are mutually connected at physical layer, emerges almost surely in general models.

Proof. See Appendix.

3.5 Approximation Formulas for the Critical Density

Since the phase transition occurs if $\lambda_{inf} > p_2^{-1}(0.5; d_{sup}, r)$ according to Lemma 4, $\lambda_c^{(2)}(d_{sup}, r)$, defined by

$$\lambda_c^{(2)}(d_{sup}, r) \stackrel{\text{def}}{=} p_2^{-1}(0.5; d_{sup}, r), \tag{3}$$

gives an upper bound of the critical density. We have found through simulation experiments that $\lambda_c^{(2)}(d_{sup}, r)$ yields the vehicle density, around which the connection probability defined in Sec. 3.6 reaches one (Sec. 4).

If $\lambda_{inf} > p_1^{-1}(0.5; d_{sup}, r)$, each edge is weakly open with probability larger than 0.5. If there exists an infinite-length path using weakly open edges only, the set of an infinite number of vehicles, mutually connected at physical layer, also emerges. Unfortunately, an edge being weakly open or not depends on whether neighbor edges are weakly open or not. The critical probability of the dependent bond percolation on the square lattice, where the states of different edges are not independent, is not always equal to 0.5. In this paper, however, we conjecture that $\lambda_c^{(1)}(d_{sup}, r)$, defined by

$$\lambda_c^{(1)}(d_{sup}, r) \overset{\text{def}}{=} p_1^{-1}(0.5; d_{sup}, r), \tag{4}$$

would yield a good estimate of the critical density. Note that $\lambda_c^{(1)}(d_{sup}, r) \leq \lambda_c^{(2)}(d_{sup}, r)$. We have found through simulation experiments that $\lambda_c^{(1)}(d_{sup}, r)$ gives the vehicle density around which the connection probability exceeds 0.5 (Sec. 4).

The two formulas, $\lambda_c^{(1)}(d, r)$ and $\lambda_c^{(2)}(d, r)$, are for the unit-length-wise critical density, which is defined as the average number of vehicles in an interval of unit length on road for phase transition. In some cases, the transmission-area-wise critical density, defined as the average number of vehicles in a square with sides of length r for phase transition, are useful. The following formulas give the transmission-area-wise critical densities;

$$\alpha_c^{(1)}(d, r) = \frac{2\lambda_c^{(1)}(d, r)r^2}{d}, \quad \alpha_c^{(2)}(d, r) = \frac{2\lambda_c^{(2)}(d, r)r^2}{d}.$$

It is easy to see that $\alpha_c^{(1)}(d, r)$ and $\alpha_c^{(2)}(d, r)$ depend only on d/x. Figure 6 show the estimates of the critical density by $\alpha_c^{(1)}(d, r)$ and $\alpha_c^{(2)}(d, r)$ as well as the critical density when vehicles are freely positioned on a two-dimensional space. It were numerically shown that the critical density for free two-dimensional space is equal to 1.4125 [6,11,9]. Comparing $\alpha_c^{(1)}(d, r)$ (or $\alpha_c^{(2)}(d, r)$) with the critical density on free two-dimensional space in Fig. 6, we see that the road constraint on vehicle positions significantly reduces the critical density especially when $d \gg r$. When d is close to r, however, the road constraint on vehicle positions makes the critical density even larger. The road constraint reduce the possibilities for having different paths between two vehicles, which would increase the critical density especially when d is close to r.

3.6   The Connection Probability

The emergence of the unbounded cluster does not ensure that all vehicles are mutually connected because some of vehicles are not necessarily contained in the unbounded cluster. However, we can conjecture that the probability of two arbitrary vehicles being connected at an arbitrary instant, which is called the *connection probability*, would rapidly change from 0 to 1 around the critical density. We have confirmed this conjecture by simulation, which will be shown in Sec. 4.

From the viewpoint of the bidirectional communications between vehicles, the *persistent connection probability*, which is defined by the probability that two arbitrary vehicles are continuously connected for some duration, is also important. As shown in Sec. 4, the *persistent connection probability* shows similar dependence on the vehicle density with the connection probability. That is, the persistent connection probability rapidly changes from 0 to 1 around some positive vehicle density.

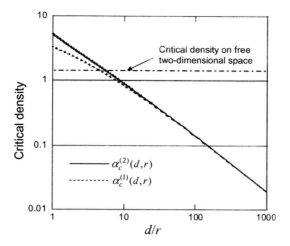

Fig. 6. Critical densities

4 Connectivity in Non-poisson-Positioning Cases

4.1 Mobility Model

Next, through simulation experiments, we investigate the connectivity under more realistic movement patterns of vehicles. In simulations, we emulated movement patterns of vehicles by NETSIM. NETSIM simulates the mobility of vehicles based on the car-following logic [2]. In NETSIM, vehicles probabilistically turn left or right at intersections, and stop at intersections when the signal is on red. The Poisson-positioning assumption obviously does not hold under the NETSIM model. For reference, we also run simulations under the fixed-speed model, where all vehicles were initially deployed on roads according to a Poisson process and moved on a road with fixed speed, which ranged from 20 km/h to 60 km/h. The speeds of vehicles on a given road were all the same[1], and vehicles did not turn left or right at intersections. The Poisson-positioning assumption seems to hold in the fixed-speed model.

4.2 Simulation Condition

In the simulation, we used a 10 km × 10 km square area, where 11 vertical and 11 horizontal roads are crossing in a lattice shape. The distances between intersections are all 1 km. We run simulations with different vehicle densities and with different transmission ranges of vehicles.

4.3 Connection Probability

Figure 7 shows the relationship between the connection probability and the vehicle density when the transmission range of vehicles r is 200 m. In the fixed-speed model,

---

[1] The speeds of vehicles on different roads are different.

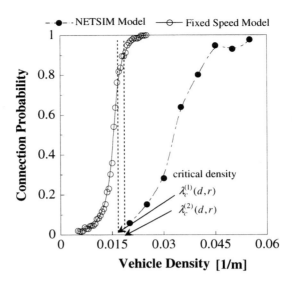

Fig. 7. Connection probability (r = 200m)

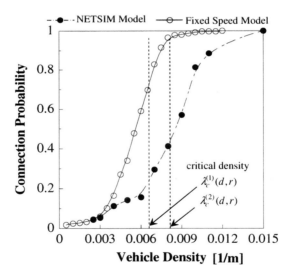

Fig. 8. Connection probability (r = 400m)

the connection probability rapidly tends from 0 to 1 around two estimates of the critical density, $\lambda_c^{(1)}$ (0.017 1/m) and $\lambda_c^{(2)}$ (0.019 1/m), and the connection probability is almost equal to 1 when vehicle density exceeds the two estimates. In particular, $\lambda_c^{(2)}$ gives the vehicle density, at which the connection probability is about to reach one, and $\lambda_c^{(1)}$($<$ $\lambda_c^{(2)}$) gives the vehicle density around which the connection probability exceeds 0.5.

This result agrees with the theoretical consequence obtained in Sec. 3. We also observe that the dependence of the connection probability on the vehicle density in the NETSIM model is very similar with that in the fixed-speed model; the connection probability in the NETSIM model also shows rapid increase when the vehicle density is around 0.02 1/m and it is close to 1 when the vehicle density exceeds 0.05 1/m. This fact suggests that the critical density still exists even in non-Poisson-positioning cases. Note that the critical density in the NETSIM model is larger than that in the fixed-speed model. We show the results when $r = 400$ m in Fig. 8, where the similar dependence of the connection probability on the vehicle density is observed, but the critical density when $r = 400$ m is smaller than that when $r = 200$ m. In the fixed-speed model vehicles were randomly positioned along the road, while in the NETSIM model a cluster emerged around the intersection along the horizontal road. The cluster in the NETSIM model was made by the action of traffic signal; vehicles on the horizontal road were waiting for the light turn to green. In the NETSIM model, clusters of vehicles often emerged at intersections and thus vehicle positions did not follow the Poisson process, which requires higher vehicle density to ensure the connectivity between vehicles.

4.4   Persistent Connection Probability

Figures 9 and 10 show the persistent connection probabilities during 10 minutes when the transmission ranges of vehicles are 200 m and 400 m, respectively. The dependence of the persistent connection probability on the vehicle density is very similar with that of the connection probability; we also see the rapid increase of the persistent connection probability as the vehicle density increases. Note that higher vehicle density is required for the phase transition (rapid increase from zero to one) in terms of the persistent connection probability compared with the connection probability. For example, in the fixed-speed model, the persistent connection probability begins to increase when the vehicle density exceeds the estimate of critical density by $\lambda_c^{(2)}$ (0.019 1/m) while the connection probability is about to reach one at the same vehicle density.

5   Deployment of Roadside Relay Stations

Deploying message relay stations (RSs) on roadside seems to improve the connectivity between vehicles. Finally, we theoretically investigate the effectiveness of deploying the roadside RSs. For simplicity, we assume that the densities of vehicles on roads are all equal to λ and the lengths of edges are all equal to d. First observe that if

$$\lambda \geq \lambda_c^{(2)}(d, r) = p_2^{-1}(0.5; d, r), \tag{5}$$

then the deployment of the RSs is not necessary because the vehicle density is over the critical density and thus the connectivity between vehicles is almost ensured without RSs. We call the region satisfying (5) the *RS-unnecessary region*.

Meanwhile, if $\lambda < \lambda_c^{(2)}(d, r) = p_2^{-1}(0.5; d, r)$, then the deployment of the roadside RSs may improve the connectivity. Now let L_{rs} be the deployment interval of RSs. Since the intensity of RSs is given by $1/L_{rs}$, the connection probability would be almost equal to 1

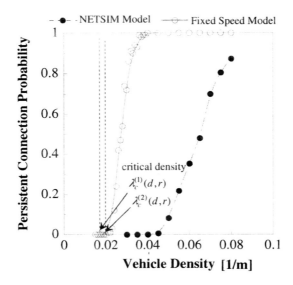

Fig. 9. Persistent Connection probability (r = 200m)

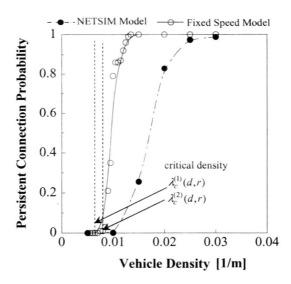

Fig. 10. Persistent Connection probability (r = 400 m)

when $\lambda + 1/L_{rs} \geq \lambda_c^{(2)}(d, r)$. This consideration yields the following guideline for the RS deployment interval in order to have the full (100-percentile) inter-vehicle connectivity:

$$L_{rs} \leq \frac{1}{\lambda_c^{(2)}(d, r) - \lambda} = \frac{1}{p_2^{-1}(0.5; d, r) - \lambda}. \qquad (6)$$

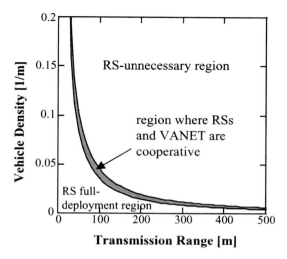

Fig. 11. RS-unnecessary and VANET-unnecessary regions

Here we note that if

$$\frac{1}{p_2^{-1}(0.5; d, r) - \lambda} < r, \tag{7}$$

then the guideline (6) requires $L_{rs} < r$, under which RSs are mutually connected and thus vehicles are also mutually connected via RSs without message relay of vehicles. In other words, in the region satisfying (7), VANET does not essentially contribute the inter-vehicle connectivity. We call the region satisfying (7) the *RS-full-deployment region*.

The above consideration clarifies that RSs and VANET are cooperative only the outside of the union of RS-unnecessary and RS-full-deployment regions, which is given below

$$p_2^{-1}(0.5; d_{sup}, r) - \frac{1}{r} \leq \lambda < p_2^{-1}(0.5; d_{sup}, r).$$

Figure 11 shows the region (hatched region) where the RS-deployment and VANET are cooperative when $d = 1$ km. We see that this region is so small. This simply illustrates that deploying roadside-relay stations to provide better connectivity between vehicles is not so effective in fixed-speed model.

6   Conclusion

In this paper, we study the fundamental characteristics of physical-layer connectivity in VANETs. We theoretically find that, under the Poisson-positioning assumption, there exists the finite critical-vehicle density, above which a large (theoretically infinite-size) set of vehicles emerges and an arbitrary pair of vehicles in the set is connected in single or multiple hops. We also consider the connectivity under the NETSIM-vehicle-mobility model where the Poisson-positioning assumption does not hold anymore.

We numerically find that, even in such non-Poisson-positioning cases, there still exists the critical vehicle density. The critical density in non-Poisson-positioning cases is, however, larger than that expected under the Poisson-positioning assumption.

We find that deploying roadside relay stations is not so effective in providing better connectivity under the Poisson-positioning assumption. However, this is not always the case if the Poisson-positioning assumption does not hold. In addition to this, in this work, we do not consider the effect that the radio-wave-propagation is obstructed by buildings at corners of intersections. If we take into account of the obstruction by the buildings, we may have different conclusions concerning the effectiveness of deploying roadside relay stations. This remains as one of future works.

Appendix

A.1   Proof of Lemma 1

An edge (say edge i) is weakly open if edge i is completely covered by a cluster of communication areas of vehicles on the straight road including edge i. The probability of the latter is known as *the complete coverage probability* in the theory of the one-dimensional coverage process. According to formula (2.23) of [8], which gives the analytical expression of the complete coverage probability, $p_1(\lambda; d, r)$ is the probability that the interval of length d is completely covered by clusters made of segment with fixed-length r. That is, $p_1(\lambda; d, r)$ is equal to the probability that edge i is completely covered by a cluster of communication areas of vehicles on the straight road including edge i, which completes the proof.

A.2   Proof of Lemma 2

If $d \leq r/2$, an edge is strongly open if at least one vehicle exists on the edge, whose probability is equal to $1 - e^{-d\lambda}$.

If $r/2 < d \leq r$, an edge is strongly open if at least one vehicle exists in interval B in Fig. 12. Even if there is no vehicle in interval B, an edge is strongly open if intervals A and C in Fig. 12 respectively contain at least one vehicle. The probability that one vehicle exists in interval B is equal to $1 - e^{-(r-d)\lambda}$, and the probability that no vehicle exists in interval B but intervals A and C respectively contain at least one vehicle is equal to $e^{-(r-d)\lambda}(1 - e^{-(d-\frac{r}{2})\lambda})^2$. Thus, (2) also holds when $r/2 < d \leq r$.

If $r < d$, an edge is strongly open if at least one vehicle exists in intervals A and C in Fig. 12 respectively and interval B in Fig. 12 is completely covered by one cluster. The probability that at least one vehicle exists in intervals A and C respectively is equal to $(1 - e^{-\lambda r/2})^2$, and the probability that interval B is completely covered by one cluster is equal to $p_1(\lambda; d, r)$. The event that at least one vehicle exists in intervals A and C respectively and the one that interval B is completely covered by one cluster are associated, so (2) also holds when $r < d$.

when $r > d > r/2$

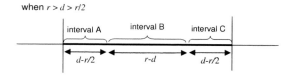

when $d > r$

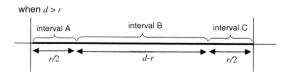

Fig. 12. Partitioning an edge into three intervals

A.3   Proof of Lemma 4

Let $p_s(i)$ be the probability that edge i is strongly open. Since $p_2(\lambda; d, r)$ is strictly increasing in terms of λ and strictly decreasing in terms of d,

$$p_2(\lambda_s; d_i, r) \geq p_2(\lambda_{inf}; d_{sup}, r).$$

Thus, if $\lambda_{inf} > p_2^{-1}(0.5; d_{sup}, r)$, then

$$p_s(i) \geq p_2(\lambda_s; d_i, r) \geq p_2(\lambda_{inf}; d_{sup}, r) > 0.5.$$

meaning that each edge is strongly open with probability larger than 0.5. Note that the general model corresponds to an inhomogeneous bond percolation because the probabilities of edges being open are different from each other. Thus, we need to prove that, if each edge is open with probability larger than 0.5, the unbounded cluster emerges almost surely even in inhomogeneous (and independent) bond percolation. To this end, let $\{X_i\}_{i \in \mathbb{N}}$ be a family of independent random variables indexed by the edge, where X_i is uniformly distributed on $[0, 1]$. We also define

$$\eta_i(p_i) = \begin{cases} 1 & \text{if } X_i > p_i, \\ 0 & \text{if } X_i \leq p_i. \end{cases}$$

We can say that edge i is open if $\eta_i(p_s(i)) = 1$. Now choose p_0 so that $p_2(\lambda_{inf}; d_{sup}, r) > p_0 > 0.5$. It is clear that $\eta_i(p_s(i)) \geq \eta_i(p_0)$ whenever $p_s(i) \geq p_0$. That is, we can couple the general model with a homogeneous bond percolation model where the edge is open with probability $p_0 > 0.5$. Since the homogeneous bond percolation model has the unique infinite-size cluster with probability one when $p_0 > 0.5$, the general model does so, which completes the proof.

References

1. Task 3: Identifying Intelligent Vehicle Safety Applications Enabled by DSRC - Interim Report (2003)
2. Aycin, M.F., Benekohal, R.F.: Comparison of car-following models for simulations. Transportation Research Record 1678, 116–127 (1999)

3. Baccelli, F., Blaszczyszyn, B.: On a coverage process ranging from the boolean model to the poisson-voronoi tessellation with applications to wireless communications. Adv. Appl. Prob. 33, 293–323 (2001)
4. Bechler, J., Storz, O., Franz, W., Wolf, L.: Efficient discovery of Internet gateways in vehicular communication systems. In: IEEE VTC 2003-Spring, pp. 965–969 (2003)
5. Dousse, O., Baccelli, F., Thiran, P.: Impact of interference on connectivity in Ad Hoc networks. IEEE/ACM Trans. Networking 13(2), 425–436 (2005)
6. Dousse, O., Thiran, P., Hasler, M.: Connectivity in ad-hoc and hybrid networks. In: Proc. of the IEEE INFOCOM (2002)
7. Grimmett, G.R.: Percolation. Springer (1989)
8. Hall, P.: Introduction to the Theory of Coverage Processes. John Wiley & Sons (1988)
9. Harada, J., Shioda, S., Saito, H.: Path coverage properties of randomly deployed sensors with finite data-transmission ranges. Computer Networks 53(7), 1014–1026 (2008)
10. Kesten, H.: The critical probability of bond percolation on the square lattice equals $\frac{1}{2}$. Commun. Math. Phys. 74, 41–59 (1980)
11. Liu, B., Towsley, D.: A study on the coverage of large-scale sensor networks. In: Proc. of the First IEEE International Conference on Mobile Ad-hoc and Sensor Systems (2004)
12. Meester, R., Roy, R.: Continuum Percolation. Cambridge University Press (2004)
13. Namboodiri, V., Agarwal, M., Gao, L.: A study on the feasibility of mobile gateways for vehicular ad-hoc networks. In: VANET 2004 (2004)
14. Resta, G., Santi, P., Simon, J.: Analysis of multi-hop emergency propagation in vehicular ad hoc networks. In: Proc. of the ACM MobiHoc (2007)
15. Shioda, S., Harada, J., Watanabe, Y., Goi, T., Okada, H., Mase, K.: Fundamental characteristics of connectivity in vehicular ad hoc networks. In: Proc. of the IEEE PIMRC (2008)
16. Sormani, D., Turconi, G., Costa, P., Frey, D., Migliavacca, M., Mottola, L.: Towards lightweight information dissemination in inter-vehicular networks. In: Proc. of the VANET 2006 (2006)
17. Sun, Y., Belding-Royer, E.M., Perkins, C.E.: Internet connectivity for Ad-hoc mobile networks. International Journal of Wireless Information Networks 9(2), 75–88 (2002)

An Energy-Delay Routing Protocol for Video Games over Multihops Ad Hoc Networks

Arnaud Kaiser, Khaled Boussetta, and Nadjib Achir

L2TI – Institut Galilée – University of Paris 13
93430 Villetaneuse, France
firstname.lastname@univ-paris13.fr

Abstract. Nowadays, with the development of networked technologies and the great expansion of video games industry, almost all video games propose a multi-player mode. Development of portables consoles which integrate 802.11 technology offers to people the opportunity to play anywhere, at any time and with anybody. However, wireless networked conditions are not always optimal and directly impact the quality of game perceived by players. In this paper, we propose a multimetric ad hoc routing protocol, based on OLSR, which improves game experience in terms of fairness among players and gaming sessions lifetime. We consider the delay and the energy as metrics to route informations through the network. We compare our routing protocol with an energy-efficient OLSR version and a delay-efficient OLSR version. We show that our routing protocol provides better performances in terms of fairness while keeping a good network lifetime.

Keywords: multihops ad hoc networks, multimetric routing, networked games, objective evaluation.

1 Introduction

Over the past fifteen years, the video games market has grown at an exceptional rate. This impressive progression was sustained by the innovation and the creativity of this industry. Among the basic ingredients in recent successful games, interactivity supported by network communications is a key element. As a matter of fact, most of nowadays popular games integrate a multiplayer mode.

Taking into consideration the popularity of LAN multiplayer games and the tremendous success of wireless networks, we believe that future game consoles will benefit from supporting MANET (Mobile Ad-hoc NETworks) mode. Indeed, MANET allows spontaneous creation of data networks by exploiting the multihops communication capacity of the mobile terminals. Moreover, all the networking functionalities (multihop routing, auto-configuration, self healing, security, etc.) are carried out by the terminals themselves in an entirely distributed way. Therefore, besides the social and cultural interest of playing with close located persons, MANET technology can allow players, to easily improvise a LAN multiplayer party without any need for an existing fixed wireless network

D. Simplot-Ryl et al. (Eds.): ADHOCNETS 2011, LNICST 89, pp. 193–208, 2012.

infrastructure. A scenario, like a group of kids equipped with MANET terminals wishing to play anywhere (e.g. in a playground, in a school bus etc.) a WLAN party will be possible.

In order to make such scenario a common based reality in the near future, several issues still have to be addressed by the research community. Several difficulties come from the inherent constraints that characterize MANET technology. In particular, the mobility of the core network, the energy limitation and the variability of shared resources. All these problems lead to a variable connectivity and potentially, to a high fluctuation in the provided Quality of Service (QoS). On the other hand, multiparty games are very sensitive to resource availability. They are very demanding on CPU and thus, high consuming on energy. In addition, the game play could experience a significant degradation caused by delays variability, which is typically the case in MANET, due to the mobility of users and to the random nature of IEEE 802.11 MAC layer.

In this work, we address the routing issue for multiplayer networked games in a multihop ad hoc network environment. We consider specifically the most popular ad hoc routing protocol. Namely, OLSR. Our aim is to increase the network life duration and improve game fairness considering OLSR and supposing a multiplayer FPS (First Person Shooter) game. We propose and analyze, through realistic experimentations and using objective metrics, a multimetric routing protocol based on energy consumption and end-to-end delay.

The remainder of this paper is organized as follows: in the next section, we briefly introduce OLSR and present the state of the art on ad hoc routing under energy and delay criteria. Section III describes our routing protocol. Section IV gives a detailed description of our experimentation scenarii. In section V, we analyze and discuss the obtained results. Finally, section VI summarizes the main contributions of this work and provides some future prospects.

2   Related Work

2.1   Ad-Hoc Routing Protocols

Routing protocols for ad hoc multihop networks can be classified into two main categories: *reactive* protocols and *proactive* protocols.

Routing protocols belonging to the first category compute a route to reach a destination only when needed. As long as a node in the network doesn't want to send data, no signaling messages are sent, leading to save energy and reduce congestion and collisions. However, when a node wants to send data, it first has to start a route discovery mechanism to find a route to reach its destination. This mechanism is time consuming and hence delays the data sending until the node has found a route.

Routing protocols from the second category periodically send signaling messages in order to discover and update the network topology. A node using this kind of routing protocol always has a route available to reach every nodes present in the network. Thus, the node can instantly send data when needed. However, signaling message used are energy consuming and increase risks of congestion and collisions.

A *hybrid* category also exists. Routing protocols belonging to this category combine both reactive and proactive algorithms.

As we are considering a time sensitive application where delay is a crucial metric, we decide to base our work on the well-known proactive routing protocol OLSR.

2.2   OLSR Overview

OLSR [1] is a proactive routing protocol, which means that it memorizes permanently paths to all discovered nodes in the network. Thus, all nodes can be reached at any time. In order to discover and update the network topology, OLSR sends periodical signaling messages known as HELLO and TC messages.

A node uses the HELLO messages to discover its neighborhood. The HELLO messages are broadcasted with a TTL (Time To Live) of 1 such that only direct neighbors receive the message. A HELLO message contains the neighbors table of the node that sent it. The neighborhood table is a list of all the neighbors known by the node. An information about the link type to these neighbors is also noticed. A link with a neighbor can be unidirectional or bidirectional. If a node receives a HELLO message from a neighbor and sees its own IP address inside, it knows that the communication with this neighbor works in both sides, so the link is bidirectional. Finally, thanks to these HELLO messages, all nodes know their direct neighbor nodes (1-hop neighbors) and their 2-hops neighbors.

The second step of the protocol is the MPR (Multi-Point Relay) selection. The MPR selection is a technique that improves broadcasting messages by allowing only a subset of nodes to forward broadcasted messages. Each node chooses a subset of nodes among its 1-hop neighbors, such that all of its 2-hops neighbors are reachable via this subset. The chosen subset is called MPR set. When a node broadcasts a message, only its MPR nodes are allowed to forward the message. Thus, the number of retransmissions of the broadcasted message is reduced. The nodes inform their neighbors that they have chosen them as MPR via the HELLO messages. The nodes that were elected as MPR, create a MPR selector table which lists all neighbors that have chosen them as MPR. As an example, let us consider the network topology presented in figure 1. C_8 has three 1-hop neighbors (C_1, C_2 and C_3) and three 2-hops neighbors (C_4, C_5 and C_6). C_8 has to choose its MPR nodes among its 1-hops neighbors in order to be able to reach nodes C_4, C_5 and C_6. C_4 and C_5 are reachable via C_1, C_6 is reachable via C_3, so let us assume that the MPR nodes of C_8 are C_1 and C_3. When C_8 broadcasts a message, C_1 and C_3 will forward it but not C_2. This reduces flooding of the network.

The next step of the protocol is to transmit the MPR selector table to all nodes in the network. To this end, the TC (Topology Control) messages are used. All MPR nodes broadcast periodic TC messages that contain their MPR selector table. The TTL value is set to 255 (maximum value) such that all nodes in the network receive it. Of course, the flooding of the TC messages uses the MPR technique.

Finally, by combining informations contained in HELLO and TC messages, the nodes have a global view of the network topology. Then, they compute the Dijkstra's shortest path algorithm to find the bests routes to reach all destinations in the network. The metric used to compute the routes is the number of hops.

2.3   Integrating Energy Consumption in OLSR

In order to reduce the energy consumption in ad hoc networks, many works were done in the literature to combine the OLSR protocol with the energy metric.

In [2], instead of the number of hops, the authors consider the residual energy of nodes to compute routes. Thus, they avoid nodes with low remaining energy, leading to increase the network lifetime.

In [3], the authors go further and also consider the energy consumed at the 1-hop and 2-hop neighbors of the node that sends a message. Indeed, as we are in a wireless environment, when a node sends a message, all its neighbors receive it, even if they are not concerned by it, leading to consume energy.

In [4], the authors base their route computing on a min-max energy algorithm. In each available route to reach a destination, they look at the node that has the lowest remaining energy. They choose the route whose lowest remaining energy node has the greatest value.

In [5], the authors exploit the Willingness field of the HELLO messages to compute their link cost. The Willingness is a value that informs if a node will forward data or not. When a node has a low remaining energy, it sets its Willingness to 0 in order to inform the other nodes that it won't forward traffic anymore. The authors also use the RTS/CTS messages in order to turn off (sleep mode) the nodes that are not concerned by the actual communication.

2.4   Integrating Delay in OLSR

As shown in our previous work [12], in the context of real time video games the delay metric is the most important one. Some works in the literature have studied the combination of the delay metric and the OLSR protocol.

In [10], the authors compute the delay between two neighbor nodes. They assume that nodes are synchronized. They timestamp the HELLO signaling messages, such that a node receiving a HELLO message can calculate the delay value of the link to its neighbor. The delay metric is then used in the Dijkstra's shortest path algorithm to compute routes.

In [11], the authors add three new signaling messages in the OLSR protocol. These messages enable to compute the end-to-end delay value between two nodes in the network, without the need of a synchronized network.

2.5   Multimetric Routing Protocol

Some works have been done to combine energy and delay metrics in a routing protocol.

In [6], the authors propose EDC-AODV (Energy Delay Constrained AODV), a modified version of the Ad-hoc On-demand Distant Vector (AODV) [13] routing protocol. Each node takes into consideration the current size of its buffer (which informs about the delay and congestion at this node, noted Q) as a first metric, and its residual energy as a second metric (noted ER). The cost of a link between two neighboring nodes is processed using the following equation:

$$cost = \alpha \sum_i \frac{1}{1 + ER_i^t} + (1 - \alpha) \sum_i (1 - \frac{1}{1 + Q_i^t}) \tag{1}$$

They use a parameter α in order to strike a balance between the two metrics. They compare their EDC-AODV routing protocol with the classical AODV routing protocol for different values of the α parameter.

In [7], the authors propose OEDR (Optimized Energy-Delay Routing), an ad-hoc routing protocol based on energy and delay metrics. They use OLSR as a base protocol and modify it. They consider the delay between two neighbors, measured thanks to timestamped HELLO messages, as the delay metric. As for the energy metric, they consider the residual energy of the nodes. They use the HELLO messages to transmit the energy and the delay values. Then, the cost of a link is the multiplication of the delay and the energy values. The Dijkstra's shortest path algorithm is finally processed using this cost to find the bests routes.

In this paper, our work consist of proposing a routing protocol, specific to real time client-server video games, which consider both the energy and delay metrics to improve the gameplay and also to increase the duration of gaming sessions. Indeed, as we have previously shown in [14], a player who has a great end-to-end delay with the game server has a bad game quality. On the contrary, a player who is close to the game server in terms of end-to-end delay has a better game quality, but his energy decreases dramatically faster because he has to forward the game traffic coming from the other players. In the next section, we describe our proposal, which is close to the one proposed in [6]. However, we decide to dynamically modify the value of the balancing parameter depending on the distance, in terms of end-to-end delay, that separates a player and the game server. If a player has a great end-to-end delay with the game server, he gives priority to the delay metric. On the contrary, a player who has a smaller end-to-end delay with the game server favors the energy metric.

3 Energy-Delay Routing Protocol

In this section, we detail our routing protocol algorithm that is based on two metrics: energy and delay. Our protocol uses a parameter, like the one presented in [6], to introduce a balance between the two considered metrics. We propose to dynamically modify the value of the parameter depending on the position of the nodes compared with the game server node.

3.1   Considered Energy and Delay Metrics

We consider the residual energy of the nodes as the energy metric. The *energy_cost* of a link is computed as follow:

$$energy\_cost_{n_s \to n_r} = 1 - RE_{n_r} \tag{2}$$

where n_s is the node which send a message and n_r is the neighbor of n_s which receives the message, and RE_{n_r} is the residual energy of the node n_r. The residual energy of the nodes is normalized such that $0 \leq RE \leq 1$.

As delay metric, we consider the delay measured on a link between two neighbor nodes. We assume that all nodes in the network are synchronized. Thus, by timestamping the OLSR HELLO signaling messages, the nodes can easily compute the delay value of the links by subtracting the timestamped value of the HELLO message from their current clock. Finally, the *delay_cost* of a link between two neighbor nodes is the delay measured on this link.

In order to inform all the nodes of the *delay_cost* and the *energy_cost* of the links, each node adds its computed values in its HELLO and TC messages.

3.2   Link Cost Function

The cost of a link between two neighbor nodes directly depends on the position of the nodes compared with the game server in terms of end-to-end delay. Hence, a node first computes its shortest path to reach the game server by considering only the delay metric. We call the total cost of this path the *delay_path_cost*.

Our goal is to find a compromise between the delay and the energy metric. However, players who have a great *delay_path_cost* should not consider the energy metric, but only focus on the delay metric. To this aim, we define a *delay_threshold*, above which we consider that the players are too far from the game server, thus very hampered. All the nodes whose *delay_path_cost* is greater than the *delay_threshold* only consider the delay metric to compute their paths. All the other nodes consider both energy and delay metrics to compute their paths. For these latter, the link cost function is defined as follow:

$$link\_cost = f.delay\_cost + (1 - f).energy\_cost \tag{3}$$

where f is a balancing factor which varies between 0 and 1. This balancing factor determines the weight of each metric. Each node computes its own balancing factor f following this equation:

$$f = \frac{delay\_path\_cost}{delay\_threshold} \tag{4}$$

with $0 \leq f \leq 1$. If f is greater than 1, we set it to 1 and thus the node will only consider the delay as link cost. This parameter varies from one node to another in function of their position compared with the game server in term of end-to-end delay. The far away from the game server a node is, the less it takes into account the *energy_cost*. On the contrary, the closest from the game server a node is, the less it takes into account the *delay_cost*.

4 Experimental Settings

In order to evaluate the performances of our multimetric routing protocol, we set up a multihop ad hoc network emulator.

Our testbed is composed of eight computers: seven clients (each one representing a player in the game) and one dedicated game server. The computers are connected in a LAN via a switch. The clients hardware configuration is as follow: a 2 GHz Core 2 Duo processor, two gigabytes of main memory, and consumer-level graphic and network cards integrated into the motherboard. The server has a 2.4 GHz Core 2 Duo processor with two gigabytes of main memory. All the eight computers run the same software configuration: Linux Ubuntu 10.04 distribution with the 2.6.32.21 kernel version.

As our computers are directly connected to AC power, we emulate the battery consumption. In the beginning of each experimentation, all the nodes are full of battery. Each time a network frame is sent or received by a node, we decrease the remaining energy of this node according to the energy consumption model presented in [9]. This model takes into consideration the size of the frames and the nodes state (transmission, reception, idle) to compute the specific amount of energy spent when sending or receiving a frame. The consumed energy is computed as follow:

$$consumed\_energy = m * s + b \qquad (5)$$

where s is the size of the frame (in bytes), m and b are constants which can be determined empirically. The constant values that we used in our experimentations are given in table 1. In order to obtain the size of the frames, we use the *pcap API* to capture the frames and recover their length. To simplify the analysis, we consider neither the energy consumed in idle mode, nor the energy consumption due to the game engine processing. We just focus on the transmission and the reception of frames. Finally, we stop our experimentations when the residual energy of a node reaches 0%.

To emulate the wireless conditions, we add some delay on each link. The delay values are chosen depending on the density of the nodes. Each node has a 10 milliseconds delay penalty per neighbor. Thus, the more neighbors a node has, the more penalized it will be. We use the *Traffic Control* (TC) and *Netem* tools available on Linux kernel to add the delay penalties.

The multihop network is emulated by using the *iptables* tool, also available on Linux kernel. Each node adds *iptables* filters, based on the MAC address, to drop all the frames that it should not have received in a real ad hoc environment. Figure 1 depicts the network topology we used in our experimentations. Values on links are the delays values in milliseconds.

Table 1. m & b values

	m (μW.s/byte)	b (μW.s)
point-to-point transmisson	0.48	431
broadcast transmisson	2.1	272
point-to-point reception	0.12	316
broadcast reception	0.26	50

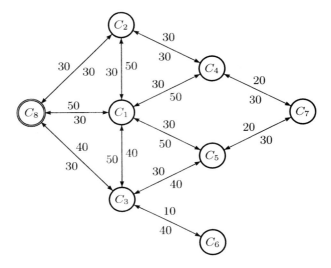

Fig. 1. The network topology used during the experimentations with delay cost of links in ms

As game application, we adopted Quake III Arena, a real-time FPS video game. Quake III Arena is a well-known multiplayer FPS which is, nowadays, still largely played over the Internet. Moreover, this game has been released to the open source, IOQuake III [8]. The game is set in *Free For All* (FFA) mode with a maximum score of 40. The goal of a FFA match is to eliminate as much enemies as possible. Each kill gives +1 point. The match ends when a player reaches the score of 40. As game quality not only depends on network quality but also on players skills, we use autonomous robots (or *bots*) on the clients side. Of course, the bots are configured in the same way, such that player's skills don't impact on game quality.

5   Results and Analysis

5.1   Energy Analysis

In figure 2, we present the energy consumption versus time while using the delay-efficient OLSR. According to the topology presented in figure 1, C_2 and C_3 are the 1-hop neighbors of the game server which belong to the shortest paths, in terms of delay, of nodes C_4, C_5, C_6 and C_7. Thus, they forward their game traffic, that is why their residual energy decreases faster. Indeed, C_3 forwards the traffic of C_5 and C_6 whereas C_2 forwards the traffic of C_4 and C_7. Until 3000 sec., we can distinguish three groups of nodes: C_2 and C_3 which forward two traffics each, C_4 which forwards one traffic (the one of C_7) and leaf nodes (C_1, C_5, C_6 and C_7) which do not forward any traffic. After 3000 sec., C_2 and C_3 reach 0% of residual energy and shut down. Then, C_1 takes over and forward the traffics of C_4, C_5 and C_7. As a consequence, its residual energy decreases faster. The only path for C_6 to reach the game server is through C_3. However, as this node is out of energy, C_6 cannot reach the game server anymore and has to leave the game. Finally, after 4600 sec., C_1 is out of energy and no other node can reach the game server. These results show that finding routes for traffic according to only the delay metric seriously reduce the game session.

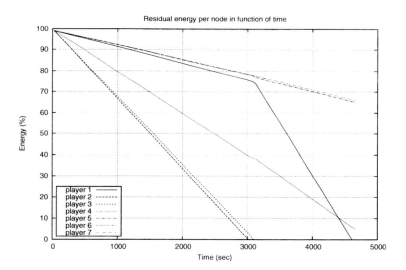

Fig. 2. Residual energy per node in function of time, considering delay-efficient OLSR

In figure 3, we present the energy consumption versus time while using the energy-efficient OLSR. Routes are now computed according to only the energy metric. We can clearly distinguish three groups of curves in this figure. Members of these groups are in fact determined by their position compared with the game server. Indeed, the first three curves are the ones of nodes C_1, C_2 and C_3, which all are 1-hop far from the game server. These three nodes forward game traffic from and to nodes C_4, C_5, C_6 and C_7, that is why their residual energy decrease faster than the other nodes. The second group of curves is composed of nodes C_4 and C_5, which both are 2-hops far from the game server. They fairly forward traffic from and to C_7. Finally, curves of C_6 and C_7 represent the third group. These two nodes are leaf nodes and do not forward any other traffic than theirselves. Thus, their residual energy decreases slower than all other nodes. This figure shows well that the traffic load is fairly distributed among the nodes of a same group to avoid excessive energy consumption of only one node. Indeed, all the players can play together up to only 3000 sec. against 4000 sec. for energy-efficient routing. Using the energy metric rather than the delay metric increased the game session from 3000 sec. to 4000 sec.

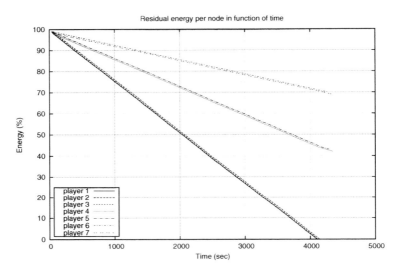

Fig. 3. Residual energy per node in function of time, considering energy-efficient OLSR

In figure 4, we present the energy consumption versus time while using our energy-delay routing protocol (with a threshold of 150 ms). In the beginning, all nodes have the same amount of energy (100%). Thus, it is the delay metric that differentiates the costs of the links. C_4 chooses C_2 and C_5 chooses C_3 to forward their game traffic to the game server because their delay cost is smaller than the one of C_1. The residual energy of C_1 thus decreases slower than the one of C_2 and C_3. If we consider the game traffic from the players to the game server, C_1 can be considered as a leaf node because it does not forward any traffic. However, its residual energy decreases faster than the ones of C_6 and C_7, which are leaf nodes too. Indeed, if we consider the game traffic from the game server to the players, C_8 has a *delay_path_cost* equals to zero (i.e. its factor $f = 0$) because it is the game server. Hence, it only considers the energy metric as link cost. As C_2 and C_3 already forward the game traffics of C_4 and C_5 respectively, and thus consume more energy than C_1, C_8 chooses C_1 to forward its game traffic to the different players. This explains why the residual energy of C_1 decreases faster than the ones of C_6 and C_7. However, after 650 sec., the delay advantage that C_2 and C_3 offer is counterbalanced by their lower remaining energy compared to the one of C_1. C_4 and C_5 then balance their game traffic between C_1 and C_2 and between C_1 and C_3 respectively, that is why the curve of C_1 becomes parallel to the curves of C_2 and C_3. The same phenomenon appears after 1100 sec. between C_4 and C_5. Indeed, at this time, C_7 starts to balance its traffic between these two nodes. Once more, these two curves become parallel. Our routing protocol tends to reduce the energy consumption on nodes that are close to the game server and have a short delay cost. Moreover, we can see that all nodes are able to play until 4000 sec., which is the same amount of time as with energy-efficient routing protocol.

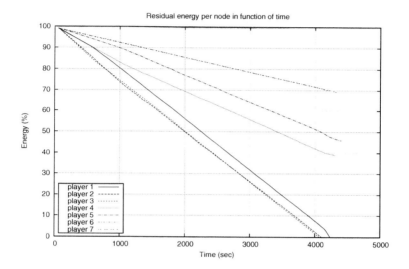

Fig. 4. Residual energy per node in function of time, considering energy-delay OLSR (threshold = 150 ms)

Finally, we plot in figure 5 the duration of a gaming session in function of the routing strategy chosen. Results clearly show that increasing the *delay_threshold* value leads to increase the gaming session. Indeed, the bigger is the *delay_threshold*, the more nodes will take into account the energy metric to compute their paths.

5.2   Score and Fairness Analysis

Figure 6 represents the CCDF (Complementary Cumulative Distribution Function) of score of players with the delay-efficient OLSR. We can distinguish in this figure two groups of curves. The first group is composed of nodes C_1, C_2, C_3 and C_6. Their curves are very close to each others. That means that there is a good fairness between them. Moreover, their probability of ending a match with a score at least equals to 30 is about 70%. The second group is composed of nodes

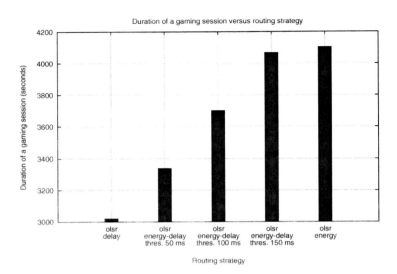

Fig. 5. Duration of a gaming session versus routing strategy

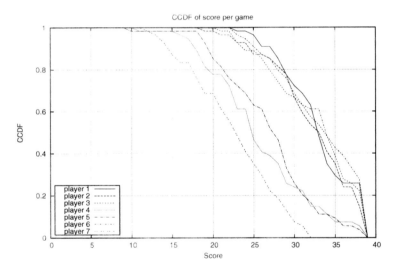

Fig. 6. Score CCDF of each player with delay-efficient OLSR

C_5, C_4 and C_7. Their probability of having a score of at least 30 is very low and their curves are more distant from those of the first group. Indeed, delay-efficient routing selects paths that have the smaller end-to-end delay. Therefore, nodes which are far from the game server or which have higher end-to-end delays are penalized. This kind of routing protocol does not provide fairness among players, so game experience of penalized players may be frustrating.

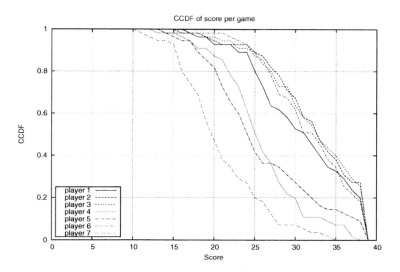

Fig. 7. Score CCDF of each player with energy-efficient OLSR

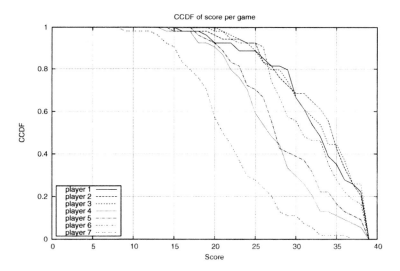

Fig. 8. Score CCDF of each player with energy-delay OLSR (threshold = 150 ms)

Figure 7 represents the CCDF of score of players with the energy-efficient OLSR. Here again, the nodes C_1, C_2, C_3, and C_6 have better probabilities of finishing a match with a good score because they are closer to the game server in term of end-to-end delay. C_7 is still the last one because it has the greater end-to-end delay. However, curves of C_4 and C_5 are closer to each other, which means that fairness between these two nodes is better than with the delay-efficient OLSR.

Indeed, C_4 and C_5 do not only choose C_2 and C_3 respectively to reach the game server but they balance their traffic between C_1, C_2 and C_3 in function of the residual energy. Thus, when they use C_1 as relay, their end-to-end delay increases. Finally, their average end-to-end delay tends to be closer and that is why their score curves are closer. We also see on that figure that the global score of each node is a little worse than with delay-efficient OLSR. This is due to the fact that only the energy metric is taken into account, so sometimes the nodes choose a path with a higher end-to-end delay. However, unfairness between C_1, C_2, C_3, C_6; C_4, C_5 and C_7 is not that much increased.

Figure 8 represents the CCDF of score of players with our energy-delay OLSR (with a threshold of 150 ms). Compared with the two others figures, we can see here that the interval between curves of C_1, C_2, C_3, C_6 and C_4, C_5 is reduced. Indeed, the probabilities to reach a score at least equals to 30 at the end of a match increased for C_4 and C_5 and slightly decreased for C_1, C_2, C_3 and C_6, making the game more fair. Except C_7, which is very far from the game server, our modified OLSR routing protocol enable to increase fairness among players.

Finally, figure 9 depicts the average score of the players in function of the routing strategy chosen. Results show that increasing the *delay_threshold* value leads to slightly decrease the average score. These results confirm the ones presented in figure 5. Increasing the *delay_threshold* value improves lifetime of game session and fairness among players but at the cost of some gaming quality (in particular for players which are close to the game server). On the contrary, reducing the *delay_threshold* value, decreases the lifetime of game session and the fairness among the players but improves the game quality.

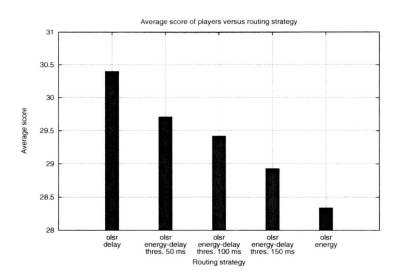

Fig. 9. Average score of player versus routing strategy

6   Conclusions and Future Work

In this paper, we focus on the energy consumption and the game quality of a real-time multiplayer video game session over multihop ad hoc networks. We propose a multimetric routing protocol based on the delay and the energy metrics. It is specialized in client-server based applications because it takes into consideration the position of the nodes compared with the game server.

We study the impact of a delay-efficient protocol and an energy-efficient protocol on the duration and the quality of gaming sessions. We showed that one improves game quality but seriously decreases the network lifetime whereas the other do the contrary. Moreover, no one of them improves the fairness among the players.

We then compare our routing protocol with the two mentioned above. We showed that it enables to find a compromise between game quality and energy consumption and also increases the fairness among the players, depending on its *delay_threshold* parameter. Setting the latter to a value close to the maximum existing end-to-end delay between the game server and the players seems to be a good compromise between lifetime and quality of gaming sessions.

Our future work consist of using a dynamic *delay_threshold* value: the game server can compute it depending on the different end-to-end delay it has with the players and share the computed value to all the players by using the routing protocol signaling messages. Also, we plan to evaluate our proposition in a mobile environment (MANET).

References

1. Clansen, T., Jacquet, P.: Optimized Link State Routing Protocol (OLSR) (October 2003), http://www.ietf.org/rfc/rfc3626.txt
2. Kunz, T.: Energy-Efficient Variations of OLSR. In: International Wireless Communications and Mobile Computing Conference, IWCMC (2008)
3. Mahfoudh, S., Minet, P.: An energy efficient routing based on OLSR in wireless ad hoc and sensor networks. In: Advanced Information Networking and Applications Workshops, AINAW (2008)
4. Benslimane, A., El Khoury, R., El Azouzi, R., Pierre, S.: Energy Power-Aware Routing in OLSR Protocol. In: International Conference on Mobile Computing and Wireless Communication, MCWC (2006)
5. De Rango, F., Fotino, M., Marano, S.: EE-OLSR: Energy Efficient OLSR Routing Protocol for Mobile Ad-hoc Networks. In: Military Communications Conference, MILCOM (2008)
6. Sanchez-Miquel, L., Vesselinova-Vassileva, N., Barcelo, F., Carbajo-Flores, P.: Energy and Delay-Constrained Routing in Mobile Ad Hoc Networks: an Initial Approach. In: 2nd International Workshop on Performance Evaluation of Wireless Ad Hoc, Sensor, and Ubiquitous Networks, PE-WASUN (2005)
7. Regatte, N., Sarangapani, J.: Optimized energy-delay routing in ad hoc wireless networks. In: Proceedings of World Wireless Congress (2005)
8. http://ioquake3.org/

9. Feeney, L.M.: An Energy Consumption Model for Performance Analysis of Routing Protocols for Mobile Ad Hoc Networks. In: Mobile Networks and Applications (2001)
10. Badis, H., Al Agha, K.: QOLSR Multi-path Routing for Mobile Ad Hoc Networks Based on Multiple Metrics: Bandwidth and Delay. In: IEEE Vehicular Technology Conference, VTC (2004)
11. Meraihi, A.N., Jacquet, P.: Le Controle du Delai dans le Protocole OLSR. Research Repport (2003)
12. Kaiser, A., Maggiorini, D., Achir, N., Boussetta, K.: On the Objective Evaluation of Real-Time Networked Games. In: Global Telecommunications Conference, GlobeCom (2009)
13. Perkins, C.E., Royer, E.M.: Ad hoc On-demand Distant Vector Routing. In: IEEE Workshop on Mobile Computing Systems and Applications, WMCSA (1999)
14. Kaiser, A., Achir, N., Boussetta, K.: Multiplayer Games over Wireless Ad hoc Networks: Energy and Delay Analysis. In: International Workshop on Ubiquitous Multimedia Systems and Applications, UMSA (2009)

An Energy Analysis of IEEE 802.15.6 Scheduled Access Modes for Medical Applications

Christos Tachtatzis, Fabio Di Franco, David C. Tracey,
Nick F. Timmons, and Jim Morrison

WiSAR Lab,
Letterkenny Institute of Technology,
Port Road, Letterkenny, Co. Donegal, Ireland
{christos,fabio,david,nick,jim}@wisar.org

Abstract. Medical body area networks will employ a range of implantable and body worn devices to support a wide range of applications with diverse QoS requirements. The IEEE 802.15.6 working group is developing a communications standard for low power devices operating on, in and around the body and medical devices are a key application area of the standard. The ISO/IEEE 11073 standard addresses medical device interoperability and specifies the required QoS for medical applications.

This paper investigates the lifetime of devices using the scheduled access modes proposed by IEEE 802.15.6, while satisfying the throughput and latency constraints of the ISO/IEEE 11073 applications. It computes the optimum superframe structure and number of superframes that the device can sleep to achieve maximum lifetime. The results quantify the maximum expected achievable lifetime for these applications and show that scheduled access mode is not appropriate for all application classes such as those with intermittent transfer patterns.

Keywords: Energy Analysis, IEEE 11073, IEEE 802.15.6, Scheduled Allocations, Wireless Body Area Network, Wireless Medical Applications.

1   Introduction

The rapid expansion of wireless technology has led to the possibility of widespread untethered medical and health monitoring. The use of wireless technology, promises benefits in terms of replacing cabling, greater flexibility in equipment placement, wider access to patient data (not limited to the bedside or wired points), patient mobility in hospital and possibly home monitoring allowing earlier patient release. There will also be opportunities for the emerging monitoring and alerting applications such as remote patient monitoring and automatic drug delivery.

The emphasis in Wireless Sensor Networks (WSNs) and Wireless Personal Area Networks (WPANs) has been low power, low cost and short range operations. The importance of low power operation is even greater in medical Wireless

D. Simplot-Ryl et al. (Eds.): ADHOCNETS 2011, LNICST 89, pp. 209–222, 2012.

Body Area Networks (medical WBANs) where devices are expected to operate over long periods without battery replacement and charging may not be feasible; i.e. implantable medical devices. Existing WPAN standards have high energy demands for medical application and insufficient QoS guarantees. IEEE 802.15.6 [1] has the potential to overcome the limitations of other standards, such as IEEE 802.15.1 [2] and 802.15.4 [3] and to allow the wider implementation and deployment of Wireless Body Area Networks (WBANs). IEEE 802.15.1 was the first standard to focus on the short range personal area networking environment and IEEE 802.15.4 traded throughput for low power operation. Previous work [4] and [5] has shown lifetime limitation of IEEE 802.15.4 for medical applications.

Recent work has considered the performance of the IEEE 802.15.6 contention based access under saturation conditions [6]. The delay and throughput limits for a single device using contention based access was examined in [7]. Both [6] and [7] considered contention based access and in this paper we extend this by examining the performance of the contention free scheduled access modes. The results presented are based on the analysis in [8]. In particular the medical device lifetimes are investigated for real application requirements from the ISO/IEEE 11073 [9]. These results are computed with a mixed integer program that finds the optimum superframe structure and the number of beacon periods through which the device could sleep to achieve maximum lifetime, while satisfying the QoS requirements (data rate and latency) for a range of applications.

The remainder of the paper is organised as follows: Section 2 gives an overview of IEEE 802.15.6. Section 3 gives an overview of the ISO/IEEE 11073 application scenarios. Section 4 presents the analysis and the mixed integer program. Sections 5.1 and 5.2 presents the sensitivity of the lifetime to the MAC parameters and the lifetime estimates respectively. Section 6 presents future work and conclusions.

2   IEEE 802.15.6 Overview

2.1   Physical Layer

IEEE 802.15.6 specification defines Narrowband (NB), Ultra-Wide Band (UWB) and Human Body Communications (HBC) physical layers and a common frame structure. The NB physical layer operates in seven different frequency bands with a variable number of channels, bit rates and modulation schemes. Our analysis concentrates on bands 6 and 7, which operate at symbol rates of 600 ksps with varying modulation schemes, coding rates and spreading factors.

2.2   Medium Access Control Layer

The IEEE 802.15.6 draft specifies a common MAC for all the supported physical layers and which can use one-hop star or two-hop restricted tree topologies. In these topologies, the hub is responsible for coordinating channel access by establishing one of the following three access modes:

- Beacon mode with beacon period superframe boundaries
- Non-beacon mode with superframe boundaries
- Non-beacon mode without superframe boundaries

The time base is divided into equal length beacon periods (also known as superframes) and each superframe is divided into allocation slots. In the first two access modes the time base is common between hubs and nodes and is decided by the hub; i.e. the hub establishes superframe boundaries and defines the number of allocation slots in it. In the first access mode, the hub communicates the superframe structure via beacon frames or Timed frames (T-Poll). The second access mode does not transmit beacons and the superframe structure is enforced through the use of Timed frames (T-Poll). In the non-beacon mode without superframe boundaries each node establishes its own time base independently.

In the beacon mode with superframe structure the hub organises the superframe in access phases, shown in Fig. 1, and allows three types of access:

1. Random access (Contention based): CSMA/CA or Slotted ALOHA for the narrowband and ultra-wide band physical layers respectively. These are the EAP1, EAP2, RAP1, RAP2 and CAP shown in Fig. 1. The EAPs are reserved for emergency high priority traffic while the RAPs are used for non-recurring transfers.
2. Improvised, unscheduled access: Post (i.e. a hub instruction) or Poll (i.e. a data request from the hub). During this mode, devices must be awake and wait for a poll or post frame from the hub, before they can transmit.
3. Scheduled access (Contention free): 1-periodic where devices exchange frames with the hub in every superframe or m-periodic where devices and hubs exchange frames every m superframes allowing the device to sleep between transfers. In this mode, devices can start their transfer when the reserved allocation slot time has commenced

Scheduled transfers, unscheduled and improvised transfers occur in the Managed Access Phases MAP1 and MAP2.

Fig. 1. Beacon mode with beacon period superframe boundaries structure

The length of these phases is variable and is defined in numbers of allocation slots. The draft defines four acknowledgement policies: 1) not acknowledged frames (N-Ack), 2) immediately acknowledged (I-Ack), 3) block acknowledged later (L-Ack) and 4) block acknowledged (B-Ack).

3   ISO/IEEE 11073 Applications

The ISO/IEEE 11073 Draft for Point-of-Care (PoC) medical devices [9] defines a range of medical application classes. Table 1 is a subset of the IEEE 11073 application classes which can be supported by the maximum data rate of 971 kbps provided by the narrowband physical layer of the IEEE 802.15.6 draft. The ultra-wideband physical layer of IEEE 802.15.6 can support application data rates up to 10 Mbps.

Table 1. Applications from IEEE 11073

Class: Data Type	Latency	Bandwidth
A: Alarms/alerts/ Positional Alerts (real-time)	**A1:**< 200ms and **A2:** <3 s	64 bytes per alarm
B: Patient State	< 3 s	64 bytes per alarm
C: Sensor watchdog/heartbeat	< 60 s	64 bytes per hour
D: Reminder	< 3 s	1632 bytes per alarm
E: Physiologic parameters (real-time) [e.g. episodic BP, HR, SpO2, ETCO2, temp]	< 3 s	20 bytes/param at **E1:** 0.5 to **E2:** 5 Hz
F: Telemetry Waveforms (real-time)	< 300ms	ECG: [**F1:** 3-lead 2.4 kbps, **F2:** 5-lead 10 kbps, **F3:** 12-lead 72 kbps], **F4:** Ventilator: 50-60 bps, **F5:** SpO2: 50-120 bps

4   Analysis

The analysis presented is for medical monitoring devices which report periodically. As such it concentrates on IEEE 802.15.6 Scheduled Access mode (1-periodic and m-periodic allocations in beacon mode with superframe boundaries) using the one-hop star topology. The device lifetimes are determined using the analytical model presented in [8] for uplink block transfers[1]. The purpose of this analysis is to determine the superframe structure and the number of beacon periods through which the device must sleep to achieve maximum lifetime for these applications. It considers the end device in a one-hop point-to-point link. This is the best case for a particular device as there are no conflicting requirements from other devices on the BAN.

---

[1] The analytical model was developed for version 1 of the draft and it was updated to comply with version 2. See discussion further in this section.

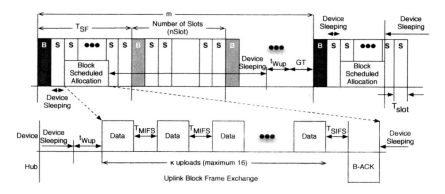

Fig. 2. Optimisation parameters. Superframe structure and periodicity m

The IEEE 802.15.6 offers a flexible superframe structure that can be adjusted by the hub to suit the communication requirements of the BAN. Fig. 2 shows the superframe structure and the device's duty cycle for an m-periodic uplink allocation. The cycle starts with the device receiving a beacon and subsequently going to sleep until the start of its allocation interval where the device wakes-up for the block scheduled allocation. After the block schedule allocation the device goes to sleep for m superframes before waking-up to receive the next beacon and the cycle repeats itself. During the block schedule allocation the device sends data to the hub in block acknowledged transfer. The maximum number of frames in a block transfer is 16 according to the IEEE 802.15.6. Each frame fragment has the maximum size of 255 bytes except for the last frame fragment which has the length required to send the remaining data. This analysis uses the maximum frame size, because it is the most efficient transfer due to the reduced header overhead under ideal channel conditions, which allows us to determine the upper bound of maximum lifetime. It may not be suitable in scenarios where the bit error rate is high and there will be a higher probability of frame corruption.

If the data to be transfered cannot fit in a single scheduled allocation, the device requests additional allocations in the same superframe and it is assumed that the device goes back to sleep between the allocations intervals.

The superframe is divided in slots and the number of slots ($nSlots$) is adjustable by the hub. To allow further flexibility the hub can adjust the duration of the slot in increments of $pAllocationSlotResolution$ (equal to 1 ms for the narrowband physical layer). The minimum slot duration $pAllocationSlotMin$ is defined equal to 1 ms for the narrowband physical layer.

The superframe duration is:

$$T_{SF} = nSlots \cdot T_{slot}$$
$$T_{slot} = (pAllocationSlotMin + L \cdot pAllocationSlotResolution) \qquad (1)$$

The parameters that control the superframe structure are $nSlots$, which can be between 1 and 256 and the slot length L, which can be between 0 and 255. These parameters ranges allow slot durations between 1 ms and 256 ms and superframe durations in the range of 1 ms to 65.536 s.

The analysis determines the optimal value of m for maximum device lifetime when the m-periodic mode is used and observing the constraints specified by IEEE 802.15.6 and radio constraints such as device warm-up times [8]. The guard time used in the analytical model of [8] has been updated to comply with the definition of [1] as follows.

The nominal synchronisation interval (SI_n) is specified to be 8 beacon period lengths (T_{SF}). The nominal guard time is $GT_n = GT_0 + 2 \cdot SI_n \cdot \delta$ where GT_0 is fixed at 61.6 μs based on data-link and physical layer parameters, while δ is the clock accuracy. GT_n should be used when the last synchronisation interval SI is less than the nominal SI_n, otherwise GT_a should be appended to it. Hence the guard time is a function of SI and after rounding to the clock accuracy (δ):

$$GT(SI) = \begin{cases} \left\lceil \frac{GT_n}{\delta} \right\rceil \cdot \delta & \text{if } SI < SI_n \\ \left\lceil \frac{GT_n + GT_a}{\delta} \right\rceil \cdot \delta & \text{if } SI \geq SI_n \end{cases} \quad (2)$$

The optimisation problem was formulated as a mixed integer program that maximises the device lifetime, assuming that no other devices operate on the BAN and finds the optimum parameters that maximise the following cost function:

$$\begin{aligned} maximise: \quad & T_{life} = \frac{Q}{I_{total}(nSlots,L,m,\Delta,\tau)} \\ where: \quad & \Delta = \frac{N_F \cdot 255 \cdot 8}{m \cdot T_{SF}}, \tau = m \cdot T_{SF} \quad (3) \\ subject\ to: \quad & \Delta \leq \Delta_{App}, \tau \leq \tau_{App} \\ & nSlots \in [1,256], L \in [0,255], m \in [1,256] \end{aligned}$$

where T_{life} is the device lifetime in years, Q the battery capacity, Δ the achieved data rate, τ the achieved delay, I_{total} the average current consumption of the device as a function of ($nSlots$, L, m, Δ, τ) and is determined as in [8], N_F the number of data frames transmitted every m superframes and T_{SF} the superframe duration. The application data rate and latency requirements are Δ_{App} and τ_{App} respectively.

5   Device Lifetime for Medical Applications

Equation 3 is solved for selected data rates and latency requirements per IEEE 11073. The solutions give the superframe structure ($nSlots$, L) and the parameter m for m-periodic allocations that maximise the device lifetime. It is important to note that more than one equivalent solution may exist. For example, for the class F2: 5-lead ECG from Table 1 with data rate of 10 kbps and latency requirement of 300 ms there are fourteen optimum equivalent solutions as illustrated in Table 2.

Table 2. Solutions for ECG 5-Lead, Data Rate 10 Kbps, Latency 0.3 s

nSlots	L	T_{SF}	m	Wake-up Period (s)	Lifetime (years)
15	0	15	20		
4	4	20	15		
5	3				
10	1				
20	0				
5	4	25	12		
25	0			0.3	0.14411
2	14	30	10		
3	9				
5	5				
6	4				
10	2				
15	1				
30	0				

For the application class shown and the other classes considered, the equivalent solutions for maximum lifetime are dominated by their latency requirement. All the parameter combinations that maximise the wake-up period result in equivalent lifetimes. However, there are a few notable exceptions. For example, solutions where the parameter m is less than 8 are sub-optimal. This is explained by the fact that the nominal guard time as specified in the draft standard is fixed and over-provisioned when the last synchronisation interval (SI) is below the nominal synchronisation interval (SI_n). In fact, the version 1 of the draft had specified the nominal guard time to be equal to 1/10 of the allocation slot (T_{slot}) and made any solution with $L > 0$ suboptimal in terms of energy efficiency, making the parameter L meaningless. The version 2 of the draft has revised the definition of nominal guard time to be proportional to the beacon transmission frequency, making L a parameter worth controlling in optimising the lifetime. This modification to the draft has, however, resulted in a similar limitation on optimising the lifetime using parameter m, i.e. optimal lifetimes have m greater than 8, unless the application's data rate forces m to be less.

Note that there are no solutions with small superframe duration (T_{SF}) in Table 2. Such solutions are not feasible because the duration of the superframe is too short for the block transfer to fit between the transmissions of two beacons. For example, a superframe with two slots and L equal to zero will result in a superframe with duration of 2 ms and the parameter m to maximise the wake-up period must be 150. In this case the duration of the block transfer is 12.69 ms and can not fit within the 2 ms superframe. The mixed integer program uses constraints to remove such solutions (not shown in Equation 3 for clarity).

5.1   Device Lifetime Sensitivity to MAC parameters

The dynamics and sensitivity of the model can be seen in Figures 3 to 5 for selected application classes (classes A and B not shown in Figures, and the results are similar to class E). The maximum lifetime against the parameter L, which is proportional to the slot length, is shown in Fig. 3. For each point in this graph the parameter L is kept constant at the values indicated on the x-axis and the other parameters (number of slots and m), are allowed to change in the mixed-integer program. The output of the integer program returns the maximum achieved lifetime for the specified value of L. The circles in the graph indicate the maximum points for each application class (i.e. the maximum of the maximum lifetimes for the given L).

The step change in maximum lifetime at certain values of L (Fig. 3), must be noted and is an outcome of meeting the latency requirements of an application

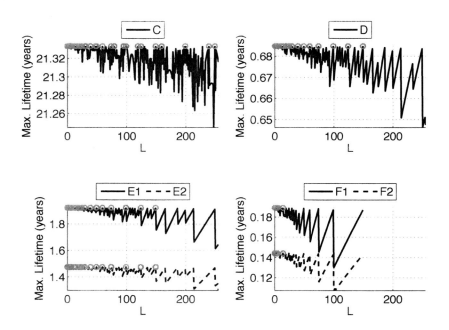

Fig. 3. Maximum lifetime versus slot length (L) for applications C, D, E1, E2, F1 and F2

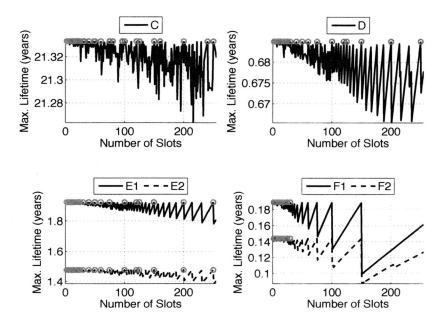

Fig. 4. Maximum lifetime versus number of slots in a superframe ($nSlots$) for applications C, D, E1, E2, F1 and F2

for a given L. For example, the 12-lead ECG requires a latency of 300 ms. A value of L=99, (so T_{slot}=100 ms) meets this latency with 3 superframes and 1 slot in each superframe. When L is increased to 100 (so T_{slot} is 101 ms), and holding the number of slots in the superframe at 1, leads m having to decrease to 2 in order to satisfy the latency requirement. This results in a more frequent duty cycle of 202 ms which increases current consumption and reduces the lifetime.

The maximum lifetime against the number of slots in a superframe is shown in Fig. 4. From the graph it can be observed that multiple equivalent solutions exist for each application. In a similar fashion to Fig. 3, a step change can be observed at certain values of $nSlot$ caused by meeting the enforced application latency requirement. The circled points in Fig. 4 show the equivalent solutions that maximize the maximum device lifetime.

The maximum device lifetime can be plotted against the parameter m as shown in Fig. 5. It must be pointed out that not all applications have feasible solutions for $m \in [1, 255]$, because high values of m result in more data building up in the device buffers and so require longer superframes for the data transfer. This combination of longer superframes and high m will violate the latency constraint of the applications, e.g. application F1: 3-lead ECG is only feasible when m is in the range of 1 to 21.

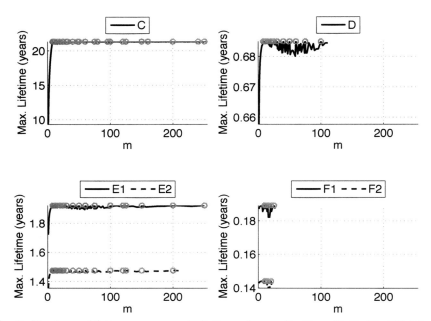

Fig. 5. Maximum lifetime versus periodicity m for applications C, D, E1, E2, F1 and F2

5.2   Device Lifetime Estimates

Fig. 6 shows the maximum achieved lifetime for variable data rates and latency requirements. From Fig. 6 it can be observed that lifetime greater than 1 year can only be achieved by applications with a latency constraint of 3 s or more.

The maximum device lifetime for applications with latency constraints of 0.2 and 0.3 s, and data rates less than 1000 bps is 51 and 76 days respectively. This low device lifetime can be explained by the fact that the superframe duration is kept low to satisfy the tight delay constraint causing devices to wake up regularly to send small chunks of data and receive beacons.

The frequent wake up cycle, results in the consumption of a significant amount of energy in beacons. This is validated in Fig. 7, which shows the percentage of energy spent in beacons. For low latency constraints and low data rates more than half of the device's energy is spent in handling beacons.

Fig. 6 also shows that at high data rates, the proportion of energy spent in transferring data dominates as illustrated by the convergence of the lifetimes for different values of application latency. This dominance is also evident in Fig. 7 where the percentage of energy consumption associated with beacons is below 10% at high data rates.

From Fig. 6 the maximum lifetime for the applications classes of Table 1 can be extracted and are summarised in Table 3. Table 3 also shows one of

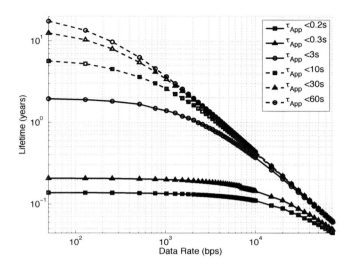

Fig. 6. Maximum device lifetime satisfying the given data rate and latency requirements

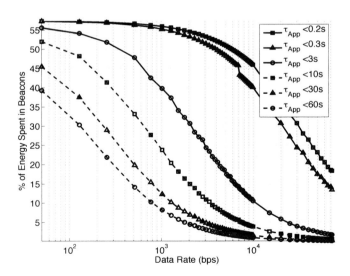

Fig. 7. Normalized energy spent in beacons

the computed optimum solutions (the one with the maximum number of slots in the superframe) for each application from ISO/IEEE 11073. The selected solutions shown are those with the maximum number of slots in the superframe. The additional slots will enable the hub to accommodate connections with other devices with the extra slots that remain free.

While it was expected that the scheduled access modes would not be suitable for intermittent data transfer, because devices with m-periodic allocations have to wake-up to receive beacons and maintain their slot allocation even if they have no data to transfer, Table 3 shows how low the lifetime would be in such cases. Use of scheduled access modes for classes such as A and D, could only be justified when high reliability and deterministic response time is required at the expense of energy usage. For class A, use of the Emergency Access Phases (EAPs) would be more appropriate, while class D could use the Random Access Phases (RAPs).

Finally, the solution for application class F3: 12-lead ECG, with data rate of 72 kbps and delay constraint of 300 ms, is only feasible when the parameter m is less or equal to 6. This is caused by the high data rate demand of the application. For m more than 6, too much data are accumulated in the device buffers and the superframe length does not fit the data exchange forcing m to reduce.

Table 3. One optimum solutions for ISO/IEEE 11073 applications of Table 1

App. Class	App. Rate	App. Latency	nSlots	L	m	Lifetime (years)
A1	2048	0.2	25	0	8	0.13095
A2	2048	0.3	30	0	10	0.19156
B	170.6	0.3	30	0	10	0.20489
C	0.12	60	250	29	8	21.3336
D	4352	3	250	0	12	0.68493
E1	80	3	250	0	12	1.92350
E2	800	3	250	0	12	1.47530
F1	2400	0.3	30	0	10	0.18928
F2	10000	0.3	30	0	10	0.14411
F3	72000	0.3	50	0	6	0.04839
F4	60	0.3	30	0	10	0.20581
F5	120	0.3	30	0	10	0.20522

6   Conclusions

Medical Devices in BANs are an important application area for IEEE802.15.6 and maximising device lifetime is a key requirement in such scenarios. The analysis and results presented provide best case estimates for device lifetime when using IEEE 802.15.6 scheduled access modes with data rate and latency constraints as defined by ISO/IEEE 11073 for medical devices. The paper has shown the optimum superframe structure and m-period for these application scenarios, which were found using a mixed integer program.

The functionality in IEEE 802.15.6; to allow devices to skip beacon periods provides flexibility and reduces energy consumption. This is, however, subject to the latency requirements of given applications which may force devices to wake-up more frequently and limits the amount of time the devices can spend in sleep state. The results presented have shown the significant extent to which these application constraints, particularly latency, can impact the device lifetime, when scheduled access modes are used.

The findings on the estimated device lifetimes (and corresponding superframe structure), such as the low device lifetime for applications with intermittent data transfer, show the importance of considering medical application requirements to select the appropriate access mode and ensure the best use of the proposed standard.

Analysis of the first draft, which specified the nominal guard time to be equal to $1/10$ of the allocation slot, made any solution with $L > 0$ suboptimal in terms of energy efficiency. Draft 2 redefined the nominal guard time to be fixed (and proportional to the nominal synchronisation interval), resulting in the optimum lifetime solutions having the device sleep for more than 8 beacon periods, unless the application's data rate forces m to be less. This use of a fixed nominal guard time to mitigate the effects of missing beacons should be reconsidered, given the impact it has on the device lifetime.

Future work will be necessary to characterise random, improvised and unscheduled access modes and subsequently investigate the scenario where multiple applications with contradictory QoS constraints operate in the same body area network. This would provide data to form policies based on application requirements and aid the hub to set the MAC parameters and achieve desired outcomes, i.e. maximum device lifetime.

Acknowledgment. This work was carried out under the auspices of Enterprise Ireland Applied Research Enhancement (ARE).

References

1. IEEE P802.15.6/D02 Wireless Medium Access Control (MAC) and Physical Layer (PHY) Sepcifications for Wireless Personal Area Networks (WPANs) used in or around a body (December 2010)
2. IEEE Standards for Information Technology - Telecommunications and Information Exchange Between Systems - Local and Metropolitan Area Networks - Specific Requirements - Part 15.1: Wireless Medium Access Control (MAC) and Physical Layer (PHY) Specifications for Wireless Personal Area Networks (WPANs), IEEE Std 802.15.1-2005 (Revision of IEEE Std 802.15.1-2002), pp. 1–580 (2005)
3. IEEE Standards for Information Technology - Telecommunications and Information Exchange Between Systems - Local and Metropolitan Area Networks - Specific Requirements - Part 15.4: Wireless Medium Access Control (MAC) and Physical Layer (PHY) Specifications for Low Rate Wireless Personal Area Networks (WPANs), IEEE Std 802.15.4-2006 (Revision of IEEE Std 802.15.1-2003), pp. 1–305 (2006)

4. Timmons, N.F., Scanlon, W.G.: Analysis of the performance of IEEE 802.15.4 for medical sensor body area networking. In: 1st Annual IEEE Communications Society Conference on Sensor and Ad Hoc Communication Networks (IEEE SECON) (October 2004)
5. Sukor, M., Ariffin, S., Fisal, N., Yusof, S., Abdallah, A.: Performance study of wireless body area network in medical environment. In: 2nd Asia International Conference on Modeling and Simulation (AICMS) (May 2008)
6. Rashwand, S., Misic, J., Khazaei, H.: Performance Analysis of IEEE 802.15.6 Under Saturation Condition and Error-Prone Channel. In: IEEE Wireless Communications and Networking Conference (March 2011)
7. Ullah, S., Kwak, K.S.: Throughput and Delay Limits of IEEE 802.15.6. In: IEEE Wireless Communications and Networking Conference (March 2011)
8. Tachtatzis, C., Di Franco, F., Tracey, D., Timmons, N.F., Morrison, J.: An energy analysis of the IEEE 802.15.6 scheduled access modes. In: IEEE Globecom Workshop on Mobile Computing and Emerging Communication Networks (MCECN) (December 2010)
9. Draft Health Informatics - Point-of-Care Medical Device Communication - Technical Report - Guidelines for the use of RF wireless technology, IEEE Unapproved draft Std P11073-00101/D5 (June 2008)

A Localized Algorithm Based on Minimum Cost Arborescences for the MECBS Problem with Asymmetric Edge Costs

Frederico Barboza and Flávio Assis

LaSiD - Distributed Systems Laboratory
DCC - Department of Computer Science
UFBA - Federal University of Bahia
Salvador, Bahia, Brazil
`fred.barboza@gmail.com, fassis@ufba.br`

Abstract. In this paper we describe a (distributed) localized approximation algorithm for the MECBS (Minimum Energy Consumption Broadcast Subgraph) problem with asymmetric edge costs, called LMCA (Localized algorithm for energy-efficient broadcast based on **L**ocal **M**inimum **C**ost **A**rborescences). Given a directed weighted graph $G = (V, E)$ with edge weight function w and a source node s, the MECBS problem consists of finding a range assignment to V such that the induced graph contains a spanning directed tree rooted at s with minimized cost. This problem can be efficiently solved for some specific cases, but it is NP-hard in the general case. To the best of our knowledge, LMCA is the first localized algorithm to the MECBS problem with asymmetric edge costs (without restricting the way how edge costs might be asymmetric). We compared LMCA with blind flooding and with two alternative solutions we designed for the problem, LMCP and LBIPAsym (a variation of LBIP for the case of asymmetric edge costs). In our experiments, LMCA outperformed these algorithms. We additionally present and evaluate two slight variations of LMCA, called LMCAc and LMCAfl.

Keywords: MECBS, asymmetric edge costs, minimum cost arborescence, localized algorithm, wireless sensor networks.

1 Introduction

In this paper we address the problem of energy-efficient broadcast in Wireless Sensor Networks (WSN). Broadcast is a useful communication primitive in different scenarios, such as in the dissemination of data or specific requests from the base station to the whole network (for example, for the distribution of cryptographic keys or synchronization packets). Since the need for conserving energy of nodes is a key issue in WSN (due to the fact that the nodes are typically operated by non-replaceable batteries), broadcasting should be performed as efficient in terms of energy use as possible.

D. Simplot-Ryl et al. (Eds.): ADHOCNETS 2011, LNICST 89, pp. 223–238, 2012.
© Institute for Computer Sciences, Social Informatics and Telecommunications Engineering 2012

Different approaches for the problem of energy-efficient broadcasting in wireless networks have been proposed. This problem consists of, given a *source node* s, determining a transmission power to each node of the network such that: (a) the resulting topology contains a spanning tree rooted at s; and (b) the sum of the costs associated with the nodes is minimized. The control of the transmission power of nodes is possible since radio transceivers commonly used in practical systems typically support transmissions at different power levels.

This problem has been formulated as the MECBS (Minimum Energy Consumption Broadcast Subgraph) problem [1]. In this paper we consider a version of this problem in which edge costs might be asymmetric. I.e. transmitting from a node u to a node v might have a different cost than transmitting from v to u. This happens, for example, in heterogeneous networks, where transmission and reception costs are dependent on hardware characteristics (specific to each node) or when the cost of *overhearing* is taken into consideration (overhearing is one of the major sources of energy expenditure due to communication in a WSN [14]). Heterogeneous networks have been less considered in the literature on energy-efficient algorithms, but they are the type of networks that is and will be used in many applications. The general MECBS problem is NP-hard [1].

In this paper we describe LMCA (Localized algorithm for energy-efficient broadcast based on Local Minimum Cost Arborescences), a localized algorithm that is an approximation for the MECBS problem with asymmetric edge costs. Although many results have been proved for symmetric versions of MECBS and some results for the general MECBS problem, to the best of our knowledge LMCA is the first localized algorithm to MECBS with asymmetric edge costs (without restricting the way how edge costs might be asymmetric). As there is no other specific localized algorithm for this problem in the literature, we compared LMCA with blind flooding and with alternative solutions we designed: one based on local computation of trees of minimum cost paths (which we call LMCP) and a variation of LBIP [5] for the case of asymmetric edge costs (which we call LBIPAsym). LBIP was designed for the version of MECBS with symmetric edge costs (for which it is a very good approximation) and thus cannot be directly applied to the version of MECBS we consider in this paper. LMCA outperformed these algorithms in our experiments. We additionally describe small variations of LMCA (which we call, respectively, LMCAc and LMCAfl) which improved slightly on the performance of LMCA in terms of energy cost in some scenarios, but which require, resp., higher processing cost at nodes and the exchange of longer messages.

This paper is structured as follows. In Section 2 we present the MECBS problem. In Section 3 we discuss related work. In Section 4 we describe the adopted system model. In Section 5 we describe LMCA and present proofs of its correctness. In Section 6 we present a performance evaluation of LMCA. Finally, we conclude the paper in Section 7.

2   The MECBS Problem

We use the MECBS problem formulation as presented in [1]. Let $G = (V, E)$ be a directed weighted graph with edge weight function $w : E \to \mathbb{R}^+$. A *range assignment* for G is a function $r : V \to \mathbb{R}^+$. The *transmission graph* induced by G and r is defined as $G_r = (V, E')$, where:

$$E' = \cup_{v \in V} \{(v, u) : (v, u) \in E \wedge w(v, u) \leq r(v)\}$$

The MECBS is then defined as follows: given a *source node* $s \in V$, find a range assignment r for G such that G_r contains a directed spanning tree of G rooted at s and $cost(r) = \sum_{v \in V} r(v)$ is minimized.

We consider that the edge weight function might be asymmetric. I.e. for two edges (u, v) and (v, u) in E, $w(u, v)$ might be different from $w(v, u)$.

3   Related Work

The MECBS problem has been extensively studied. However, most work concentrates on versions of the problem with symmetric edge costs $(w(u, v) = w(v, u))$. Algorithms that are centralized (e.g., BIP [10]), distributed but not localized (e.g., [13]) and localized (RTCP and RBOP [8], LBOP, LBOP-T and RBOP-T [9], TR-LBOP and TRDS [6] and LBIP [5]) for specific versions of the problem have been proposed. In particular, BIP is a very efficient centralized approximation algorithm [5,15] with a $\Omega(n)$ performance ratio [18].

The general MECBS problem is NP-hard [1]. This problem was also proved to be inapproximable within $(1 - \epsilon) \ln n$ for any $\epsilon > 0$, unless $P = NP$ (n denotes the number of nodes) [2,16,1].

For the general case, there are few approximation algorithms. Centralized algorithms were proposed in [18,7,13]. The algorithms presented in [7] and [13] provide logarithmic approximations to MECBS and improves the approximation ratio of the algorithm presented in [18]. The algorithm in [7] provides a $2(ln(n - 1) + 1)$ approximation ratio. The algorithm in [13] improves slightly on this result, with a $3/2(ln(n-1)+1)$ performance ratio. As there is no sublogarithmic approximation to the problem, these algorithms are asymptotically optimal.

To the best of our knowledge, distributed algorithms that consider asymmetry are only presented in [19,4]. In [19] the authors present a centralized and a distributed algorithm to construct a strongly connected broadcast arborescence with bounded transmission delay. The algorithm is not localized (it is based on distributed algorithms for calculating shortest paths, minimum weight directed spanning trees and depth-first search). In [4], edge costs are defined by multiplying the transmission power by the node's *energy unit cost*, thus restricting the way how edge costs might be different. The algorithm described in the paper (multi-dimensional case, $\alpha > 1$) [4] is not localized as well.

Additionally, in [11], although the authors define a version of the problem with directed graphs and potentially asymmetric edges costs, the distributed algorithm presented is based on the GHS minimum cost spanning tree algorithm, which assumes undirected graphs. In [15], the authors model the different transmission levels of transceivers (in a homogeneous environment). Asymmetry could be modelled by including all the transmission levels of all radio devices used in a particular setting. However, the number of such levels would be very large if we consider, for example, asymmetry due to hearing costs (the restriction of $\Theta(log(n/logn))$ ranges assumed in the paper would not apply in a general case).

Thus, to the best of our knowledge, LMCA is the first localized approximation algorithm to the MECBS problem with asymmetric edge costs.

4   System Model

A wireless sensor network is represented by a strongly connected directed graph $G = (V, E)$ with edge weight function $w : E \rightarrow \mathbb{R}^+$, where V is the set of nodes, E represents the set of communication channels and $\mathbb{R}^+$ is the set of nonnegative real numbers. We associate a *process* with each node. A process is a finite state automaton that models the behaviour of a node. Each process has a unique identifier. So we have processes $p_1, p_2, ..., p_n$, where $n = |V|$. One of the processes is the *root* process (or simply *root*). The node associated with the root process is the root node. Since there is a one-to-one relationship between processes and nodes, we will use the terms *process* and *node* interchangeably.

Processes communicate with each other by exchanging messages. Edge $(p, q) \in E$ iff process q can receive messages from process p. We assume that each node knows the set of processes in its two-hop neighbourhood. We do not restrict how edge costs are defined. Edge costs might be asymmetric, i.e. $w(p, q)$ might be different from $w(q, p)$, for any two nodes p and q. The communication relationship, however, is symmetric (if u can hear a message from v, v can also hear a message from u, when both transmit at full power). We assume that each node can adjust its transmission power to any value from 0 to a maximum. The graph induced when all nodes transmit at maximum power is strongly connected.

We assume an asynchronous system model. I.e. there is no known upper bound on the time a message takes to arrive at the destination and there is no known upper bound on the time a process takes to execute a single step. Channels and nodes are assumed to be reliable. A message sent by a node eventually arrives without modification at the receiver.

5   The LMCA Algorithm

5.1   Algorithm Overview

LMCA works incrementally. Starting from the root, each process p_i calculates a minimum cost arborescence rooted at p_i on the graph that represents its two-hop neighbourhood (as explained right below, nodes that are known to have already been covered will be ignored). We use Edmonds's algorithm to find the minimum cost arborescence [3]. Process p_i uses the calculated arborescence to define: (a) the cost associated with it (i.e. $r(p_i)$) and its associated transmission power; (b)

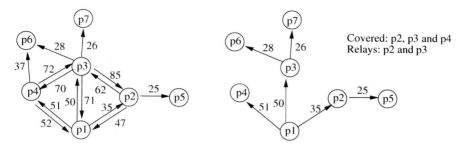

Fig. 1. Example of LMCA

the set of processes that become *covered* by it, i.e. that are reached by p_i when it transmits with the defined transmission power; and (c) the next processes to continue the algorithm. These processes are called *relay processes* (or simply *relays*). The algorithm is repeated in the same way by each relay process. The list of processes in p_i's neighbourhood that are known by p_i to have already been covered is transmitted to the next relays. Thus these processes can be ignored in the local calculation of the relays' minimum cost arborescences.

Each node p_i determines the relay and covered processes as follows. Process p_i chooses a process p_j among its children in the minimum cost arborescence for which $w(p_i, p_j)$ is the highest. Let us call this node $highest_i$. Process p_i will adjust its transmission power to the minimum power necessary to reach $highest_i$. All processes p_k in p_i's one-hop neighbourhood for which $w(p_i, p_k)$ is less than or equal to $w(p_i, highest_i)$ are the *processes covered by* p_i. The other processes in the arborescence are the *uncovered processes*, according to p_i's view.

We call *bridges* the edges (q, s) in the minimum cost arborescence rooted at p_i which have a covered process as tail (q) and an uncovered process as head (s)[1]. The relay processes will be those processes that are tails of bridges.

Figure 1 illustrates how a process (p_1) determines bridges and relays. The left part of the figure shows the graph that represents p_1's two-hop neighbourhood. Processes p_2, p_3 and p_4 are one-hop neighbours of p_1. An arrow from node p_i to node p_j represents the edge (p_i, p_j). The numbers beside the arrows represent the costs of the corresponding edges.

The right part of Figure 1 represents the tree built by process p_1. Process p_4 is p_1's child in the tree for which the cost of the edge from p_1 to it is the highest (i.e. p_4 is $highest_1$). The transmission power associated with p_1 is the minimum power needed to reach p_4. The cost associated with p_1 is the cost of the (p_1, p_4) edge. The nodes covered by p_1 are p_2, p_3 and p_4. Nodes p_5, p_6 and p_7 are uncovered. The bridges are edges (p_2, p_5), (p_3, p_6) and (p_3, p_7). Therefore, the relays will be processes p_2 and p_3.

After having determined the relays, process p_i broadcasts a RELAY message, using the minimum power needed to reach $highest_i$. This message contains a list of the processes that are known to be covered and those that were chosen as

---

[1] For an edge (u, v), we call u and v, resp., the *tail* and the *head* of the edge.

relays by p_i. The nodes that are known by p_i to be covered are those in its two-hop neighbourhood that are covered by p_i or by some other node, as indicated on the list of covered nodes present either in the first RELAY message received by p_i or in an ALREADYRELAY message (see below). Note that all processes that will hear a RELAY message are covered. A process, say p_j, that receives this message from process p_i will be in one of the following states:

- p_j *has already been a relay or it is the root*: if p_i chose p_j to be a relay, p_j replies with an ALREADYRELAY message, informing that it has already been a relay. This message contains the set of covered nodes in p_j's two-hop neighbourhood. If p_i did not choose p_j to be a relay, p_j just ignores the message.
- p_j *is not the root, it has not been a relay and it is on the list of relays*: p_j will continue the algorithm (repeating the steps described above with its own local information). p_i becomes the parent of p_j.
- p_j *is not the root, it has not been a relay and it is not on the list of relays*: p_j was not chosen by p_i to be a relay. As p_j is covered, the cost associated with it remains zero. p_i becomes the parent of p_j.

When process p_i receives an ALREADYRELAY message, it updates the set of covered processes and executes the local procedure again to find a new set of covered nodes, relays and a new transmission power. The new transmission power will be the maximum between the current and the new one.

This algorithm is presented in Figure 2, where p_i represents a generic process. All processes execute the same algorithm. We assume that p_i already knows the $G_i^{2h} = (V_i^{2h}, E_i^{2h})$ graph, i.e. the graph that represents its two-hop neighbourhood. Procedure FINDLOCALMCA represents the main part of the algorithm: elimination of nodes already covered (Fig. 2, lines 1-2); calculation of the local minimum cost arborescence rooted at p_i (represented by the EDMONDS procedure in Fig. 2, line 3); determination of $highest_i$ (Fig. 2, line 4); determination of p_i's cost (Fig. 2, line 5); determination of the new covered and uncovered nodes (Fig. 2, lines 6-7), bridges and relays (Fig. 2, lines 8-9); update of the set of covered nodes in p_i's two-hop neighbourhood (Fig. 2, line 10); and the broadcast of a RELAY message (Fig. 2, line 11), using the power associated with the current value of $myCost_i$.

Lines 12-14 of Fig. 2 represent the actions performed by p_i on starting the algorithm. Lines 15-17 of Fig. 2 represent the actions performed by p_i when it receives an ALREADYRELAY message. Lines 18-25 of Fig. 2 represent the actions performed by p_i when it receives a RELAY message. It either: replies with an ALREADYRELAY message; executes FINDLOCALMCA and sets its parent; or simply updates its parent, as described above.

Full Coverage

The algorithm, as described above, does not guarantee full coverage (i.e. that all nodes become covered at the end of the algorithm). In our experiments (see Section 6), however, the algorithm did not cover all nodes only in very rare

Let $G_i^{2h} = (V_i^{2h}, E_i^{2h})$ be the graph that represents p_i's two-hop neighbourhood

$OneHopNeighbours_i \leftarrow \{q : (q \in V_i^{2h}) \wedge ((p_i, q) \in E_i^{2h})\}$

$Covered_i \leftarrow \emptyset \quad myCost_i \leftarrow 0 \quad parent_i \leftarrow nil \quad NewCovered_i \leftarrow \emptyset$

$IAmRelay_i \leftarrow false$

Procedure FINDLOCALMCA

1    $V_i \leftarrow (V_i^{2h} \setminus Covered_i) \cup \{p_i\}$

2    $E_i \leftarrow E_i^{2h} \setminus \{(q, r) : ((q, r) \in E_i^{2h}) \wedge ((q \notin V_i) \vee (r \notin V_i))\}$

3    $MCA_i(V_{MCA_i}, E_{MCA_i}) \leftarrow$ EDMONDS (p_i, G_i)

4    $highest_i \leftarrow$ any member of the set $\{q : ((p_i, q) \in E_{MCA_i}) \wedge$
             $(\nexists r : ((p_i, r) \in E_{MCA_i}) \wedge (cost(p_i, r) > cost(p_i, q)))\}$

5    $myCost_i \leftarrow max\{myCost_i, cost(p_i, highest_i)\}$

6    $NewCovered_i \leftarrow \{q : (q \in OneHopNeighbours_i) \wedge (cost(p_i, q) \leq myCost_i)\}$

7    $Uncovered_i \leftarrow V_i \setminus (NewCovered_i \cup \{p_i\})$

8    $Bridges_i \leftarrow \{(q, s) : ((q, s) \in E_{MCA_i}) \wedge (q \in NewCovered_i) \wedge$
             $(s \in Uncovered_i)\}$

9    $RelayProcs_i \leftarrow \{q : (q \in NewCovered_i) \wedge (\exists r \in V_i : (q, r) \in Bridges_i)\}$

10    $Covered_i \leftarrow (NewCovered_i \cup Covered_i) \cap V_i^{2h}$

11   Send RELAY($Covered_i$, $RelayProcs_i$) using power defined by $myCost_i$

end

12   **on** starting LMCA

13   **if** $((p_i = root) \wedge (\exists$ uncovered node in $OneHopNeighbours_i))$ **then**

14   FINDLOCALMCA

end

15   **on** receiving ALREADYRELAY ($pCvrd$) from p_j

16    $Covered_i \leftarrow Covered_i \cup pCvrd$

17   **if** $(\exists$ uncovered node in $OneHopNeighbours_i)$ **then** FINDLOCALMCA

end

18   **on** receiving RELAY ($pCvrd$, $pRelays$) from p_j

19   **if** $((p_i = root) \vee (IAmRelay_i))$ **then**

20   **if** $(p_i \in pRelays)$ **then** Send ALREADYRELAY($Covered_i$) to p_j

   else

21   **if** $(p_i \in pRelays)$ **then**

22        $Covered_i \leftarrow pCvrd$

23        $IAmRelay_i \leftarrow true$

24   FINDLOCALMCA

25      $parent_i \leftarrow p_j$

end

Fig. 2. Algorithm executed by process p_i (Part I) - Main part

situations. Full coverage can be guaranteed by making each node check (after a certain period of time) if it has been covered. If it has not, it simply asks one of the covered nodes in its one-hop neighbourhood for covering it. The chosen neighbour adjusts its transmission power in order to cover the requesting

OneHopNeighbours$_i$ and *myCost$_i$* are as defined in Fig. 2.

```
1   on timeout { Only executed if p_i is not covered yet }
2       CoveredNeighs_i ← {q : (q ∈ OneHopNeighbours_i) ∧ (q is covered)}
3       if (CoveredNeighs_i = ∅) then
4           restart timeout
        else
5           RelayNeighs_i ← {q : (q ∈ CoveredNeighs_i) ∧ (q is a relay)}
6           if (RelayNeighs_i ≠ ∅) then
7               p_r ← any member of RelayNeighs_i
            else
8               p_r ← any member of CoveredNeighs_i
9           send COVERREQUEST to p_r
10          parent_i ← p_r
    end
11  on receiving COVERREQUEST from p_j
12      myCost_i ← max{myCost_i, cost(p_i, p_j)}
13      Covered_i ← {q : (q ∈ OneHopNeighbours_i) ∧ (cost(p_i, q) ≤ myCost_i)}
14      IAmRelay_i ← true     { p_i becomes a relay (if it has not been yet) }
    end
```

Fig. 3. Algorithm executed by process p_i (Part II) - Enforcing coverage

node and thus becomes a relay (if it has not been one yet). It is shown in Section 5.2 that any uncovered node will eventually have a covered node in its neighbourhood.

This extension is represented in Figure 3, for a generic process p_i. While a process is not covered yet, it periodically verifies if some of its neighbours has already been covered (Fig. 3, lines 1-4). The set of covered neighbours is represented by *CoveredNeighs$_i$* (Fig. 3, line 2). If *CoveredNeighs$_i$* is empty, the process simply restarts a timer, to execute this verification again in the future (Fig. 3, lines 3-4). Otherwise, process p_i chooses a covered neighbour to cover it. It chooses one neighbour that is a relay, if there is any (Fig. 3, lines 5-7). The set of relay nodes is represented by *RelayNeighs$_i$*. If there is not any, it chooses one of the covered (but not relay) nodes (Fig. 3, line 8). The chosen neighbour, represented by p_r, should be one that minimizes the overall broadcast cost. Process p_i sends a message to process p_r, asking p_r for adjusting its power to cover it (Fig. 3, line 9). Process p_r becomes p_i's parent (Fig. 3, line 10).

When a process p_i receives a COVERREQUEST message from a process p_j, it adjusts its power to cover p_j (Fig. 3, lines 11-12). Process p_i updates its set of covered nodes and becomes a relay, if it is not one yet (Fig. 3, lines 13-14).

A process p_i obtains information about which of its neighbours have been covered or are relays by exchanging specific messages with its neighbours. We do not specify this message exchange here.

Induced Graph

LMCA induces a graph, $G_r = (V, E_r)$, where:

$$E_r = \bigcup_{p \in V} \{(p, q) : ((p, q) \in E) \wedge (w(p, q) \leq myCost_p)\}$$

I.e. G_r contains all processes as vertices and all edges (p, q) such that node p covers node q. This graph might be different from a minimum cost arborescence of the whole original graph. It might contain more than one edge with the same node as head.

Observe that LMCA uses only knowledge about its two-hop neighbourhood, so it is localized. Note that a message to be broadcast by an application can be piggybacked in the RELAY messages or forwarded to a node as a reply to a COVERREQUEST message (thus avoiding an extra delay and overhead to execute LMCA before actually broadcasting an application message).

The cost of the algorithm executed locally by each process is dominated by EDMONDS. Edmonds's algorithm runs in $O(E_i^{2h} + V_i^{2h} log V_i^{2h})$ time [3].

5.2   Correctness

LMCA shall satisfy termination, full coverage and the induced graph, G_r, must contain a directed spanning tree rooted at the root node. These properties are represented by the lemmas and theorems presented in this section.

We refer to the two parts of LMCA as: (a) Part I, represented in Figure 2, where processes incrementally calculate local minimum cost arborescences and determine covered and relay nodes; and (b) Part II, represented in Figure 3, which is needed to guarantee full coverage of nodes.

Lemma 1. *Eventually all processes become covered.*

Proof. Full coverage is simply guaranteed by Part II of LMCA. Suppose, by contradiction, that the execution of the algorithm reaches a (global) final state where some of the nodes are covered and some are not (we assume, for simplicity, that the root node is covered at the beginning of the algorithm - so there is always at least one covered node). As the graph induced when all nodes transmit at maximum power is strongly connected, there would be at least one uncovered node that is neighbour of a covered one in this graph. As a node executes Part II periodically until it becomes covered, all uncovered nodes that are neighbours of covered nodes will become covered. By repeating this argument, all nodes will eventually become covered.

Lemma 2. *LMCA eventually terminates, i.e. each process reaches a final state, at which no transitions are possible.*

Proof. As all nodes eventually become covered (lemma 1), in all executions of LMCA each node is either (a) relay (including the root) or (b) a covered but non-relay node. In case (a), the execution of the node terminates, because each node executes FINDLOCALMCA only a limited number of times as, each time a process (re-)executes it, it either chooses new relays or eliminates at least one of its neighbours (which was chosen relay, but has already been one). By this argument, each node might only receive a bounded number of RELAY messages. Furthermore, each node might receive a bounded number of COVERREQUEST messages as well (each one-hop neighbour that sends such a message does it only once, as channels and processes are reliable). In case (b), a covered non-relay node becomes covered either passively (as a consequence of the execution of FINDLOCALMCA by some relay node) or actively (by executing Part II of LMCA). Thus, each node receives at most a bounded number of messages (RELAY messages from its relay neighbours).

Theorem 1. *When LMCA terminates, the graph induced by it, $G_r = (V, E_r)$, contains an arborescence rooted at the root node.*

Proof. We must show that there is a path in G_r from the root node to each other node in the graph. As all nodes are covered, all nodes will have a parent node, except the root. First we show that G_r does not have any cycle. Suppose, by contradiction, that there is a cycle $\langle p_{i_1}, p_{i_2}, ..., p_{i_m} \rangle$, where $p_{i_1} = p_{i_m}$, $m \geq 2$, and p_{i_j} is the parent of $p_{i_{j+1}}$. As all nodes in the cycle are parents of some other node, they are all relays. As p_{i_k} is parent of $p_{i_{k+1}}$, p_{i_k} became a relay before $p_{i_{k+1}}$. Thus, transitively, p_{i_1} became relay before p_{i_m} which became relay before p_{i_1} (a contradiction). As there are no cycles in G_r, the reverse paths $R = \langle q_{i_1}, q_{i_2}, ..., q_{i_r} \rangle$, where q_{i_k+1} is the parent of q_{i_k} in G_r ($k \geq 1$) ends at the root node (i.e. q_{i_r} is the root node, since it is the only node that has no parent). Thus, there is a path from the root node to each node in the graph (just follow R in the opposite direction).

6   Evaluation

6.1   Compared Algorithms

As discussed in Section 3, we are not aware of any other localized algorithm for the problem of MECBS with asymmetric edge costs, as considered in this paper. Therefore in order to evaluate the performance of LMCA we compared it with blind flooding and with two alternative solutions we designed, as variations of, respectively, LMCA and LBIP [5]. We call them LMCP (Localized algorithm for energy-efficient broadcast based on **L**ocal **M**inimum-**C**ost **P**aths trees) and LBIPAsym (**LBIP** for graphs with **Asym**metric edge costs).

In blind flooding each node that receives a message simply broadcasts it with maximum power. It corresponds to a situation with no specific power control.

LMCP is a simple variation of LMCA where each node p_i calculates a tree of minimum cost paths (from itself to nodes in its two-hop neighbourhood) instead of a minimum cost arborescence. It can be proved that LMCP guarantees full coverage of the graph. Let $T_{sp} = (V, E_{sp})$ be a shortest-paths tree rooted at the root node, calculated over a maximum power graph. The proof is based on the fact that the edges in T_{sp} will belong to the trees calculated locally by the nodes.

LBIPAsym is a variation of LBIP [5]. LBIP is known as a very good approximation algorithm for the version of MECBS with symmetric edge costs. As we are assuming that edge costs might be asymmetric, LBIP cannot be directly applied. In LBIP, each process constructs locally a tree (as in LMCA) and each tree induces a broadcast cost. This local tree is constructed iteratively as follows. For a set of already covered nodes, a new uncovered node u is inserted in the tree that is: adjacent to a covered node, say v; and the edge connecting u and v is the one which results in the lowest increment in the broadcast tree so far. In LBIPAsym, the only difference is that we consider only the directed edges from covered nodes to uncovered nodes when choosing a new node to be inserted in the tree.

We additionally investigated the impact of modifying LMCA in two different ways, generating two slight variations of the algorithm, which we call, resp., LMCAc and LMCAfl. LMCAc performs an additional processing when determining the relay nodes, in order to try to decrease their number. In LMCAfl, when a node p_i sends a RELAY message, this message will now contain a list with *all* nodes that p_i knows to have been covered so far, i.e. the list might now include nodes that are not in p_i's two-hop neighbourhood.

6.2 Description of the Experiments

As in this paper we are interested in the cost of the final range assignment, we have implemented a specific Java program for the experiments. The nodes were distributed over a 500m x 500m area. We varied the density of the network. We made experiments with 12, 25, 50, 75 and 100 nodes, randomly spread over the area. All nodes are stationary. For each network configuration (number of nodes), 100 different scenarios were generated.

LMCA is independent of any specific edge cost function. For the experiments, we adopted a cost function based on the energy model described in [17]. Energy is spent by nodes during transmission and reception states (the energy spent during processing is ignored).

For each (u, v), $cost(u, v)$ denotes the energy spent by the network when u transmits with the minimum power necessary to reach node v. We consider that this cost involves the energy spent by u to transmit and the energy spent by all nodes that hear the transmission (reception cost). $cost(u, v)$ is thus defined as:

$$cost(u, v) = cf(u) + \gamma(u).d(u, v)^\alpha + \sum_{\forall s:(s \neq u) \wedge (d(u,s) \leq d(u,v))} cr(s) \qquad (1)$$

where: $cf(u)$ is the (fixed) energy spent by the transmitter electronics at node u; $\gamma(u)$ is a parameter characteristic of the transceiver and the channel [12]; $d(u, v)$ is the distance (in meter) between u and v; α is the path loss exponent $(2 \leq \alpha \leq 6)$ [12]; and $cr(s)$ is the reception cost of node s.

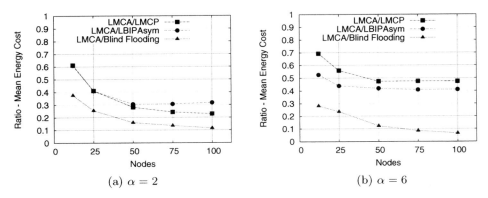

Fig. 4. Ratio of the mean energy cost of LMCA and, resp., LMCP, LBIPAsym and Blind Flooding

We used the following values: $cf(u) = 48$ nJ/bit, $\gamma(u) = 16.1$ pJ/bit/m^2 and $cr(v) = 236.4$ nJ/bit. For each scenario, we used first $\alpha = 2$ and then $\alpha = 6$. Maximum transmission range was 30 units. These values were based on characteristics of the CC2420 transceiver. Since the reception cost of nodes is used in the cost function, $cost(u, v)$ and $cost(v, u)$ might be different (asymmetric costs).

6.3   Experiment Results

First we describe a comparison between LMCA and blind flooding, LMCP and LBIPAsym in relation to energy cost (see Section 2). Figure 4 shows the ratio between the mean energy cost of LMCA and, respectively, the mean energy cost of LMCP (line with squares), LBIPAsym (line with circles) and blind flooding (line with triangles). Figure 4(a) represents the results of the experiments for $\alpha = 2$. Figure 4(b) represents the results of the experiments for $\alpha = 6$. Each point in the graphic represents the ratio between the mean energy cost of LMCA and each of the other algorithms, considering 100 scenarios. We see that LMCA outperformed LMCP, LBIPAsym and blind flooding. For $\alpha = 2$, the ratio decreases with the increase in network density, with the exception of a very little increase in the ratio between LMCA and LBIPAsym from 50 to 100 nodes (from 0.30 to 0.31). For example, in the scenarios with 100 nodes, the cost of LMCA was 11.5% of the cost of blind flooding, 22.8% of the cost of LMCP and 32.0% of the cost of LBIPAsym. For $\alpha = 6$, the ratio decreased with the increase in network density, but the ratio between LMCA and, resp., LMCP and LBIPAsym remained stable for 50 or more nodes. Thus, according to the experiments, calculating locally a minimum cost arborescence (LMCA) provided better results than calculating locally trees of minimum cost paths (LMCP). The adaptation of LBIP to graph with asymmetric edge costs performed worse than LMCA as well.

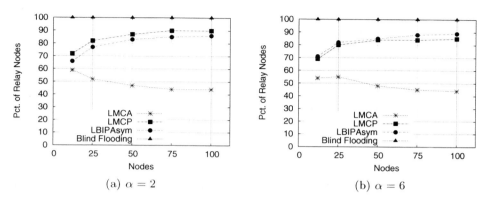

Fig. 5. Mean percentage of relays: LMCA, LMCP, LBIPAsym and Blind Flooding

Figure 5 represents the percentage of relays for LMCA, LMCP, LBIPAsym and blind flooding (for $\alpha = 2$ and $\alpha = 6$). The percentage of relays for blind flooding is always 100%, as each process locally broadcasts a received message. We see that, differently from LMCP and LBIPAsym, in LMCA the percentage of relay nodes decreases with the increase in the number of nodes in the network. The behaviour of the algorithms for the cases of $\alpha = 2$ and $\alpha = 6$ was similar.

We additionally evaluated whether there would be an improvement in the results of LMCA if (a) we tried to decrease the number of relays by considering the coverage of nodes which are relay candidates and (b) by passing more information about covered nodes between relays. As previously stated, we call these variations LMCAc and LMCAfl, respectively.

More specifically, the difference between LMCAc and LMCA is the following. Recall that $RelayProcs_i$ is the set of relays chosen by process p_i in LMCA (see Figure 2). In LMCAc, process p_i further processes $RelayProcs_i$ removing from this set nodes whose children in the local minimum cost arborescence are covered by other nodes in the set. I.e. a node v is removed from $RelayProcs_i$ if there is another node u in the set that covers v's children when u transmits with the power defined by LMCA (induced by the local tree). This process is illustrated in Figure 6. This figure represents the tree locally built by node s (minimum cost arborescence rooted at s). According to LMCA, processes u and v will be relays. But, as the range of u includes v's children, v is removed from the set of chosen relays ($RelayProcs_i$).

In LMCAfl, each node p_i, instead of informing to the next relays the list of covered nodes in p_i's two-hop neighbourhood, it includes in this list the set of *all nodes* that p_i knows to have already been covered (so far, in the execution of the algorithm).

Figure 7 shows the ratios of the mean energy cost, number of exchanged messages, size of the list of covered nodes and percentage of relay nodes between LMCA and LMCAc, for the cases of $\alpha = 2$ and $\alpha = 6$. For $\alpha = 2$, all the ratios

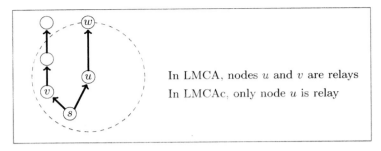

Fig. 6. Example of LMCAc (tree built at node s)

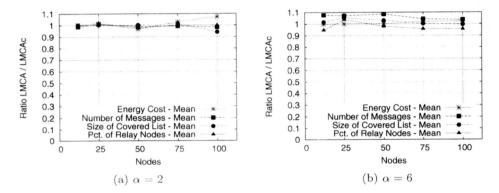

(a) $\alpha = 2$ (b) $\alpha = 6$

Fig. 7. Impact of further processing the set of candidate relay nodes (LMCAc)

are very close to 1, except for the case of 100 nodes, where the mean size of the list of covered nodes is smaller for LMCA and LMCAc exhibited smaller energy cost. For $\alpha = 6$, the ratios of the mean number of messages, size of the list of covered nodes and percentage of relay nodes varied slightly more than for the case of $\alpha = 2$. These ratios, however, remained in the range between 0.95 and 1.1. The ratios related to energy cost, however, remained very close to 1. Thus, the performance in terms of energy cost was practically the same for both algorithms, but LMCA exchanged more messages. Recall that LMCAc requires more local processing at each node.

Figure 8 shows the ratios of the same parameters (total energy cost, number of exchanged messages, size of the list of covered nodes and percentage of relay nodes), but now for LMCA and LMCAfl. For both values of α (2 and 6), the mean size of the list of covered nodes was higher for LMCAfl (as expected) and the mean percentages of relay nodes used by LMCA and LMCAfl were very close. For $\alpha = 2$, LMCAfl resulted in a mean energy cost that is either very close or lower than the mean energy cost of LMCA. LMCA, however, had a light improvement on the number of exchanged messages, when the number of nodes was 100. For $\alpha = 6$, the energy cost was roughly the same, but LMCA

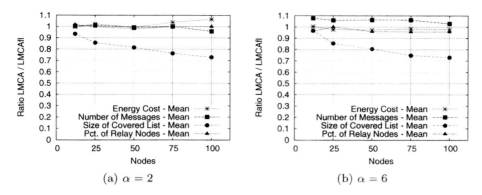

Fig. 8. Impact of transferring more information about covered nodes between relays (LMCAfl)

resulted in more message exchange (although the ratio was always less than 1.1). The performances of the algorithms were equivalent, but LMCAfl requires longer messages to be sent between nodes.

7 Conclusion

In this paper, we presented LMCA, a localized algorithm for the MECBS problem with asymmetric edge costs. We are not aware of any other localized algorithm for this version of the problem. We think that this version of MECBS is very relevant it models scenarios in heterogeneous sensor networks.

To evaluate the performance of LMCA, we compared it with blind flooding and variations of LMCA and LBIP that we designed, called resp. LMCP and LBIPAsym. In our experiments, LMCA outperformed these algorithms, achieving 1% and 8%, 22% and 48%, and 32% and 41% of the costs of, respectively, blind flooding, LMCP and LBIPAsym, for the cases of $\alpha = 2$ and $\alpha = 6$.

We analysed additionally the impact of further refining the choice of relay nodes, by taking into consideration the coverage of relay candidates, and of transferring more information about covered nodes between relays. The performance of these variations was slight better in some scenarios, but at the cost of either further processing by the nodes or the exchange of longer messages. For $\alpha = 6$, the performances of these algorithms and LMCA were equivalent.

References

1. Clementi, A.E.F., Crescenzi, P., Penna, P., Rossi, G., Vocca, P.: On the Complexity of Computing Minimum Energy Consumption Broadcast Subgraphs. In: Ferreira, A., Reichel, H. (eds.) STACS 2001. LNCS, vol. 2010, pp. 121–131. Springer, Heidelberg (2001)

2. Clementi, A.E.F., Crescenzi, P., Penna, P., Rossi, G., Vocca, P.: A worst-case analysis of an MST-based heuristic to construct energy-efficient broadcast trees in wireless networks. Technical Report 010, University of Rome "Tor Vergata", Math Department (2001)

3. Korte, B., Vygen, J.: Combinatorial Optimization - Theory and Algorithms, 4th edn. Springer (2008)

4. Ambühl, C., Clementi, A.E.F., Ianni, M., Rossi, G., Monti, A., Silvestri, R.: The range assignment problem in non-homogeneous static ad-hoc networks. In: Proc. of IPDPS 2004 (2004)

5. Ingelrest, F., Simplot-Ryl, D.: Localized broadcast incremental power protocol for wireless ad hoc networks. Wireless Networks 14 (2008)

6. Ingelrest, F., Simplot-Ryl, D., Stojmenović, I.: Optimal transmission radius for energy efficient broadcasting protocols in ad hoc and sensor networks. IEEE Trans. on Parallel and Distr. Systems 17(6) (June 2006)

7. Calinescu, G., Kapoor, S., Olshevsky, A., Zelikovsky, A.: Network Lifetime and Power Assignment in ad hoc Wireless Networks. In: Di Battista, G., Zwick, U. (eds.) ESA 2003. LNCS, vol. 2832, pp. 114–126. Springer, Heidelberg (2003)

8. Cartigny, J., Simplot-Ryl, D., Stojmenovic, I.: Localized minimum-energy broadcasting in ad-hoc networks. In: Procs. of INFOCOM (2003)

9. Cartigny, J., Ingelrest, F., Simplot-Ryl, D., Stojmenovic, I.: Localized LMST and RNG based minimum-energy broadcast protocols in ad hoc networks. Ad Hoc Networks 3 (2005)

10. Wieselthier, J.E., Nguyen, G.D., Ephremides, A.: Energy-efficient broadcast and multicast trees in wireless networks. Mobile Network and Applications 7(6), 481–492 (2002)

11. Čagalj, M., Hubaux, J.-P., Enz, C.: Minimum-energy broadcast in all-wireless networks: Np-completeness and distribution issues. In: MobiCom 2002, pp. 172–182. ACM, New York (2002)

12. Rappaport, T.S.: Wireless Communications: Principles and Practice, 2nd edn. Prentice-Hall (1996)

13. Ghosh, S.K.: Energy efficient broadcast in distributed ad-hoc wireless networks. In: Procs of the 11th IEEE Int. Conf. on Computational Science and Engineering (CSE 2008), São Paulo, Brazil (July 2008)

14. Misra, S., Mohanta, D.: Adaptive listen for energy-efficient medium access control in wireless sensor networks. Multimedia Tools and Applications 47(1), 121–145 (2010)

15. Calamoneri, T., Clementi, A., Monti, A., Rossi, G., Silvestri, R.: Minimum-energy broadcast in random-grid ad-hoc networks: Approximation and distributed algorithms. In: Procs. of MSWiM 2008. ACM Press (2008)

16. Wan, P.-J., Calinescu, G., Li, X.-Y., Frieder, O.: Minimum-energy broadcasting in static ad hoc wireless networks. Wireless Networks 8, 607–617 (2002)

17. Heinzelman, W.B., Chandrakasan, A.P., Balakrishnan, H.: An application-specific protocol architecture for wireless microsensor networks. IEEE Trans. on Wireless Comms 1(4), 660–670 (2002)

18. Liang, W.: Constructing minimum-energy broadcast trees in wireless ad hoc networks. In: Procs. of MOBIHOC 2002, Switzerland. ACM (June 2002)

19. Li, Y., Thai, M.T., Wang, F., Du, D.-Z.: On the construction of a strongly connected broadcast arborescence with bounded transmission delay. IEEE Transactions on Mobile Computing 5(10), 1460–1470 (2006)

Author Index

CPSIA information can be obtained at www.ICGtesting.com
Printed in the USA
LVOW110807290413

331269LV00022B/100/P